FLEXIBLE EMPLOYMENT

Flexible Employment

The Future of Britain's Jobs

Shirley Dex
Lecturer in Management Studies
University of Cambridge

Andrew McCulloch

Research Assistant
University of Cambridge

First published 1997 by
MACMILLAN PRESS LTD
Houndmills, Basingstoke, Hampshire RG21 6XS
and London
Companies and representatives
throughout the world

ISBN 0–333–68214–9 hardcover

A catalogue record for this book is available
from the British Library.

This book is printed on paper suitable for recycling and
made from fully managed and sustained forest sources.

10 9 8 7 6 5 4 3 2 1
06 05 04 03 02 01 00 99 98 97

Printed in Great Britain by
The Ipswich Book Company Ltd
Ipswich, Suffolk

To Roger Sewell,
who knows about these things

Contents

List of Tables   viii

List of Figures   xii

Preface   xiii

Acknowledgements   xv

1   Introduction   1

Part I Employers and the Labour Market

2   Employers' Use of Flexible Work   15
3   The Labour Market of Flexible Jobs   28

Part II Individuals

4   Individuals in Flexible Work in Britain in the 1990s   45
5   Characteristics of Individuals in Flexible Jobs   64
6   Changes in Flexible Work in Britain during the 1980s   90
7   Flexible Jobs over the Lifetime   104

Part III Households

8   Flexible Jobs and Households   135

Part IV Britain's Jobs in the World Economy

9   How does Britain Compare with other Industrialised
    Countries?   153
10 The Future of Britain's Jobs   173

Appendix: The British Household Panel Study Data   191

Bibliography   197

Index   203

Lists of Tables

2.1　Elements of non-wage labour costs in Britain in the 1990s　17

3.1　Men's non-standard employment by industry, LFS 1994　29

3.2　Women's non-standard employment by industry, LFS 1994　30

3.3　Men's non-standard employment by occupation, LFS 1994　31

3.4　Women's non-standard employment by occupation, LFS 1994　31

3.5　Managerial duties of all jobs ever held by Wave 3 (retrospective) BHPS sample of men and women　34

3.6　Men's non-standard employment by region, LFS 1994　37

3.7　Women's non-standard employment by region, LFS 1994　37

4.1　Profile of non-standard forms of employment among men of working age in Britain in 1994, LFS　56

4.2　Profile of non-standard forms of employment among women of working age in Britain in 1994, LFS　57

4.3　Reason for holding a temporary job by sex and self-defined hours of work, LFS 1994　60

4.4　Employment in flexible working arrangements, LFS 1994　61

5.1　Profile of non-standard forms of employment by age of working-age men in 1994, LFS　65

5.2　Profile of non-standard forms of employment by age of working-age women in 1994, LFS　67

5.3　Attitudes to mother working by job status at Wave 2 for employed men and women in BHPS sample　71

5.4　Attitudes to women working by job status at Wave 2 for employed men and women in BHPS sample　71

5.5　Most important aspect of a job: per cent who say job security is most or second most important by economic activity status: BHPS Wave 1　73

5.6　Satisfaction scores by status of job: BHPS Wave 2　73

5.7　General health questionnaire (GHQ score) by job status at Wave 2 for employed men and women in BHPS sample　75

5.8　GHQ mean score by type of job: BHPS 1991 Wave 2　75

5.9   Highest educational qualifications by job status at Wave 2 for employed men and women in the BHPS sample   76

5.10   Hourly earnings quartiles by job status at Wave 2 for employed men and women in the BHPS sample   78

5.11   Mean hourly gross pay of men and women by category and age group at Wave 2 of BHPS   79

5.12   Periods of unemployment by job status at Wave 2 for employed men and women in the BHPS sample   81

5.13   Percentage of working life spent unemployed by job status at Wave 2 for employed men and women in the BHPS sample   81

5.14   Housing tenure by job status at Wave 2 for employed men and women in BHPS sample   83

5.15   Lone parent status by job status at Wave 2 for employed men and women in BHPS sample   85

5.16   Whether individual is a carer for someone inside the household by job status at Wave 2 for employed men and women in BHPS sample   85

5.17   Household income quartiles by job status at Wave 2 for employed men and women in BHPS sample   86

5.18   Financial situation by job status at Wave 2 for employed men and women in BHPS sample   87

6.1   Changes in non-standard forms of work over time for men as per cent of employed men of working age, LFS   94

6.2   Changes in non-standard forms of work over time for women as per cent of employed women of working age, LFS   95

6.3   Total extent of flexible work by age for men and women not in full-time education, over time, LFS   98

6.4   Whether or not individual has a second job, LFS   100

6.5   Tenure durations with current employer, over time, LFS   102

7.1   Experience of flexible jobs in entire working life of men and women in BHPS sample   106

7.2   Number of flexible jobs of varying kinds held by BHPS sample of men and women up to Wave 3   107

7.3   Numbers of flexible jobs over working life by age group at Wave 3: BHPS   108

7.4   Percentage of working life spent in various flexible states for men and women with at least one flexible job, BHPS   110

7.5   Percentage of time spent in flexible jobs by numbers of
      jobs held for BHPS sample of men and women up to
      Wave 3   111
7.6   Age of individuals at first entry into flexible jobs and
      leaving all flexible jobs by type of job – BHPS
      samples of men and women at Wave 3   119
7.7   Marital status of first entry into flexible jobs by type
      of job – BHPS samples of men and women   120
7.8   Economic activity status prior to first occurrence of
      flexible job of men and women in BHPS at Wave 3   121
7.9   Number of unemployment periods before first entry into
      flexible jobs by type of job – BHPS samples of men
      and women at Wave 3   124
7.10 Reasons why left last job, before first and all entries into
      flexible jobs by type of job – BHPS samples of men
      and women   125
7.11 Whether had previous unemployment experience before
      temporary job, by whether a successful move made at the
      end of temporary job BHPS samples of men and women
      at Wave 3   129
7.12 Highest educational qualification according to whether
      individual makes a successful transition out of temporary
      work, BHPS sample of men and women at Wave 3   129
7.13 Duration of full-time job for those who successfully left
      temporary jobs, BHPS   130
8.1   Current experiences of flexible work in BHPS households
      at Waves 1 and 3   136
8.2   BHPS households' past experiences of flexible work up
      to Wave 3 BHPS   137
8.3   Number of flexible jobs ever experienced in BHPS
      households up to Wave 3   137
8.4   Number of individuals with current flexible jobs by type
      of household at Wave 1 BHPS   139
8.5   Individuals with any flexible jobs by household type at
      Wave 1 BHPS   141
8.6   Husbands' and wives' detailed job status at Wave 2 BHPS   142
8.7   Employed husbands' and wives' summary job status at
      Wave 2 BHPS   144
8.8   Husbands' and wives' past statuses, BHPS up to Wave 2   144
8.9   GHQ mean scores of husbands and wives by economic
      activity status: BHPS Wave 1   146

8.10   Housing tenure of household according to whether
household contains any individuals with a flexible job:
Wave 1 BHPS   147

8.11   Household income quartiles by household type by whether
household contains any individuals with a flexible job:
BHPS Wave 1   148

9.1   Changes in trade union membership as percentage of
wage and salary earners in selected countries over time:
1970–90   155

9.2   Part-time employment in selected OECD countries:
1979–92   157

9.3   Women's share of part-time employment 1979–92   158

9.4   Average hours worked in reference week by part-timers
in selected OECD countries   160

9.5   Temporary workers as a percentage of total
employment 1983–91   162

9.6   Demographic composition of employees in temporary
jobs in 1991   162

9.7   Share of persons having a temporary contract because
they could not find a permanent job   163

9.8   Percentage of temporary contracts covering a period of
training, 1987   164

9.9   Self-employment's share of total employment in selected
OECD countries: 1979–90   166

9.10   Percentage of short enterprise tenure employment in
selected countries 1985–91   170

A1.1   Definitions of categories of non-standard forms of
employment created from LFS and BHPS data   194

A1.2   BHPS wave responses of individuals   195

A1.3   Levels of missing values on selected aspects of jobs
recalled as part of Wave 3 job listing   195

A1.4   Flexible jobs in the BHPS data up to Wave 3   196

List of Figures

7.1	Men in permanent employment, BHPS	113
7.2	Women in permanent employment, BHPS	113
7.3	Women in full-time permanent employment, BHPS	114
7.4	Men self-employed throughout the year, BHPS	116
7.5	Women in part-time employment, BHPS	116
7.6	Temporary employment (men and women), BHPS	117
7.7	Women's temporary employment, BHPS	117
A1.1	Involuntary part-time work, 1984–94, LFS	192
A1.2	Temporary employment as a proportion of all employees, 1984–94, LFS	193
A1.3	Involuntary temporary employment, 1984–94, LFS	193

Preface

This topic has a very personal significance to me. I married into a career of flexible work in 1985 and since then it has dominated our family life. My husband's succession of fixed-term contracts in hospital medicine meant that we had to move around the country several times since then: from Stoke-on-Trent to Manchester, from Manchester to Norwich, from Norwich to Cambridge. I managed to hold on to my permanent full-time job and was granted leave to roam around the country picking up jobs here and there as I went. Some of the readers of this book may have met me at times along this trail and asked, 'and what are you doing now?' in a puzzled tone, being none the wiser after I had told them. I have tried to juggle with this uncertainty. I have spent a lot of time 'keeping my options open', commuting long distances to work, and at times missing opportunities to further my own status and career in order for us to live together with the hope that we might both find jobs at the end of the trail. I sadly miss a friend who understood in Cathie Marsh, also married to a hospital medic, before she died.

We have found the uncertainty of whether and where the next contract will be an enormous strain. In addition there's the strain and stress of moving house regularly, managing to make some friends just about the time when you have to move again, finding your way round new shopping centres, new nurseries and schools and settling the kids in, and telling everyone you've changed your address. These problems are common to jobs which require mobility and are not necessarily 'temporary' or uncertain. Some of the issues raised are also common to dual-career couples.

The uncertainty of many flexible jobs adds another dimension to the stress, for the individual and their family. It is the never knowing whether you are staying or going, whether to work at making friends, spend time choosing somewhere to live where you would like to stay and become attached to, and constantly having to look through the job adverts, pleasing your bosses whose references you depend on, and so on. People could say, well you knew what you were getting into when you chose your career. The trouble is, you often don't. You don't know how difficult it will be to get the next job. It might have been easier when you started out than it has become when you face it. And you don't know everything about yourself and how you will cope with uncertainty coupled with the responsibilities of family life. Anyway, some individuals who have an entrepreneurial spirit may cope just fine, but many don't, and there is still their partner to consider. Our journey through this uncertainty was ended by my husband changing his career since his stand on various ethical issues in the health service lost him the final prize of a consultant's job. He hadn't pleased the bosses enough.

I am in no doubt that the productivity of my own work has been lowered over the past few years by all of the events linked to our participation in the flexible economy. I am fairly sure that my husband's work has suffered as well. For every flexible job, potentially two people may be working at lower than their best because of the stressful conditions of many such jobs. A lot of this book is about statistics. I hope readers will not forget that the lives of real people lie below the figures about flexible work, parts which can sometimes get lost in a presentation of statistics, important as the overall picture is.

Shirley Dex
April 1996

Acknowledgements

The research contained in this report was largely carried out as part of two contracts: one for the Equal Opportunities Commission on the effects of deregulation on women's employment, the other, for the Employment Department, was an analysis of flexible work in the retrospective employment histories of individuals in the British Household Panel Study. We wish to thank the Equal Opportunities Commission and the new Department for Education and Employment for allowing us to use material contained in these reports. We also wish to thank Dave Perfect for editorial input to our work. The views expressed in this report are those of the authors and do not necessarily represent the views of the Commission or of the Department for Education and Employment.

We wish to acknowledge the ESRC Data Archive at the University of Essex for providing access to the Labour Force Survey data. This research was also part of the scientific programme of the ESRC Research Centre on Micro-Social Change at the University of Essex which collects the British Household Panel Study. We also wish to thank Peter Robinson for supplying data to us to enable us to reproduce his graphs on temporary and part-time employment.

Shirley Dex
Andrew McCulloch

1 Introduction

Has the notion of a job for life disappeared? Undoubtedly there have been changes in the nature of jobs in Britain since the 1970s. Some commentators have called the changes a revolution, and a casualisation of the labour market (Social Justice Commission report; Hutton, 1995). Others have suggested this characterisation vastly overstates the changes which have taken place (Robinson, 1995); flexible jobs are argued to represent the voluntary preferences of many people. However, there is no doubt that this is a topical issue and on the agenda of politicians who are concerned about the lack of 'feel-good' factor in the British electorate.

Flexible work is now a familiar phrase used to describe some of the changes which have been occurring in Britain's structure of employment, competitiveness and regeneration. It is used as a descriptive term, a prescriptive term, and even as a term of abuse. It is used interchangeably with 'non-standard forms of employment', 'atypical work' or 'marginal work'. It is attached to jobs, firms and labour markets at local and national levels. It has come to be associated of late with the deregulating labour market changes brought about by Mrs Thatcher's government although in fact some of the elements of flexible employment have much longer histories.

Flexible work means a variety of different things, but at its most basic it is a description of a change in the distribution of labour market jobs, away from standard full-time permanent employee contracts, and towards a growth in various types of non-standard employment forms. Increased flexibility has been viewed as positive and prescriptive by government policy which has regarded labour market deregulation and the growth of flexible jobs as being part of the same process (Watson, 1994). Deregulation has been an attempt to free the labour market through the greater use of jobs with non-standard conditions of employment; for example, part-time workers (especially those working less than 16 hours per week), seasonal, casual, fixed term contracts and other temporary workers and freelancers. Also, the implication is that these jobs will be shorter than those of earlier generations; individuals will need to be flexible and have a succession of jobs over their lifetime.

During the 1980s, the regulatory framework for the labour market in Britain underwent a series of changes, changes which have been

1

described as promoting labour market deregulation. The rationale for the package of new measures is aptly captured in the Employment Department's overall aim: 'To support economic growth by promoting a competitive, efficient and flexible labour market' (Employment Department Group, 1991). This aim is also seen as a vital element if Britain is to survive in the increasingly competitive product markets of Europe and the rest of the world. As well as documenting some of these changes, previous commentators have questioned whether they are likely to achieve the ends of greater efficiency, or the macro-economic goals they are meant to offer the British labour market. There has been some discussion of both employers' and individuals' views about these changes. The impact of labour market fragmentation on pay has been examined by Rubery (1992) and Industrial Relations Services (1992).

Interest in marginal workers in the European Community has been increasing (Meulders and Plasman, 1992). There are many labour market changes which are giving the impression that labour markets are being restructured away from stable permanent (male) jobs, towards more unstable temporary (female) jobs. There is the overall growth in women's employment, the growth in part-time work in services, increases in self-employment, declines in men's full-time employment in manufacturing industries and an associated decline in unionisation, increases in male unemployment, and the expectation that stiffer competition in the Single European Market is likely to produce pressures to reduce costs, pay and job security. If these non-standard forms of employment increase some individuals will be suffering downturns in their conditions of work and their pay and security. The Social Charter, of course, was designed partly to protect workers from these potential changes.

Britain's move towards greater amounts of flexible work necessitates our asking a number of questions.

- Are flexible jobs truly inferior in comparison with the standard full-time permanent contracts of employment? If so, what are the implications of this inferiority for individuals and households?
- How are flexible jobs distributed between different groups and households in Britain?
- How does flexible work affect gender inequalities in the labour market?
- Is there a feel-bad factor associated with flexible jobs?
- Does flexible work help to cause unemployment or does it help the unemployed to leave unemployment behind?

- Do employers need this sort of flexibility? Are such jobs necessary if Britain is to survive in global markets?
- What are the disadvantages to Britain, its working population and the business community of going further down the route of flexible employment?

In this book we begin to tackle these questions. We present the latest statistics and evidence on the extent of flexible work, how it is distributed and how it is affecting Britain's working population. We also begin to place the structure of employment in 1990s Britain in the context of her competitors in the industrialised world.

We examine whether employers are changing their employment practices in the light of the new climate in labour market relations, the ways in which they are doing so and the reasons for their actions. We also examine flexible jobs from the individual's and the household's perspectives, providing an overview of the relative levels of non-standard or flexible work using large-scale nationally representative surveys. We document some of the characteristics of these jobs and the employees who hold them. Trends in the growth of flexible work in recent years are also documented, although unfortunately the available large-scale sources do not allow us to investigate all types of flexible work. Lastly, we examine flexible work in the context of the national and cross-national labour markets along with some of the policy implications this raises.

DEFINING 'FLEXIBLE WORK'

While flexible work is a much discussed topic, it can mean different things to different people. In order to be clear about the aspects of flexible work with which we are concerned in this book, we outline the list of possibilities below. The following types of jobs may be characterised as being flexible:

1. self-employment including subcontractors and freelancers but excluding the self-employed with employees;
2. part-time work, especially jobs with very low hours which do not ensure eligibility to the National Insurance system and thus to many state benefits and, prior to 1995, to employment protection legislation;
3. temporary work;
4. fixed-term contract work;

5. zero-hours contract employment;
6. seasonal work;
7. annual hours work, shift work, job sharing, flexitime, Sunday working, overtime, term-time only work or compressed working weeks.
8. working at home;
9. teleworking;
10. term-time working;
11. Sunday working;
12. job sharers.

Firms have been considered to be moving towards increased flexibility in a number of ways. The reasons for these changes vary, but for many they can be encapsulated as reflecting a desire for greater efficiency:

Numerical flexibility – the ability of firms to adjust the number of workers they wish to pay according to the demand for labour, as assessed by the demand for its goods and services. (Flexible work items 1, 2, 3, 4, 5, 6, 8, 10, 11, 12);

Functional flexibility – the ability of firms to transfer labour between tasks. Sometimes this requires that job demarcations be broken down. (This could be associated with any of the other flexible items or be carried out separately.)

Labour market flexibility or labour mobility – the ease with which labour can transfer between regions, industries and organisations according to changes in economic conditions. (Flexible work items 1 and 9);

Working time flexibility – the number and timing of work hours from week to week, day to day, or year to year. This type of flexibility is a particular form of numerical flexibility. (Flexible work items 2, 5, 6, 7, 8, 9, 10, 11, 12);

Place of work flexibility – covers flexibility to work outside the employer's workplace, either at home or from home, as a teleworker or as a more traditional homeworker. (Flexible work items 1, 2, 5, 6, 8 and 9);

Clearly there are some links between these different forms of flexibility and the job characteristics they imply. This is partly illustrated in the list of 'flexible work' items which are attached to most of these meanings of flexibility. Our data allow us to document the ways in which, and extent to which, numerical flexibility is appearing in individuals' working lives. Also, we are able to examine how flexible work affects households as well as individuals. However, we are not able to provide any quantitative evidence about zero-hours contracts (item 5) on the list of flexible work forms because they are not yet separate categories coded by any of the major surveys.

POST-FORDISM

Flexibility is one of the major themes describing the phase of post-Fordist production in the global economy. In this phase of economic development, capital's capacity to increase productivity under the old system of production is argued to have failed. New technologies coupled with increasing competitive pressures characterise the new organisational structures of post-Fordist production. Large hierarchical bureaucracies give way to smaller conglomerations of small companies linked through informal networks which concentrate on producing goods and services for specialist niche markets (Amin, 1994). Industrial districts are spawned (Piore and Sabel, 1984). The growth of subcontracting, self-employment and temporary work are types of employment which characterise this phase of production. Flexible practices within firms mirror the flexibility between firms. However, flexible practices within firms have been argued to be a new form of social control over workers (Gottfried, 1992).

The gender implications of post-Fordism were initially neglected, largely because the theory originated from descriptions of the changes occurring in men's skilled manual work in manufacturing. Research has since begun to investigate gender relationships more fully (Walby, 1989; Acker, 1992; Smith, 1993). The rhetoric of flexibility in these jobs was found not to coincide with the reality of them; men and women have been found to experience flexibility differently as a result of the different positions they occupy in the social structure (Smith, 1993); flexible practices in the workplace have been found to build on, as well as create, gendered subcultures (Gottfried and Graham, 1993); flexibility in the workplace often ends up reinforcing rather than helping to dismantle gender and class hierarchies in the workforce (Walby, 1989).

An alternative framework for understanding the rise of flexible employment comes from a regulative and institutional framework which, like post-Fordism, assumes that a cross-national perspective is required for a more complete understanding.

A FRAMEWORK FOR THE ANALYSIS OF LABOUR MARKET FLEXIBILITY

Rubery (1989) has done most to elaborate a regulative framework in which labour market flexibility can be understood. She outlined four main sets of economic and social institutions which structure an employment system. The four components are, the system of labour market regulation, the labour market system, the industrial system and the system of social reproduction.

The first component, the system of labour market regulation, includes legal and voluntary regulation. The legal element defines 'employees', 'employee rights', and who is eligible for paying tax, etc. The voluntary element consists of making standards across industries or at national levels, union demarcations and agreements, employer and union attitudes, and legal restraints on voluntary behaviour.

The second component, the labour market system, consists of labour market flows, access to employment for those out of employment, non-standard employment forms, labour supply conditions and non-standard employment, training systems, and the stocks and flows of skilled workers.

The third part, the industrial system, consists of the structure of industry, the sectoral shares, the size distribution of firms and vertical and horizontal integration, as well as employer policies and strategies for competitiveness. Employer policy covers the variability of product demand, technological conditions, managerial ethos and the impact of labour market conditions on policy.

Lastly, the system of social reproduction includes the systems of income maintenance and child-rearing and family systems. It covers how far the state and family support young children, the unemployed and the elderly, the regulations on supplementing benefit income through casual work, social attitudes towards labour force participation and state and market provisions of services for child-rearing.

These components have clear links with certain traditional categories of labour market analysis: the supply side (labour market system), and the demand side (industrial system). Discussions by economists would usually take the legal and policy framework as given, exogenous, and leave it largely in the background. Similarly, the system of reproduction would tend to be neglected in a consideration of economic restructuring. What is important about Rubery's framework is that all of these elements are brought into the picture. The implication is that it is not possible to understand restructuring, labour market flexibility and marginalised workers, without all of the elements being considered together. This view will be demonstrated to be a useful one through the analysis presented in this paper. That all of these components need to be considered together becomes very obvious when women and marginal workers are the focus. This book can only begin to assemble part of the necessary data that a thorough consideration of all of these components would necessitate. However, it is a start.

REGULATORY CHANGES

A number of changes to the regulations which affect the labour market took place over the 1980s. Blanchflower and Freeman (1994, table 2.2) list them under four headings: reductions in union power; changes in the welfare state to give increases to work incentives; reductions in government's role in the labour market; and enhancing self-employment and skills. In Chapter 2 we discuss the labour market regulations operating in the 1990s which affect the costs to employers of different types of standard and non-standard contracts of employment. Here we review the way regulation and changes in the regulatory framework in Britain have affected the way bargaining over pay and conditions is carried out. The changes amount to increases in decentralisation, and of course changes in the way regulations are made also affect the outcomes of pay and conditions.

Probably the main change in the framework has come from the decline in trade union coverage and the associated increasing fragmentation of the system of pay determination in Britain in the 1980s (Beatson, 1993; Beatson and Butcher, 1993). A range of more specific measures have contributed to these changes. Employers have been encouraged to end national collective bargaining; compulsory competitive tendering has been introduced for contracts in the public sector; there have been restrictions on secondary trade union action; there has been the abolition of the fair wages clause which required firms working as subcontractors for central or local government to pay the 'going-rate'; the Wages Councils have been abolished; and legislation which prevented women from carrying out night work and restricted their amount of overtime has been repealed.

These changes have resulted in a marked increase in the range of pay settlements (Brown, 1987) and a widening in the structure of pay differentials (Rubery, 1989). However, this micro-level pay variation, with pay varying according to the ability to pay of individual firms, has not been matched by macro-level pay flexibility. The fact that average real wage growth has outstripped growth in productivity is arguably caused by average earnings not varying with the ability to pay of the whole economy. Studies have also shown that the union mark-up on wages stayed approximately constant through the 1980s (Blanchflower and Freeman, 1994).

As far as individual employee rights are concerned, little changed from the passing of the 1978 Employment Protection (Consolidation) Act to 1994 when employment protection legislation changed. There has not been time for the most recent changes to have an impact. This study, therefore, is set in the context of the employment protection legislation which was in place from 1975.

With the exception of some extensions to the eligibility rules for maternity leave, qualifying periods for employment protection remained largely unchanged from 1978 to 1994. Under the terms of this legislation, those who were contracted to work for 16 hours or more per week had the right to receive redundancy payments if they had two years' continuous service with the same employer (those who were contracted to work between 8 and 16 hours per week generally had this right after five years' continuous service and those working less than eight hours per week had no rights). Those working 16 hours or more per week also had the right to take an unfair dismissal case.

The most recent employment protection legislation, as part of the Trade Union Reform and Employment Rights Act 1993, has removed the hours threshold for entitlement to employment protection. Consequently, many part-time jobs which were previously uncovered are now covered. The rights to statutory maternity leave have recently been changed. Under this legislation that came into effect after February 1995, all women, irrespective of length of service or hours of work are now entitled to a minimum period of 14 weeks' maternity leave. This improves the position of many women employed part-time who formerly would not have been eligible. The rights of part-timers have also improved through a series of court cases which have ruled that the statutory exclusions of part-time workers working less than 16 hours per week, in respect of redundancy and unfair dismissal rights, were directly discriminatory.

It is instructive to note, however, that at least two European studies have found that Britain has the least amount of regulation among European countries (Brunhes, 1988; Emerson, 1988). However, the relative absence of legal regulation does not mean that institutional pressures are absent in British labour markets. Such pressures are likely to be specific to individual organisations and arise from custom and practice in particular establishments.

The benefit system has increased the pressure on men, in particular, to accept flexible jobs. Unemployed men are now encouraged to take part-time employment or risk losing their benefit. Since 1992, the unemployed have been required to take any reasonable job providing it offers at least 16 hours work (previously 24 hours) per week, or risk losing benefit. Other more minor institutional pressures are reviewed in Rubery (1994).

European Commission Directives and judgements in the European Court of Justice can also affect the status and legal position of flexible work in Britain. There have been a series of directives which, if enacted, would improve the rights of part-time and temporary workers. Women's rights to maternity leave have recently been improved following a directive on maternity leave, as described above. European law has ruled that it is indirectly discriminatory to treat part-timers differently from full-timers. The Equal Opportunities Commission (EOC) brought a case under European law which successfully challenged the exclusion of part-timers from unfair dismissal and redundancy pay rights.

The introduction of flexible forms of work within the public sector appears to have occurred alongside the protection of status, conditions, contracts and union collective bargaining for a privileged core workforce (Rubery, 1989).

Some would argue that these changes in the framework preceded the growth in flexible work forms and have facilitated them. Others argue that flexibility and deregulation are separate notions.[1] As Rubery (1989) and Deakin (1988) have pointed out, the system of labour market regulation, both legal and voluntary, is the framework which shapes the employment contract. This determines the incentives and opportunities for employers to develop forms of employment which lie outside the normal regulatory framework. One argument in favour of deregulated markets is that high levels of regulation provide incentives for employers to create employment forms which lie outside the coverage of regulation. If this were the primary motivation for nonstandard working contracts, we might expect deregulation to be associated with shrinking amounts of flexible work. This sort of reasoning might explain the relative lack of change in temporary work in Britain. It does not help to explain the large increases in part-time work or in self-employment. There is, in any case, little evidence to suggest that unions have actively resisted the development of flexible work (ACAS, 1988).[2]

Firms in Britain appear to have a greater ability and opportunity than firms in other countries to introduce flexibility without the need to create special employment forms which facilitate the evasion of regulation. Explanations of the growth of part-time and self-employment cannot therefore be wholly attributed to the legal employment protection system. Rubery (1994) has argued that incentives to use part-time, temporary or self-employed workers are also likely to come from the fiscal system and from the industrial relations system. For example, there are fiscal incentives for firms to use the self-employed and some part-timers and some temporary workers since they can avoid paying national insurance contributions, sick pay and fringe benefits for these workers.

DATA SOURCES

We draw upon a variety of sources. For the employer's perspective we draw on published studies and surveys. For the individual's perspective we have carried out our own analyses of the nationally representative quarterly Labour Force Survey and the first three waves of the British Household Panel Study 1991–93. The British Household Panel Survey Wave 3 (1993) retrospective history provided the data for the lifetime perspective on individuals' and households' experiences of flexible jobs. Statistics about the labour markets of other industrialised countries come largely from the OECD statistical material and from another employer's survey. The two British large-scale nationally representative surveys which we have analysed are described in a little more detail below.

Labour Force Survey

The Labour Force Survey (LFS) is a household sample survey of around 60 000 households. Before 1984 it was conducted every two years. Between 1984 and 1991 it was carried out annually, and since 1992 it has been carried out quarterly. The LFS questionnaire covers a wide range of employment-related questions. These questions allow an investigation to be made of the extent of different forms of non-standard employment in Britain. We have used the Spring 1994 version of the LFS for our most recent picture of flexible work; earlier years, 1975, 1981 and 1986, are used to show how flexible work has been changing over time. Unfortunately, some of the relevant questions have changed during the life of the survey so it has not always been possible to provide a series over the 1980s on all particular forms of flexible work.

The precise definitions used for the types of flexible job that it is possible to examine from the LFS and from other data are set out in Appendix Table A1.1.

British Household Panel Study

The British Household Panel Study (BHPS) allows us to investigate flexible work in Britain in a number of ways. A summary of the details of the survey, its size and response rates are provided in the Appendix. Each panel wave contains information which enables us to identify flexible work of the following kinds: self-employment, part-time work, low-hours work, second jobs, temporary and fixed term contracts, and home work.

In addition, at Waves 2 and 3, the survey collected a retrospective employment status and job history in which self-employment, part-time and temporary work are all distinguishable in the past employment of the surveyed individuals. Individuals were allowed to define these states for themselves (see Table A1.1). The value of this record is that it enables us to see how many and which individuals have experienced flexible work at some time in their work history, at what point they experienced it, how long they spent in this state, and how it fits into their overall career pattern. Individuals in the BHPS sample at Wave 3 recalled in total of the order of 32 000 past jobs when they were interviewed. Unfortunately, individuals did not always remember all of the details of every job, or their start and end dates. Details of the extent to which individuals remembered the various aspects of their jobs are described in the Appendix.

A further benefit of the BHPS data is that this information on flexible work is available for all adult household members. This means that it is possible to match up flexible work experiences within households to see whether such experiences accumulate within households, or whether one individual's flexibility is matched by a more permanent position for a spouse or another household member.

PLAN OF THE BOOK

The book is divided into a number of parts. These cover the different aspects of the issues which flexible work raises. In Part I there are two chapters which examine the role flexible work plays for employers in the economy (Chapter 2) and the types of jobs which are flexible jobs in British labour markets (Chapter 3). In Part II four chapters review the extent to which individuals are holding flexible jobs in Britain in the 1990s (Chapter 4), the characteristics of individuals who are in flexible jobs (Chapter 5), how this aggregate picture changed over the 1980s (Chapter 6), and how flexible jobs have appeared through the lifecycle of individuals (Chapter 7). Part III contains only one chapter which takes a household perspective on the experience of flexible jobs (Chapter 8). This is a vital but often neglected level of examining issues. Many of the issues that flexible jobs raise for individuals are issues that households and not just individuals are forced to address. Part IV contains two chapters which tackle the place of Britain in the global economy, the policy issues and the future of Britain's jobs. Chapter 9 focuses on how Britain's jobs compare with those of other industrialised countries. Chapter 10 draws together some conclusions about the questions which were raised at the outset of the book. The forecasts for the structure of Britain's jobs in the year 2000 and its implications for policies and economic strategies are also considered in the concluding chapter.

Notes

1. McLaughlin (1994) makes this point. However her main argument is that the jobs which are created alongside deregulation are actually contributing to inflexibility in the labour market because they are helping to entrench polarisation and segmentation.
2. An ACAS survey of private manufacturing firms found union-recognised plants with relatively high levels of multiple forms of flexibility.

Part I
Employers and the Labour Market

2 Employers' Use of Flexible Work

Much of the literature on employers and flexible work emerged from a number of founding studies. Atkinson (1984) and Atkinson and Meager (1986) introduced the term 'flexible firm' to the literature in Britain which discussed how firms were changing to face up to competitive pressures. Piore and Sabel (1984) were US researchers making similar points on a much broader canvas about global markets. The picture painted by these studies was of employers seeking to invest their available resources on a 'core' staff of permanent, full-time, largely male employees and using a 'periphery' group of temporary, part-time, largely female and poorly paid workforce to fill in the gaps on a short term basis, and at the lowest possible cost. The periphery group would probably be denied the conditions of employment, the fringe benefits, and other advantages of the full-time employees. This framework has been much disputed (Pollert, 1991). However, it is clear that some changes have been occurring. There have been studies in Britain to test out whether this framework accords with employers' views of their strategies. We review these studies below, but first we consider the relative costs and benefits of flexible, non-standard forms of employment in comparison with the so-called core jobs. We consider them in theory and by measurement. The case for employers adopting strategies to increase their use of flexible jobs rests on there being clear advantages to their doing so – advantages which are not outweighed by disadvantages of pursuing such strategies.

THE CASE FOR FLEXIBLE EMPLOYMENT IN THEORY

Hill et al. (1989) have offered some points of theoretical reasoning about employers' decisions to create flexible jobs: Flexible employment is likely to increase or be generated

- where there are anticipated changes in output, relative factor prices or production technology;
- where there are unanticipated changes in output, relative factor prices or production technology;

15

- where there is an absence of alternative employment opportunities;
- or where there is no resistance to the changes.

Anticipated changes could be responded to by altering existing employment opportunities. This means that unanticipated changes are the most likely candidates driving a desire for flexibility; flexibility then becomes an instrument to reduce fixed costs and thereby cope with uncertainty. A flexible employment contract offers the possibility of transferring the uncertainty from the employer onto the employee, although this transfer will only be possible where alternative and better employment offers are absent. Uncertainty is likely to lead to the desire for manpower flexibility and slack or unorganised labour markets provide the oppportunity for the desire to be realised.

RELATIVE COSTS OF DIFFERENT FORMS OF EMPLOYMENT

What are the costs of employment? There is of course individuals' pay, the most substantial item. But in addition, the regulatory framework for the labour market imposes a range of other non-wage costs on employers. Some of these will be mandatory because they are legislated for; some of them will be the subject of negotiation and some will be voluntary on the part of employers, although they might be necessary to keep the workforce from having too high turnover. We list in Table 2.1 the various kinds of non-wage labour costs which typically apply in Britain. The same items can appear under each of the broad headings. This is because there is often a statutory minimum set, for example, for maternity leave entitlement, but then particular employers can agree after negotiation with a union to improve on the statutory benefits offered by their firm. On the other hand, in non-union establishments, the decision to improve on the statutory minimum package of benefits may be voluntary.

Commentators are clear that the legal position of atypical workers is inferior to those with regular and permanent employee status contracts (Dickens, 1992). The de facto position of workers with non-standard contracts is also much worse than for those with standard contracts. We review the main differences in the legal and de facto position of atypical workers below.

In terms of the legal position we can consider a number of elements of non-wage costs; firstly national insurance contributions (although this arguably is a wage cost); statutory sick pay; maternity leave en-

Table 2.1   Elements of non-wage labour costs in Britain in the 1990s

Type of cost to employer	Items
Unavoidable fixed costs	Recruitment and turnover Training
Mandatory/Statutory legislation	National insurance contributions Redundancy pay Maternity leave/pay Sick pay
Negotiated	Pension contributions Holiday pay Maternity pay/leave improvements Sick pay improvements Other benefits
Voluntary	Pension contributions Holiday pay Private health insurance Other benefits

titlement; unfair dismissal and statutory redundancy entitlements.

The national insurance contributions which employers pay for their employees were subject to a lower earnings limit, £56 per week in 1994. Employers did not pay contributions for employees earning below this amount. This means that low-hours part-timers will be cheaper to employ per hour than full-timers. The same earnings thresholds apply to eligibility for statutory sick pay and statutory maternity leave. Temporary workers on contracts of less than three months' duration are not entitled to statutory sick pay. On these latter two benefits to employees, the state bears the majority of the cost of these statutory schemes, but they still involve a cost to employers and a disruption to work which could both be avoided by employing low-hours part-timers. The cost to employees of not participating in the social security system in this way can be considerable; they lose entitlement to unemployment benefit and state pensions as well as to maternity leave, and statutory sick pay when they are ill.

Eligibility to maternity leave, unfair dismissal rights and redundancy pay, up to 1994, has also been subject to both an hours rule and a continuous service rule. Those who worked 16 or more hours per week had to have worked for their employer for at least two years to be eligible for these benefits; those who worked between 8 and 15 hours per week had to have worked for their employer for at least five years. A number of other non-standard forms of work are also ineligible for these benefits; those on annualised hours, and those on zero-hours or on-call contracts. Neither do voluntary overtime hours count towards the hours requirements. Since 1979, the length of service condition of eligibility for many benefits has been increased from six months before 1979 to one year in 1979 to two years in 1985. This means that many part-timers and many temporary workers have not been eligible to receive these benefits, which do not therefore impinge on employers' non-wage costs. It has become progressively more difficult for temporary workers to be entitled to many benefits. The hours conditions for these benefits was abandoned in 1994/5, but the two years service requirement remains.

The 1988 Labour Force Survey data found that 55 per cent of all part-time employees were not covered by the main employment rights through a combination of hours and length of service requirements compared with 29 per cent of full-timers.

We can see, therefore, that the statutory requirements for entitlement to some of the major employment-related benefits disadvantage part-time and temporary workers. Studies have also shown that part-timers and temporary workers are in fact disadvantaged when it comes to many of the negotiated or voluntary benefits employers give to their employees. Horrell et al. (1989), Marsh (1991) and Wood and Smith (1989) found that part-timers were less likely than full-timers to have access to accommodation, time off, meal subsidies, recreational facilities, staff housing loans, discount purchases, share participation/profit sharing schemes, private medical insurance, and use of company cars, as well as to paid holidays and occupational pension schemes. Temporary workers were also less likely than part-timers to be receiving the fringe benefits on this list. In 1991, of those employees whose employer had a pension scheme, 82 per cent of full-time permanent men were members of the scheme, compared with 81 per cent of men in part-time permanent and 50 per cent of men in temporary jobs. For women, 73 per cent of those employed in full-time permanent, compared with 47 per cent in part-time permanent and 49 per cent in temporary jobs were members of the scheme.[1]

It is difficult to put a figure on these fringe benefits, but it is clear that, based on average total costs, temporary workers cost employers the least amount per hour, followed by part-timers, and that full-time permanent employees cost employers the most in terms of the total cost per employee per hour paid out. Clearly there are financial incentives to employers to create non-standard forms of jobs.

Recent case law in the European Court has granted new rights to part-time workers which will improve their position. They are now entitled to pro rata benefits with full-timers for occupational pension contributions. Although this will eliminate for employers some of the savings of employing part-timers over employing full-timers, the differential in relative costs will remain from differences in the list of other entitlements.

Against the potential savings of employing workers with non-standard contracts of employment, employers must balance a set of costs of adopting such policies. Recruitment costs will be higher the higher the turnover of staff, and temporary jobs are likely to add to recruitment costs. If staff morale and motivation are affected by a more insecure environment, these can increase staff turnover as well as affecting productivity. Clearly these costs act as a brake on employers who might otherwise abandon permanent contracts for their employees.

EMPLOYER STUDIES

A number of studies of employers' labour use strategies have considered elements of flexible work. Since these have argued that the different forms of work should be treated separately, it is best to summarise their findings under the separate headings. It is worth making one general point about the results of the 1987 Employers' Labour Use Strategies (ELUS) survey. At that time there was little evidence that, with the exception of temporary work, employers used flexible work forms in any other than traditional ways for the type of work in question. New strategies were found in a small minority of establishments, where the use of flexible labour was already high. As a whole, however, very few firms could be said to have a strategy for using labour at all. They responded primarily pragmatically to product market demands.[2] Surveys for the period 1990 to 1994 by IRS (1994b) confirmed this impression. They found that it was more common for employers to look for greater flexibility in the use of permanent full-time workforce than to achieve flexibility by using non-standard workers. The researchers who analysed the ELUS survey predicted that the use of flexible work was unlikely to increase because of changes in firms' labour use strategies, although it might rise because of structural changes in demand with increases in the sectors traditionally using flexible work forms.

There are a number of reasons why this may not fully represent the changes which are occurring in the labour force. The large-scale reorganisations in the public sector and the effects on workers' contracts did not seem to be anticipated by the ELUS researchers (McGregor and Sproull, 1991; Hunter and MacInnes, 1991). Other recent surveys are drawing attention to increases in non-standard forms of employment, (IRS, 1994a; Reed, 1995; IM, 1994). However in most cases the results are based on extremely small samples which are far from providing a representative picture. Proctor et al. (1994) have pointed out that some of the earlier debate over Atkinson's work, and this applies to the work on the ELUS survey, has rested on an unnecessarily narrow meaning of the term 'strategy'. This has taken strategy as 'plan'. They argue that strategy can also be regarded as the 'patterns' in decision-making, in which case new strategies might be found to be more widespread. The Neathey and Hurstfield (1995) study has confirmed that new practices are being adopted in the retail and finance industries, although many employers would not call these new strategies.

Part Time

The ELUS survey of 1988 found that 85 per cent of establishments had at least one part-time employee.[3] Dex, Walters and Alden (1993) and McGregor and Sproull (1991) reviewed the reasons employers gave for using part-time workers. These included the need to meet peak periods in production or distribution, and the inability to get full-time workers of the desired quality. Surveys have found that employers have not, to any great extent, given the cost advantages of part-time workers as their reason for employing them (Beechey and Perkins, 1987; McGregor and Sproull, 1991). Part-time employees are obviously popular among employers, who regard their (hourly) productivity as often being higher than that of equivalent full-timers (McGregor and Sproull, 1991).

Cross-national comparisons have examined why British employers like part-time employment more than would appear to be the case in other countries. In the case of France employment regulation and pro rata pay and conditions make part-time employment less flexible or attractive for employers where it can also be seen as disruptive to the normal organization of work, (O'Reilly, 1994). However studies of retail supermarkets find that the pressures of competition are making part-time employment more attractive in France as well as in Britain as a way of matching labour requirements more precisely to customer shopping habits (Gregory, 1987).

The most recent study by Neathey and Hurstfield (1995) of non-standard workers in finance and retail in Britain suggests that part-time work for women with small children may not increase in the future. This study points out that employers are now using zero-hours contracts to seek even more flexibility from their workforces which the more traditional flexible workers, part-time married women with small children, may be unable to fulfil.

Temporary Work

Casey's (1988) analysis of the use of temporary work by employers in 1984 found that one-fifth of establishments used temporary workers and 6–7 per cent of establishments were high users. There was no evidence that this percentage had increased between 1980 and 1984. The ELUS survey in 1988 found that 34 per cent of establishments had at least one temporary employee and 20 per cent had at least one agency temp.[4] Service industries and large firms were more likely to use temporary workers, although manufacturing industries were more likely to use agency temporary workers. Temporary work was over-represented in small establishments which accounted for 50 per cent of all temporary workers (but only 37 per cent of all jobs). It was also over-represented in the South East. This was especially true for agency temporary work, 72 per cent of which was located in this region. There was no evidence that establishments were less likely to use temporary work where they had a dominant market position, where they were insensitive to competitors' pricing decisions, or where they were more capital intensive. The use of temporary work was less likely where activity in the establishment was declining, and where unions were stronger. The use of temporary work was found to be unrelated to establishments' use of other forms of flexible work. Millward's (1995) analysis of the Workplace Industrial Relations Survey (WIRS) also found that different types of non-standard workers were used in different types of workplace rather than being concentrated in the same type of workplace.

McGregor and Sproull (1991) showed that temporary workers were usually employed for established reasons. Temporary workers can be used to hold down the firm's wage bill, to match labour use to fluctuations in demand, to reduce non-wage costs, to cover work of limited duration (e.g. seasonal, or one-off contracts), or to provide short-term cover. There are cases of private sector temporary contracts being used to exclude employees from fringe benefits and thereby reduce costs.[5]

Since this could be done legally in Britain without using a temporary contract, using such contracts in this way may be a device to avoid industrial relations problems.

The analysis of the 1993 LFS found that the sectors in which temporary work is concentrated vary throughout the year. In the summer, 12 per cent of male employees in agriculture, forestry and fishing were temporary. In contrast, in spring, the largest proportion of male temporary workers, 8 per cent, was in other services. An IRS survey (IRS, 1994b) in 1993 found that two-thirds of employers did not have fixed-term contract workers, but among those who did they had been increasing the size of this workforce. Those employing fixed-term contract workers employed on average 2.5 per cent of their workforce on such contracts. Professional and clerical workers were found to be the most common occupational groups. In common with part-time working, other sorts of temporary job tend to be more junior and less skilled positions (IRS, 1994a).

A sizeable proportion of temporary contracts in Britain are in the public sector (IRS Employment Trends 539 1993). Escott and Whitfield (1995) have examined the reasons for using temporary workers in local government. A temporary contract in the public sector can be more of a signal that such posts are not permanent.

Some studies have also examined whether agency temporary work should be distinguished from other types of temporary work, even though it comprises a minority of temporary jobs. It is unclear in law and in employment protection legislation whether agency temporary workers should be classified as employees or as the self-employed for contractual purposes, whereas for tax purposes they are viewed as employees. However, in other respects their characteristics seem very similar to those of other temporary workers and they are difficult to distinguish in studies (McGregor and Sproull, 1991). Moreover, the distinctions between temporary workers and part-timers are not always clear to employers.[6] Temporary employment was the one area of flexible work where new strategies of employers were found to be in use in 1987; even so, only a small minority of employers were using such strategies.

Self-employment and Subcontracting

The 1988 ELUS survey found that 75 per cent of establishments used some subcontractors.[7] The ACAS (1988) survey found that in 1987, 77 per cent of organisations used outside contractors and as many as

90 per cent of manufacturers subcontracted. The 1990 Workplace Industrial Relations Survey (WIRS) found that 16 per cent of establishments employed freelancers.[8] The ACAS survey established a significant relationship between the use of subcontracting and firm size, such that it was the larger firms, over 500 employees, who made the most frequent use of subcontracting.

The self-employed are to be found concentrated in construction, distribution, hotels, repairs and other services. These industries cover 62 per cent of the self-employed. Self-employment rates differ by industry. The shifts in industry distributions help to explain some of the 1981–91 increase in self-employment, but by no means all of it. Industry variations also help to explain some of the regional differences in rates of self-employment. Self-employment is higher in East Anglia and Wales than in other regions (Campbell and Daly, 1992).

The main reasons that employers subcontract work to the self-employed, rather than take on an employee, vary according to the type of work being considered. In the case of professional services, the demand for this work may not be sufficient to warrant having a permanent employee to do the work. Freelancers were found to be employed especially in mechanical engineering, construction, business services and in higher education in the 1990 WIRS survey (IRS, 1994b). However, there have been few studies of the use of the self-employed and the results of one study which examined this issue did not reach any firm conclusions. Certainly, up to 1987, there was no evidence that establishments had new and formal strategies for employing more of the self-employed.[9]

Campbell and Daly examined the reasons for the apparent increase in self-employment in the 1980s. Seven potential explanations were examined. No single one fully explained the nature of all of the changes. Changes in the structure of demand with increases towards sectors where self-employment is more common did contribute to the explanation.[10] Similarly, there was some evidence supporting the other explanations, that technological advances, the fragmentation of larger firms, the economic cycle, demographic changes, start-up capital increases and government policies promoting self-employment have helped to increase self-employment. On the effects of the business cycle, some studies have found that self-employment increases in periods of unemployment and other studies have found it decreases.[11]

Homework

A survey of a random sample of 1000 employers found that one in ten had at least one home-based worker (Huws, 1994a). Rubery and Wilkinson (1981) examined the factors that employers considered when deciding whether to use homeworkers and outworkers. They found that employers took account of a wider range of factors than cheapness. These included whether the capital equipment fits domestic circumstances; the frequency of small bottlenecks; a shortage of factory space; having insufficient in-workers with appropriate skills, and a shortage of time for in-workers to train new in-workers. In the case of some industries, for example the fashion industry, homeworkers in Britain have been used in preference to cheaper overseas labour because of the short lead time which requires quick turnaround of the sewn garments in a rapidly changing market with increasingly customised products (Phizacklea, 1990). Hakim (1985) found that firms using freelance and outworkers were more profitable than those which did not use such forms of labour. Even though the lower cost of homeworkers may not be the main reason for their use, there clearly are cost advantages to employers. For example, Bisset and Huws (1984) found that few traditional homeworkers had any fringe benefits attached to their contract, even though the majority worked more than 16 hours per week.

Telework

A survey of a random sample of employers found that one in twenty had at least one staff member dependent on working at home and dependent on IT. The Reed (1995) survey found that 14 per cent of firms were using teleworkers in 1995. IDS (1994) suggested that between 5 and 15 per cent of firms were using teleworkers and numbers depend upon the definition used. There are often relatively few teleworkers in any one firm. Telecottages, largely in rural areas, are increasing but they are in their early stages of development (IDS, 1994). In 1994 there were 90 but it is not clear how many have a long-term future. Some studies have found telework to be concentrated in financial and business services (IRS, 1994b), and in the public sector (IRS, 1994b) whereas others have found most use of teleworking in manufacturing (Reed, 1995) and least in health. Teleworkers are also concentrated in the South East. Studies agree that the larger the organisation, the more likely it is to use this as well as other forms of non-standard forms of employment. The differences between the results on the size of teleworking show up the problems of generalising from what, in some cases, are very small sample sizes and the extremely low response rates which characterise these surveys.

The advantages to employers of teleworking are seen by IDS (1994) and Haddon and Lewis (1994) as being a reduction in overheads, productivity improvements, and help in recruiting and retaining staff. Huws's (1994) survey of employers' use of teleworking found its main advantage to be its flexibility and convenience and its ability to reduce costs and solve travel problems. Managers expressed high levels of satisfaction with teleworkers whom they thought were more productive, more reliable, more loyal, produced better work and had lower rates of turnover and absenteeism than on-site workers (Huws, 1994).

There have been some notable attempts to try out teleworking and it is from these studies that we have the most information about this form of work. The European Union is also promoting teleworking (IDS, 1994). The IDS (1994) study and Haddon and Lewis (1994) review the trials instigated by British Telecom, a leading insurance group, Digital Equipment and others. While many were satisfied with the outcomes and thought the advantages to employees were significant, other lessons were learnt from these exercises. Teleworkers need to be restricted to those who can work alone in a motivated way and to those who do not miss the social relationships at work too much. There is often less saving on office space and overheads than might at first appear since employees still need to come into the workplace regularly. Also, some managers obviously find the management issues more difficult to handle. The early predictions that telework would be a huge growth area are now thought to have been unrealistic, partly because of the disadvantages to employees.

Sunday Work

Before the liberalisation of the law on Sunday trading, an employers' survey was carried out in Britain which focused on the extent to which employers used Sunday work and their reasons for doing so (Bosworth, 1994). The survey found that the use of Sunday work was extensive and only 18 per cent of establishments did not use Sunday working of any kind. Some establishments used it where their main service or production took place on Sunday, and in other cases it was a secondary activity which occurred on Sunday, for example maintenance which could not be carried out during weekdays. Some establishments were regular users of Sunday work, and some were only occasional users.

There were significant differences in the use of Sunday working by industry: non-manufacturing industries were far more likely to undertake their main production activity on Sunday, unlike manufacturing industries. Larger establishments were more likely than smaller ones to use Sunday work, either as their main or as secondary activities. There were regional differences in the extent of usage of Sunday work. The use by establishments of Sunday work was positively associated with their use of part-time workers, temporary workers and non-permanent full-timers. Sunday work appeared to be on the increase.

Zero-hours Contracts

Zero-hours contracts are a relatively new form of non-standard contract, although they are similar to on-call employment contracts which have a longer history. In a zero-hours contract, the employee agrees to be available for work, but is only called to work when the employer has work for them to do. The employee is usually only paid for the hours actually worked. The practices of a fast-food restaurant chain hit the headlines in 1995 where a worker was laid off during the day every time the restaurant was quiet, and taken back on when custom picked up. This form of employment is largely uncovered by employment legislation and the non-wage costs to employers of zero-hours contracts must be the lowest possible.

Currently, there are no national statistics on the extent to which employers are using this form of contract. Neathey and Hurstfield (1995) have carried out case-study research on a number of organisations using these contracts in the retail distribution and insurance industries. Employers have found these contracts appealing since they give them the maximum amount of flexibility in matching their labour force to the demands of customers. The advent of detailed computerised accounts of the variations in customer demand and competitive pressures have made it possible and have pushed companies to seek ever more flexible workforces.

CONCLUSIONS

This review of the research has identified a number of important points from earlier studies of flexible work, as well as indicating some areas where there are gaps in our understanding. It shows that it is unwise to regard all types of flexible work as homogeneous. There are clearly major differences in the reasons why employers have decided to take or create the various kinds of non-standard flexible jobs. There are however, some major problems of definition which relate to most of these forms of work. It is difficult to define unequivocally teleworking, homework, self-employment and even part-time employment. The same is true of the newer forms of non-standard employment like zero hours contracts, as shown in the Neathey and Hurstfield (1995) study. The definitions adopted will influence the extent to which statistics suggest that there have been changes in the extent of such work, as we will see in other chapters.

The evidence on employers' strategies up to the mid-1980s suggested that relatively few employers had formal strategies to create non-flexible jobs either to reduce non-wage labour costs or fringe benefits, or to make their employees more vulnerable by not being covered by employment protection legislation. However, if studies took a wider view of the meaning of strategy, they might find more evidence that changes are being implemented. Since the 1980s there have been a number of firms which have hit the headlines by restructuring their workforces with these aims in mind. It is likely that studies in the 1990s would find more evidence of this behaviour and the Neathey and Hurstfield (1995) study of deregulation supports this view. On the other hand, some of the recent surveys of employers which have claimed that the use of non-standard forms of work have increased are based on extremely small samples; they should be regarded as entirely preliminary.

Notes

1. These figures were calculated from an analysis of Wave 1 of the British Household Panel Study.
2. McGregor and Sproull (1991) and Hunter and MacInnes (1991) both make this point.
3. See McGregor and Sproull (1991).
4. See McGregor and Sproull (1991) and IRS (1994b).
5. Rubery (1994) and IRS (1995) describe some examples.
6. See Casey (1988) and McGregor and Sproull (1991).
7. See McGregor and Sproull (1991) and IRS (1994b).
8. See IRS (1994b).
9. See McGregor and Sproull (1991).
10. This is the theory offered by Piore and Sabel (1984) which suggests that modern economies are inevitably moving towards flexible specialisation in both product demand and labour use strategies.
11. For example Taylor's (1994) findings suggest that self-employment increases as vacancies increase and the economy is on the upswing. Campbell and Daly (1992) review studies which have found the opposite relationship.

3 The Labour Market of Flexible Jobs

In this chapter we analyse the characteristics of different types of employment contract and flexible work. We compare the flexible work categories with permanent full-time jobs. We examine men and women separately because the labour market is, to a large degree, segregated and segmented by gender. A range of characteristics are considered to see how far there are cross-sectional associations between certain characteristics and certain types of job. This part of our analysis uses mainly the Spring 1994 Labour Force Survey data. Industry, occupation, union membership, the durations of the jobs and their regions are all examined. Since these tables have all been published in an earlier publication, Dex and McCulloch (1995), we refer the reader to that source for the documentation of the statistics described here.

INDUSTRY – 1994 LFS

The extent of the different forms of employment in each broad industry group is displayed for men and for women in Tables 3.1 and 3.2. Industries vary considerably in the extent to which they use various forms of flexible work. At an aggregate level, agriculture is notable in having 44 per cent of its male employment as flexible employment, largely because it has a high proportion of self-employment. The other industries where men's flexible employment is high are construction (47 per cent), other services (25 per cent) and distribution (28 per cent). In most of these industries, self-employment accounts for a high percentage of men's flexible employment, although not to the same extent as in agriculture and construction. However, in the distribution and other service industries the percentage in men's part-time employment is also relatively high (15–16 per cent of men's employment in each industry). The percentage of men in temporary employment in other services is also relatively high (8 per cent of the industry employment).

There are some other notable pockets of men's flexible employment although they do not necessarily add up to a large total flexible percentage. Energy and water have a high percentage in temporary em-

Table 3.1   Men's non-standard employment by industry, LFS 1994.

Men – row per cent*

Industry	FT perm.	PT	Temporary all	season./ casual	fixed term	Self- empl.	N '000	Any flexible
Agriculture	39.8	8.3	2.7	1.5	1.0	51.1	342	43.7
Energy & water	90.9	0.5	6.1	0.2	4.8	1.9	293	7.6
Minerals, ores	91.1	1.7	3.6	0.4	2.2	3.4	495	7.7
Metals & other	90.1	1.4	3.1	0.3	1.8	4.8	1647	7.4
Manufacturing	85.5	4.1	2.3	0.9	0.7	7.9	1295	11.1
Construction	45.7	3.5	3.3	0.3	2.4	46.8	1616	46.6
Distribution	62.7	15.9	3.8	2.3	0.8	18.8	2374	27.5
Transport	78.7	5.3	3.8	1.2	1.5	12.6	1202	18.1
Banking & insurance	72.5	5.9	3.8	0.5	2.0	19.4	1594	19.6
Other services	71.0	14.9	8.3	1.5	5.9	9.7	2608	25.0
All	71.5	8.1	4.4	1.1	2.4	17.0	13 470	22.7

* Do not add up to 100% since categories are not comprehensive, and not mutually exclusive.
FT – Full-time : PT – Part-time

ployment (6 per cent) and other services have a high percentage of fixed-term contracts (6 per cent) many of which are likely to be in the public sector services.

The picture for women is similar in some respects, but there are also major differences (Table 3.2). In every industry a higher proportion of female than male employment is flexible. Thus whilst there are clearly differences in the extent to which industries use and create flexible jobs, they are always more likely to employ women than men in these jobs.

Agriculture has the highest percentage of women's flexible employment (68 per cent of employment in this industry). This is similar to men. However, while self-employment was high among women employed in agriculture, as it was among men, part-time work makes an even more significant and most important contribution to the total amount of women's flexible employment in this industry; in contrast part-time work was much less important for men in agriculture. The other industries which had large percentages of women in flexible jobs were distribution (65 per cent), other services (57 per cent), and construction (49 per cent). In general, it is a large amount of part-time women's employment which gives industries their high scores for flexible jobs,

Table 3.2 Women's non-standard employment by industry, LFS 1994

Women – row per cent*

Industry	FT perm.	PT	Temporary all	season./ casual	fixed- term	Self- empl.	N '000	Any flexible
Agriculture	22.7	49.0	4.6	4.0	0.6	34.1	110	68.1
Energy & water	68.7	23.9	9.5	2.4	4.8	1.1	66	30.6
Minerals, ores	77.8	14.5	6.0	0.7	3.9	2.8	156	21.4
Metals & Other	73.2	22.0	5.2	1.1	2.7	2.6	427	26.0
Manufacturing	67.3	27.0	3.8	2.0	0.9	7.6	730	31.4
Construction	50.5	43.9	3.4	0.4	2.2	8.5	180	48.5
Distribution	32.2	60.4	5.2	3.4	1.1	8.7	2489	64.5
Transport	63.7	29.0	4.4	1.6	1.4	3.4	336	33.5
Banking & insurance	62.2	30.2	5.5	0.9	2.1	7.7	1400	36.5
Other services	41.6	51.8	9.2	1.6	6.3	5.5	4799	57.3
All	46.5	46.5	6.9	1.9	3.7	6.8	10 697	51.7

* Do not add up to 100% since categories are not comprehensive, and not mutually exclusive.

FT – Full-time : PT – Part-time

and in the case of agriculture, self-employment. Women's temporary jobs were at their highest proportions in energy and water, as for men, and other services. Fixed term contracts had their highest percentage in other services.

OCCUPATIONS – 1994 LFS

The distribution of the different forms of employment in each major occupation group are displayed for men and women in Tables 3.3 and 3.4. Occupations varied considerably in the extent to which they contained various forms of flexible work. The occupation groups with the largest overall percentages of flexible jobs for men were skilled trades (31 per cent of the occupation in flexible jobs), health professionals (26 per cent), other associate professionals (33 per cent), managers in agriculture (30 per cent) and other sales (48 per cent). The lowest levels of flexible jobs were in industrial plant (11 per cent), corporate managers (5 per cent), and science and engineering associate professionals (13 per cent).

Table 3.3 Men's non-standard employment by occupation, LFS 1994

Men – row per cent*

Occupation	FT perm.	PT all	Temporary season./casual	fixed term	Self- empl.	N '000	Any flexible
Corporate managers	89.5	2.0	1.5	0.1	1.2	3.1	1729	4.9
Managers in agriculture	44.1	4.5	0.6	–	0.5	53.0	797	29.8
Science & engineering professionals	81.0	3.3	5.4	0.1	4.6	11.8	547	15.3
Health professionals	38.7	5.0	16.8	–	16.4	43.6	117	26.1
Teaching professionals	80.0	10.0	11.2	1.4	8.5	4.0	379	19.2
Other professionals	64.3	4.5	4.8	0.1	3.5	27.9	427	20.3
Science + engineering assoc. professionals	85.2	2.7	5.7	–	5.0	6.5	468	13.0
Health associate professionals	78.9	5.6	5.1	–	4.2	11.6	89	15.2
Other associate professionals	62.2	13.9	4.0	0.5	3.3	27.8	622	33.3
Clerical & Secretarial	83.2	7.7	7.9	1.6	3.9	1.9	893	15.1
Skilled	64.6	4.1	2.7	0.5	1.8	31.0	2865	30.7
Protective & personal services	80.4	15.3	5.6	2.9	1.8	2.5	803	18.8
Buyers & Brokers	80.0	4.6	0.5	0.2	0.1	16.0	304	15.4
Other sales	48.0	36.0	7.1	4.3	1.4	11.5	371	47.6
Industrial Plant, Drivers & machine operators	88.7	2.9	4.9	1.0	2.1	4.5	962	10.5
Other elementary	74.6	5.8	4.3	1.6	1.1	18.1	966	23.8

* Do not add up to 100% since categories are not comprehensive, and not mutually exclusive.
FT – Full-time : PT – Part-time
+ includes skilled construction, skilled trade and other skilled.

Table 3.4 Women's non-standard employment by occupation, LFS 1994

Women – row per cent*

Occupation	FT perm.	PT	Temporary all	season./casual	fixed-term	Self- empl.	N '000	Any flexible
Corporate managers	75.0	19.1	3.2	0.2	2.4	4.1	808	23.1
Managers in agriculture	44.3	21.0	0.8	0.3	0.3	44.3	428	36.6
Science & engineering professionals	69.2	12.7	17.8	0.7	17.1	6.9	73	30.1

continued on page 32

Table 3.4   continued

Occupation	FT perm.	PT	Temporary all	season./ casual	fixed-term	Self-empl.	N '000	Any flexible
Health professionals	40.4	27.2	16.9	–	16.9	31.5	65	47.1
Teaching professionals	62.0	22.3	20.0	1.6	16.3	4.6	635	39.4
Other professionals	67.4	20.7	7.9	–	6.6	7.9	222	29.7
Science + engineering assoc. professionals	66.3	23.2	10.1	–	10.1	5.6	99	33.2
Health associate professionals	53.9	40.4	6.5	0.5	4.2	4.3	592	45.3
Other associate professionals	56.4	29.0	6.0	0.7	4.4	20.0	449	41.9
Clerical & Secretarial	58.6	36.3	5.5	1.1	2.5	2.8	2750	40.0
Skilled	63.9	26.9	3.7	2.2	0.9	14.1	306	34.7
Protective & personal services	30.7	62.8	8.1	3.6	3.3	5.2	1584	68.2
Buyers & Brokers	68.3	27.0	2.3	0.9	0.7	11.3	107	30.4
Other sales	20.4	76.9	4.9	3.1	1.1	2.4	1081	79.0
Industrial plant drivers & machine operators	66.1	27.8	8.7	3.9	3.0	2.4	434	33.8
Other elementary	37.2	42.8	4.1	2.5	1.6	21.1	91	57.7

* Do not add up to 100% since categories are not comprehensive, and not mutually exclusive.
FT – Full-time : PT – Part-time
+ includes skilled construction, skilled trade and other skilled.

Skilled construction, health professionals and managers in agriculture were all occupations with a high proportion of self-employed men. The health professionals occupation also had the highest proportion of male temporary employment (17 per cent of all male employment); most of this was fixed-term contract employment. A very high proportion (36 per cent) of employment in other sales was part-time, compared to the average for male employment of 8 per cent.

In addition, in some occupations which had a lower level of flexible employment overall, certain types of non-standard jobs were of importance. For example, 15 per cent of male employment in personal and protective services was part-time. Similarly, 11 per cent of male employment for teaching professionals was temporary (compared to an average of 4 per cent) and more than one quarter of those in other professional occupations and in skilled occupations were self-employed. Fixed-term contracts accounted for most temporary employment in teaching professional occupations.

Where men are employed in flexible occupations, women tend to be flexibly employed also. For example, managers in agriculture (37 per cent of women's employment in the occupation), health professionals (47 per cent), other associate professionals (42 per cent) and other sales (79 per cent) were occupations with high proportions of women in flexible jobs, as they were for men. However, there are also occupations where a much higher proportion of female than male employment is flexible. For example, 58 per cent of female employment in other elementary occupations was flexible, compared to only 24 per cent of male employment. Similarly, 68 per cent of female employment, but only 19 per cent of male employment, in protective and personal services was flexible. The occupations which had the lowest female flexible employment were corporate managers (23 per cent), science and engineering professionals (30 per cent) and buyer and broker occupations (30 per cent); in these occupations, male flexible employment was also well below average.

The occupations with high female flexible employment mostly had high female part-time employment. Other sales (77 per cent of female employment part-time), personal services (63 per cent) and other elementary occupations (43 per cent) all had above average levels of female part-time employment. Other elementary occupations also had a high proportion of female self-employment. Some occupations, e.g. managers in agriculture and health professionals, had below average levels of female part-time employment, but very high levels of female self-employment. Twenty per cent of female teaching professional jobs were temporary, most of these being fixed-term contracts.

This comparison between women's and men's occupations shows that in some occupations, female and male flexible employment is of a similar nature. For example, self-employment accounts for a high proportion of flexible employment for managers in agriculture for both women and men; self-employment and fixed-term contract employment are significant for male and female health professionals; and higher proportions of male and female part-time employment are found in other sales and personal services than in any other occupations. However, in other occupations, women are in flexible jobs and men are not. For example, 27 per cent of female health professionals worked part-time, compared to only 5 per cent of their male equivalents; 16 per cent of female teaching professionals, but only 9 per cent of males, were on fixed-term contracts; 17 per cent of female science and engineering professionals were on fixed-term contracts compared with 5 per cent of males.

Table 3.5 Managerial duties of all jobs ever held by Wave 3
(retrospective) BHPS sample of men and women

Men – row per cent

Occupation	FT perm.	FT temp.	PT perm.	PT temp.	Self-empl. perm.	Self-empl. temp.	Total	N
Manager	89.1	1.4	1.5	0.3	7.6	0.2	100	3252
Foreman/ supervisor	89.2	4.1	1.6	1.2	3.5	0.4	100	9218
Not manager/ supervisor	81.3	8.3	6.2	4.2	–	–	100	1650

Women – row per cent

Occupation	FT perm.	FT temp.	PT perm.	PT temp.	Self-empl. perm.	Self-empl. temp.	Total	N
Manager	76.5	1.5	14.8	1.2	5.8	0.1	100	2587
Foreman/ supervisor	67.5	4.3	21.8	4.8	1.4	0.3	100	12570
Not manager/ supervisor	40.6	5.9	43.3	10.2	–	–	100	2142

SUPERVISOR – 1992 BHPS

Table 3.5 gives another dimension to the occupational classification of
jobs. It shows whether or not managerial duties were attached to the
jobs. This question helped to classify the occupations of the jobs, but
it is also a separately recorded piece of information about each of the
reported jobs in the retrospective BHPS histories. For men and women,
flexible jobs were more common among jobs which did not have any
managerial or supervisor responsibilities. In the case of women's jobs
without manager or supervisor status, the majority of jobs were flexible, and mainly permanent part-time; this was not the case for men.
On the whole, men's flexible jobs did not appear to have manager or
supervisor status, except for permanent self-employed jobs. Women
could be managers and supervisors to a greater extent than men partly
because they were in permanent part-time jobs.

UNIONISED JOBS – LFS 1993 CROSS-SECTION

The extent to which flexible jobs were unionised jobs can be examined in the LFS data. The percentages of union or staff association

members among individuals holding different types of jobs are displayed in Dex and McCulloch (1995, p. 77, table 5.5) for 1993.[1] Full-time permanent jobs have the highest percentages of union members; 41 per cent of men in such jobs and 39 per cent of women in 1993. It is interesting to note this apparent equality between men and women in union membership rates when similar jobs are being compared. Women's total union density rates are usually below those of men. Part of the explanation for women's lower overall rates is therefore the types of jobs that they hold.

Women's flexible jobs had higher rates of union membership than those of men; 15 per cent of men in flexible jobs and 23 per cent of women were union members. Women's higher union membership rate than men is maintained in the various part-time jobs, although men's rates of union membership were higher than those of women in fixed-term temporary work and all sorts of self-employment. For women, after full-time permanent jobs, union membership rates were highest in part-time employment followed by temporary employment. Women's union membership rate was extremely low among self-employed women. For men, union membership rates were lowest among men in self-employment, a bit higher in part-time employment and higher again in temporary jobs. The ranking of rates across the different kinds of flexible jobs varied therefore between men and women.

It is clear that flexible forms of employment have gone alongside lower levels of union membership in these jobs, and possibly also lower levels of union coverage of such jobs.

EMPLOYER TENURE – 1994 LFS

We are interested in the extent to which flexible jobs are higher turn-over jobs. The mean durations (uncompleted) of time spent with the current employer for the various types of non-standard jobs are displayed for men and women in Dex and McCulloch (1995, pp. 82–3, tables 5.9 and 5.10). It is notable that all of the non-standard types of employment, with the exception of the self-employed with employees, had considerably higher proportions with short tenure than was the case for full-time permanent jobs. This is the case for both men and women. For example, 42 per cent of male temporary workers and 21 per cent of male part-timers had been with their employer for less than 6 months, compared to only 6 per cent of men in full-time permanent jobs. Similarly, 33 per cent of female temporary workers and

12 per cent of female part-timers had experienced less than six months' tenure, compared to only 6 per cent of women in full-time permanent jobs. Moreover, whereas 60 per cent of men in full-time permanent employment had been with their current employer for more than five years, only 28 per cent of men in part-time employment had experienced such long tenure. Women in full-time permanent employment were also more likely to have had long tenure than those in part-time work, but the percentage difference was less striking. Not surprisingly, far fewer temporary than permanent workers had been with the same employer for more than five years. However, for both sexes, the self-employed with employees were more likely than the full-time permanent employed to have had long tenure. This is not to say that all of these non-standard jobs will only last such a short time, but flexible jobs are clearly higher turnover on the basis of these figures.

It is evident from these figures that job turnover is higher in flexible employment than in full-time permanent jobs. It is also clear that the finding noted above that women have a higher turnover rate overall than men may be misleading. These data show that there are great similarities in the distributions of men's and women's tenure for full-time permanent jobs, although women always appear to have shorter tenure than men when they are both in flexible jobs. It is notable that the self-employed with employees have much in common with full-time permanent employees, and are a more stable workforce than any other group. Seasonal/casual jobs have the highest turnover, perhaps not surprisingly, and turnover appears to be higher among men than women in such jobs.

REGIONS – 1994 LFS

The extent of different types of non-standard jobs in the regions of Britain are set out for men and women in Tables 3.6 and 3.7. The overall percentages of each region's workforce who were in flexible jobs in 1994 show relatively little variation across regions, especially in the case of men. The figures range from 18 per cent of men in flexible jobs in the Rest of Scotland to 27 per cent of men in Inner London and the South West. Outer London, and Wales also have high percentages for men's flexible work and West Yorkshire, the West Midlands Conurbation and Merseyside also have low percentages.

There was probably more variation in the extent of part-time and self-employment across the regions. Inner London and Tyne and Wear

Table 3.6 Men's non-standard employment by region: LFS 1994

Men – row per cent*

Region	FT perm.	PT	Temporary			Self- empl.	N '000	Any flexible
			all	season./ casual	fixed- term			
Tyne & Wear	71.0	10.9	7.0	1.5	4.3	11.8	246	22.4
Rest of North	69.7	7.7	5.9	1.3	3.5	14.7	431	21.7
South Yorkshire	72.2	7.7	5.1	0.6	4.2	13.9	270	21.8
West Yorkshire	74.8	7.7	4.4	0.7	2.6	13.1	511	19.3
Rest of Yorkshire	70.6	8.7	4.9	1.4	2.8	16.2	397	22.5
East Midlands	73.4	7.0	3.3	0.7	1.8	16.1	1017	20.2
East Anglia	70.9	8.4	4.1	1.4	2.2	17.6	542	23.5
Inner London	67.5	11.3	5.8	0.8	4.0	17.5	570	27.2
Outer London	67.5	8.3	4.4	0.9	2.1	20.1	1036	26.1
Rest of South East	70.2	8.1	4.3	1.0	2.4	18.8	2781	24.0
South West	66.6	9.6	3.5	1.2	1.5	21.4	1180	26.7
West Midlands Con.	75.4	7.4	3.4	0.7	2.0	13.7	598	19.0
Rest of W. Midlands	72.9	7.3	3.8	1.3	1.8	15.9	686	20.4
Greater Manchester	73.3	8.0	4.0	1.0	2.4	15.4	594	21.3
Merseyside	75.0	8.2	4.9	2.1	2.0	12.2	275	19.3
Rest of North West	72.9	7.4	4.8	1.6	2.3	15.5	574	20.6
Wales	67.0	8.5	4.3	1.3	2.2	20.7	639	25.3
Strathclyde	74.2	6.9	6.6	1.4	4.2	11.3	496	19.8
Rest of Scotland	75.7	6.4	4.1	0.6	2.6	14.0	725	17.8
All	71.1	8.1	4.4	1.1	2.5	16.9	13 576	22.7

FT – Full-time : PT – Part-time

Table 3.7 Women's non-standard employment by region: LFS 1994

Women – row per cent*

Region	FT perm.	PT	Temporary			Self- empl.	N '000	Any flexible
			all	season./ casual	fixed- term			
Tyne & Wear	46.1	47.7	5.9	0.9	3.7	3.9	202	52.5
Rest of North	42.0	51.3	8.4	3.0	3.9	5.6	350	56.3
South Yorkshire	41.2	51.2	8.0	1.6	4.7	4.8	223	56.9
West Yorkshire	46.6	47.8	6.5	1.4	3.4	4.6	411	51.9
Rest of Yorkshire	38.4	53.5	5.3	1.6	2.5	6.7	306	58.2
East Midlands	45.8	47.9	6.6	1.9	3.5	6.0	791	52.2
East Anglia	44.2	47.2	7.3	2.7	3.2	8.2	419	53.7
Inner London	57.0	30.8	11.2	2.3	6.4	9.0	475	40.8
Outer London	54.3	37.4	6.6	1.2	3.8	7.9	827	44.1
Rest of South East	46.4	47.0	7.4	2.2	3.8	7.6	2172	51.9
South West	41.7	49.6	6.1	1.8	3.2	9.7	932	55.6
West Midlands Con.	49.2	45.1	6.0	2.0	3.2	4.2	455	49.3

continued on page 38

Table 3.7   continued

Region	FT perm	PT	Temporary all	season./ casual	fixed-term	Self-empl.	N '000	Any flexible
Rest of W. Midlands	43.0	50.8	6.2	2.2	3.1	7.7	533	54.5
Greater Manchester	48.5	44.1	6.2	1.4	4.1	5.2	482	50.3
Merseyside	45.9	49.5	5.6	1.0	3.4	3.7	231	52.6
Rest of North West	45.4	48.6	6.2	1.4	3.9	5.8	459	52.6
Wales	43.6	49.3	7.1	2.5	2.9	6.6	494	54.3
Strathclyde	49.0	44.9	6.9	1.7	4.5	4.2	404	49.4
Rest of Scotland	44.9	47.3	6.1	1.4	3.4	5.5	576	52.7
All	48.8	46.5	6.9	1.9	3.7	6.8	10 751	51.7

had the largest percentages of men in part-time employment and the Rest of Scotland had the lowest percentage. Men's percentage of self-employment was highest in the South West, Wales and Outer London, and lowest in Strathclyde, Merseyside and Tyne and Wear.

Men's temporary employment was at its greatest percentage in Tyne and Wear and Strathclyde and at its lowest in the East Midlands and the West Midlands conurbation. In all of these regions, it was fixed-term temporary employment that constituted the majority of temporary jobs. The percentages of seasonal/casual temporary employment exhibited less variation across regions.

Regional variations were greater for women than for men. The total percentages of flexible jobs ranged from 41 per cent at its lowest in Inner London and 44 per cent in Outer London to 58 per cent in the Rest of Yorkshire. Other regions with high percentages of women in flexible jobs were South Yorkshire and the Rest of the North. The regional profile of women's flexible jobs differed, therefore, from that of men's distributions. As we might expect, the extent of women's part-time employment in each region tended to determine the overall ranking. Women's percentage of part-time jobs was greatest in the Rest of Yorkshire (54 per cent of the female regional employment), South Yorkshire and the Rest of the North. The percentages of female part-time jobs were at their lowest in Inner and Outer London.

The percentages of women in temporary jobs did not vary greatly except that they were considerably higher in Inner London than in all other regions. Temporary work was lowest in the Rest of Yorkshire and Merseyside. As for men, most temporary jobs were fixed-term contracts.

There was slightly more regional variation in women's self-employment from its lowest in Tyne and Wear and Strathclyde to its highest in the South West and Inner London.

LOCAL LABOUR MARKET CONDITIONS – 1992 BHPS

The BHPS has travel-to-work-area (TTWA) unemployment rates matched in to the data so that it is possible to examine the conditions operating in local labour markets in which jobs are located. The figures are displayed in Dex and McCulloch (1995, p. 88, table 5.13). The TTWA unemployment rates have been grouped into low, medium and high in 1992. The distributions of jobs of different status through the different conditions of TTWA were fairly similar. However, there were a few differences. Full-time permanent jobs, whether men's or women's, were slightly less likely than other jobs to be in labour markets with low unemployment rates. In contrast, self-employed men's jobs and to a lesser extent part-time permanent men's jobs were more likely to be found in local labour markets with low unemployment rates. Self-employed men's jobs were also less likely to be found in local labour markets with high unemployment rates. For women, the self-employed were similarly more likely to be found in labour markets with low unemployment rates and less likely in areas with high unemployment rates.

This link of self-employment to more buoyant labour markets is not surprising in view of the fact that small businesses are often expected to be at the forefront of, and the engine for economic growth. However, the link between flexible work and better local labour market conditions does not extend to all types of flexible work. Men's temporary work and women's part-time permanent jobs were not located disproportionately in local labour markets with more favourable employment conditions.

CONCLUSIONS

This analysis has suggested that flexible jobs do appear to be associated with certain job-related and labour market characteristics. Flexible jobs were found to be more common in certain industries and occupations than in others. On the whole, the industries and occupations which employed a high percentage of men also employed a high percentage of women in non-standard jobs. But in addition, women were employed in flexible jobs in a range of other industries and occupations. Industries which had a high percentage of male self-employment tended to have a high percentage of male flexible employment; similarly, industries with a high percentage of female part-time employment tended to have a high percentage of female flexible employment. However, part-time employment or fixed-term contract employment could also contribute significantly to male flexible employment in some industries, as could self-employment to female flexible employment.

Four industries – agriculture, construction, distribution, and other services – had above average levels of male flexible employment. All of these except construction also had above average levels of female flexible employment. However, women always had higher percentages of flexible jobs, and more of the flexible jobs which have the poorest conditions and rewards. Self-employment, where men tend to predominate, often results in higher than average income, certainly in comparison with part-time employment. Thus women's under-representation in self-employment could have resulted in lower income overall.

In some occupations, men and women are employed in the same types of flexible jobs. For example, self-employment accounts for almost all male flexible employment in skilled construction and managers in agricultural occupations and most female flexible employment in these occupations; self-employment and fixed-term contract employment contribute significantly to flexible employment for both male and female health professionals; and part-time work is the main source of flexible employment for both sexes in personal services and other sales occupations. However, in some occupations, women are employed in flexible jobs, but men are not. For example, part-time employment is an important source of female, but not male, flexible employment for health-associated and other elementary occupations.

Part-time jobs were primarily women's jobs. Women stayed in permanent part-time jobs for similar lengths of time as they did in permanent full-time jobs. Temporary jobs had shorter durations. Temporary jobs were far less likely to be unionised.

This examination of the job-related characteristics of non-standard forms of employment has shown that there are some similarities in the status and characteristics of the flexible jobs held by men and women. However, in all sectors, women were more likely to be employed in non-standard jobs. They were also concentrated in disadvantageous types of flexible jobs. The sectors which had the highest proportions of flexible jobs were those which have been growing fastest (distribution and other services), or those which have been subjected to government public sector reorganisation. We may predict, therefore, that there will be further increases in the extent of flexible jobs in the future, although possibly not on the scale of the 1980s' increases.

Flexible jobs were found to be more common in certain regions of Britain. Self-employment was also more common in areas with buoyant labour market conditions; this was also the case for men's permanent part-time jobs and women's self-employed and temporary jobs.

This analysis of all jobs ever held by BHPS sample members up to Wave 3 has shown that flexible work has occurred in British labour markets since the second World War in certain occupational and industrial niches. Its more extensive use in certain industries, agriculture, hotels and catering, education and the rest of the services, has been common to both men and women. More variation can be seen in the occupations of flexible jobs by gender. However, while there were pockets of flexible jobs in professional occupations, by far the majority of temporary and part-time jobs appeared at the bottom end of the occupational hierarchy in unskilled or personal service occupations. A large proportion of both men and women managers were self-employed.

Temporary jobs were shorter in duration, although there were a few surprisingly long temporary jobs held by both men and women and lasting more than five years.

Notes

1. Union membership was not available for the 1994 LFS.

Part II
Individuals

4 Individuals in Flexible Work in Britain in the 1990s

In this chapter we examine the extent to which individuals were in non-standard forms of work in Britain in 1994. We are interested to ascertain how many men and women were in flexible jobs of various kinds. Some estimates of the extent of flexible work have already been made by researchers and by the Employment Department (now Department for Education and Employment) and there is a body of literature which we review below. On the whole, each study has used a different set of categories to define 'flexible work' and they have used different data sets for different years. One recent estimate by the Employment Department using the Labour Force Survey for 1993 estimated that 38 per cent of all people in employment (27 per cent of men and 52 per cent of women) were in the flexible workforce. This constituted 9696 thousand people: 3730 thousand men and 5966 thousand women (Watson, 1994). The definition on which these figures is based includes as flexible work, full-time temporary, part-time permanent, part-time temporary, full-time and part-time, self-employed, on a government scheme and unpaid family workers. Robinson (1994) suggests that flexible work constituted 40 per cent of the workforce.[1] Earlier figures for the 1980s calculated the extent of flexible work as in the region of 30–35 per cent of the workforce.[2] This study will adopt its own definition of non-standard jobs, as outlined below. First we review the existing studies on individuals' reasons for accepting flexible jobs of various kinds.

EXISTING STUDIES

These studies give insight into why individuals take up flexible jobs. Clearly, for many, there are some advantages in having a flexible job. But there are also some disadvantages.

Part-timers

In Britain, part-time work has had a distinct life-cycle aspect; women start to work part-time when they return to work after childbirth, as reviewed in Dex et al. (1993). However, this picture is beginning to change.[3] Taking a part-time job has been a way of combining employment and the responsibility for child care. At least part of the reason that a woman has chosen the part-time option is to structure her job around the availability of her partner or a close relative to provide free or cheap child care. Child care is then affordable at the low wages which many part-time jobs offer. Thus part-time employment is more prevalent for women at certain ages, between 25 and 39, and for women with dependent children. Many women have suffered downward occupational mobility by taking a low level part-time job after childbirth (Dex, 1992). In addition, part-time employment is less common among ethnic minority women (Naylor, 1994). Part-time employment has been growing among men; many male part-timers are students (42 per cent) but the percentage is still small relative to men's employment in total (Naylor, 1994).

Some research has drawn attention to the preference of many women for part-time work, and the satisfaction they often appear to derive by working part time (Watson and Fothergill, 1993). On average, 80 per cent of women say they work part time because they do not want a full-time job (Naylor, 1994); this percentage is higher for women with dependent children. Hakim (1993) has called the women who are in this position 'grateful slaves'. However, the questions used by the Labour Force Survey (LFS) on which these statistics are based are rather open to criticism.[4] Giving the answer that they did not want a full-time job begs the question 'Why don't you want a full-time job?' In the 1990 LFS 66 per cent gave the response 'Do not want a full-time job'. A more extended set of categories was used in the National Opinion Polls (NOP) Omnibus survey for 1990. Then, 14 per cent of part-timers would like a full-time job but domestic commitments would make full-time work difficult; 31 per cent were working part time to allow more time to spend with their children; 14 per cent had no need to work for financial reasons but worked part time through choice; 13 per cent needed to earn money but earned enough working part time so had no wish to work full time; 10 per cent gave some other reason. These results suggest that some of those stating that they wanted to work part time have chosen this option, but that others were constrained by domestic commitments.

Dex (1988) attempted to unravel the preference versus constraint issue using the Women and Employment Survey data. This work shows that there are important variations within the women's part-time workforce, and that the notion of being a voluntary part-timer is simplistic and unsatisfactory if it excludes women who feel some pressure to work or only to work part-time because of constraints. It was clear that a woman's decision to work part-time was heavily constrained by the presence of children and child care problems. In a multivariate analysis, attitudes were found to have a significant but extremely small effect on women's choice of working hours. The problem of child care, in the context of women's low earnings, was found to be an important constraint.

Further work on women's low paid jobs has reinforced these conclusions. Nearly two-thirds of low paid women (most of whom were working part time) thought that they did not have any choice over their current job. Many women in low-paid part-time jobs were found to be desperate to earn money (Dex, Lissenburgh and Taylor, 1994). Women with low levels of satisfaction about their pay were more likely to be low paid. Also, 50 per cent of the low paid thought they were paid less than they deserved. It is clear that the preference some women have for part-time work needs to be set alongside the important constraints that many women also feel. As Brannen et al. (1994) suggest, findings of satisfaction among women workers need to be set in context.

In addition women part-timers have been found to have more traditional attitudes than full-timers, to be less financially dependent on work, to have had less difficulty coping with work, to have had different reasons for working, and to have attached different importance to aspects of work (Martin and Roberts, 1984; Dex, 1988).

Some cross-national comparisons have investigated why women work part-time more in Britain. O'Reilly's (1994) comparison of Britain and France suggested that the supply side factors which were important in explaining French women's lower part-time participation rates were the higher level of educational qualifications and training of French relative to British women, the fact that it is more difficult to find part-time child care in France, and cultural factors. Cultural differences mean that part-time employment in France is not offering women the flexibility they want. French women want to have Wednesday afternoon off work but not fewer hours spread over the week. There are also tax and social security incentives for low hours part-time work in Britain which are absent in some other countries, (Dex and Shaw, 1986; Dex et al., 1993).

Self-employed

Far more men than women are self-employed although self-employment has been increasing among both men and women. The percentage rate of increase has been faster for women than for men. The self-employed are concentrated in the 35–49 years age group. They are more likely than employees to be married or cohabiting, and to be educated to A-level, especially where they themselves have employees. Self-employment rates are also higher among women who have dependent children, and among certain ethnic minority groups, notably Asians (Campbell and Daly, 1992). Women were over-represented among the low-earning self-employed, (Meager et al., 1994). Those who work alone have been found to have different characteristics from those who have employees. There is a greater dispersion of incomes among the self-employed than among similar groups of employees (Meager et al., 1994).

Those entering self-employment during the 1980s were formerly employees. Approximately one-half of the self-employed previously had jobs; one-third were previously unemployed, and a quarter had been economically inactive. These values varied from year to year through the 1980s, partly through changes in the business cycle. Also, men were more likely to have entered self-employment from being employees or unemployed, whereas women were more likely to have been employees or inactive (Hakim, 1989; Campbell and Daly, 1992). Survival rates in self-employment have been found to be higher when individuals have entered from jobs and become self-employed in an area in which they have some previous experience (Carter and Cannon, 1988). Meager et al.'s (1994) analysis of the 'new' recent entrants to self-employment found that women have been an increasing share of the 'new' self-employed; there are more young people, relative to all self-employed; and they are disproportionately in certain service sector activities, low-earning jobs, low value-added personal services and some higher earning business and financial services.

There has been relatively little examination of the household characteristics of the self-employed. However, people with self-employed spouses have been found to be more likely to be self-employed themselves than those who did not have spouses with self-employed status, and the offspring of self-employed parents are also more likely to be self-employed (Curran and Burrows, 1989; Taylor, 1994). Carter and Cannon (1988) found that approximately three-quarters of the self-employed had some family connection with self-employment during their lifetime. Also, those who have received gifts and/or inheritances have been found to more likely to run their own business (Blanchflower and Oswald, 1991). Examination of the relationship between spouses has found no evidence that one partner is 'kept on the books' in order to gain a tax advantage. It seems more likely that, in many instances, both work long hours running the same business.

The reasons that people become self-employed include a combination of pull and push factors. However, by far the most cited of the reasons is the attraction of independence and being one's own boss. Between one and two-thirds of entrants to self-employment gave this reason (Hakim, 1989). Smaller percentages stated that they were attracted to self-employment because of its challenge, the freedom to choose when to work, and the freedom of whom to work for. The financial motivation was much less emphasised than the independence, choice and freedom given by self-employment.[5] However, there is econometric evidence which suggests that the potential earnings from self-employment does affect this decision.[6] A more in-depth investigation of individuals' reasons for becoming self-employed found that the widely cited wish for independence means different things to different people (Carter and Cannon, 1988). It can mean a way of offering more career opportunities (young ambitious); a rejection of an authority figure (drifters); the avoidance of the frustrations of a conventional career (older high achievers); the desire for part-time employment to fit in with domestic circumstances (women returners) or the wish to be part of a family business where self-employment is the normal way of life (traditionalists). Carter and Cannon (1988) argue that women can fit into any of these categories; women do not just fit the restricted few groups described by Goffee and Scase (1985). Another important point made by Carter and Cannon is that self-employment is dynamic and that the motivation for being self-employed can change over time.

The push factors for an individual becoming self-employed include having been made redundant, being unemployed, having had a series of temporary short-term jobs and seeking to avoid the insecurity of this position, being discriminated against (especially for ethnic minorities), and having a mid-career review (Scase and Goffee, 1987). However, negative push factors were rarely the sole reason for becoming self-employed; there were usually pull factors at work as well (Carter and Cannon, 1988). Even many of those who have failed in their self-employed business are not put off from another attempt.[7] Thus we should not be surprised that some individuals have had more than one experience of self-employment. The lack of capital appears to be a constraint which prevents some who would like to become self-employed from doing so (Blanchflower and Oswald, 1991).

Homeworkers

The 1993 LFS survey suggests that there were then 662 000 homeworkers in the UK, 179 000 men and 466 000 women. The majority were self-employed or worked in a family business and 113 000 were employed by an outside organisation. A large proportion of women homeworkers are from ethnic minorities (Huws, 1994). Cragg and Dawson (1981) summarised the reasons why women are homeworkers. They argued that it is a form of work which women can perform while they have dependent children at home or while they are in ill health. Women who are unable to take on employment in the workplace for language or cultural reasons may also be able to work as homeworkers. Allen and Wolkowitz (1987) added other reasons for homeworking. These were that it is a form of work which can be combined with caring for elderly or disabled relatives and that it can be part of the traditions of communities, but not just ethnic minority communities. For example, sewing and cooking at home would be traditional activities for some groups of women.

A need for income combined with a requirement to be at home to look after children was the reason that the large majority of homeworkers gave for working from home in Huws's (1994) study. The disadvantages of working at home to these women were the very low pay, the isolation, the environmental hazards, and the mess it creates. One in ten of these homeworkers also suffered health problems from homework; neck or back ache and eye strain were commonly cited.

Bisset and Huws (1984) found that some new homeworkers attached importance to the less tangible benefits of homeworking than those in more traditional homeworking jobs. For example, they appreciated the flexibility to schedule their work and the reduction in the stress of commuting to work. Laurie and Taylor (1992) found that homeworkers in the British Household Panel Study had more traditional attitudes than other employees.

Teleworkers

There are now new forms of working at home, teleworking. This poses definitional problems. This group are distinguished from more traditional homeworkers by their use of computers and telecommunications equipment for their job. But there are issues about how much time they should spend at home in order to qualify as a teleworkers. One study has suggested that only those working for more than 50 per cent of their work time at home should be classified as teleworkers. Currently there are no reliable statistics on the extent among the workforce of teleworking. The main advantages of telework for employees have been argued to be savings on commuting time and increased flexibility or autonomy at work. However studies have shown that the disadvantages are also significant; namely those of feeling isolated at home and missing the social contact of office life (IDS, 1994; Haddon and Lewis, 1994). Studies of the teleworking trials in the 1980s found that this form of work has implications for work satisfaction and motivation, supervision, roles and gender issues, the organisation of time and space, family support and self-discipline.

Temporary workers

The 1993 LFS found that approximately 6 per cent of employees were in temporary work but this rose to 7 per cent in the summer. What individuals mean by a temporary contract can differ. In reporting that their job is temporary, they are unlikely to be referring to a strict legal concept and they may not have the same view of their state as their employer. It is important to remember that surveys which ask about temporary work use different definitions, as Casey (1988) pointed out. Temporary work also overlaps with self-employment, part- or full-time employment. The majority of individuals who have temporary status (70 per cent in the 1984 Labour Force Survey) are in seasonal/casual jobs and over half of temporary workers are part-timers; in some industries the percentages are much higher. The reasons why workers, largely women, take up temporary jobs will overlap, therefore, with the reasons why they become part-time and, to a lesser extent, self-employed. Temporary workers are younger than average workers or are over retirement age. Their reasons for taking temporary jobs also appear to vary by their age.

Casey (1988) found from 1984 data that 44 per cent of male and 29 per cent of female temporary workers had temporary jobs because permanent jobs were not available. This was the single most important reason given by men. It is a measure of involuntary temporary work. Those who had previously been on a government training scheme before taking a temporary job all took temporary jobs for this reason. Casey also suggested that this percentage of involuntary temporary workers had been growing, even if the percentage of temporary jobs overall had not shown much change. Also, 16 per cent of male and 37 per cent of female temporary workers did not want a permanent job. This was the most important reason for women. Taking a temporary job in order to get training was important to the younger age groups.

An Institute of Personnel and Development study suggests that some people may choose temporary work over permanent work because they do not want to commit themselves for an extended period, because a temporary post may be seen as a first step towards a permanent post, and because in occupations with scarce skills, short-term contracts may provide the potential for a continual upward negotiation of salaries and benefits, (Brewster et al., 1993).

Comparisons between Flexible Workers

Some comparisons can be drawn between the various types of non-standard forms of work. In terms of their hourly pay part-timers and temporary workers have often been found to receive approximately the same hourly pay as full-time permanent staff, (IRS, 1994b); agency temporary staff and self-employed subcontractees tend to get higher rates of pay, and homeworkers get lower rates of pay. All of the non-standard types of jobs have been found to receive fewer fringe benefits; sick pay, holidays, holiday pay, pensions, share options, overtime premia, and shift premia, as reviewed in Chapter 2 (Marsh, 1991; IRS, 1994b; Dickens, 1992). In the receipt of fringe benefits, fixed term contract staff and permanent part-time staff appear to do better than part-time temporary staff and they do better than those on zero hours contracts (IRS, 1994b; Neathey and Hurstfield 1995).

This review of the research has identified a number of important points from earlier studies of flexible work, as well as indicating some areas where there are gaps in our understanding. It shows that it is unwise to regard all types of flexible work as homogeneous. There are clearly major differences in the reasons why individuals have decided to take or create the various kinds of non-standard flexible jobs. As mentioned already, there are some major problems of definition which relate to most of these forms of work.

Individuals were often found to have entered self-employment to gain independence, fulfilment or autonomy at work, although it could also be in response to having been made redundant or unemployed. Women's entry into part-time work was often associated with a certain point in their lifecycle, that is when they became responsible for child care. But it was also linked for many to the need to make a contribution to household income for spending on essential goods. Entry into temporary jobs sometimes followed unemployment and was thought to be a way of gaining training. Individuals might also take a temporary job because they could not get a permanent one. However, in some cases they did not want permanent jobs.

Flexible work, in its numerical form, has elements which are viewed positively both by individuals and employers. This is particularly the case for self-employment and part-time employment. Nonetheless there can be disadvantages which arise from flexible jobs in the short and long term. For example, flexible jobs may have lower levels of earnings and limited access to fringe benefits, promotion prospects and training. Commentators have thought that, on balance, workers experience most of the disadvantages (IDS, 1994; Haddon and Lewis, 1994; IRS, 1994a, 1994b; Dickens, 1992). Dickens shows how these disadvantages can go far beyond the workplace and current earnings into workers having worse promotion prospects, less pay progression, fewer training opportunities, less eligibility for state benefits, less coverage by employment protection legislation, and lower pensions in later life.

We can now proceed to our own analysis of the extent of flexible work in Britain in the 1990s.

DEFINITION ISSUES

It is possible to argue about the definitions of flexible work and what should and should not be included. It has been suggested that permanent part-time employment, mostly carried out by women, was a more traditional form of employment. It should therefore not be included in assessments of the extent to which the labour market has been restructured (Hakim, 1987; Robinson, 1995). Most commentators, while having some sympathy with this argument, do not exclude permanent part-time employment from the calculations. Some researchers take issue with the definitions which underlie the official sources of data in a more fundamental way, and with the calculations based upon them. Felstead (1991) argued that many of the increases in self-employment do not represent increases in independence and entrepreneurial control, since they are controlled forms of self-employment. Felstead was discussing franchisees, but others have made the same points about homeworking (Allen and Wolkowitz, 1986, 1987), construction (Rainbird, 1990) and taxi-cab driving (Russell, 1983).

In this chapter we first use the Labour Force Survey for Spring 1994 to provide a more detailed picture of some aspects of non-standard work than has been done previously. We have not included the self-employed with employees as flexible workers. On the whole, we have concentrated on the paid workforce and we do include part-time permanent as a non-standard form of employment. Nor have we specifically examined homeworking, although the vast majority of homeworkers are included in our calculations of the extent of flexible work since they are covered under the headings of self-employment, part-time or temporary employment.[8]

The analysis is further complicated by the fact that some of the categories can be defined in a variety of ways. For example, it is possible to use a definition of part-time work which the individual has defined for her or himself; or it is possible to use a definition based on their working hours per week. Moreover, their actual or usual hours worked, with or without overtime and with or without paid and/or unpaid overtime, can be used. The actual definitions used to construct the various categories are set out in Appendix Table A1.1. We present alternative definitions in some cases. However, all the definitions used build upon the basic definitions underlying the Labour Force Survey data. We do not attempt, nor are we able, to separate out the self-employed who have genuine autonomy in their employment from those who do not.

It is important to note that the categories of non-standard flexible employment which we use are not mutually exclusive. 'Temporary employment' includes full- and part-time temporary work for example. Part-time work includes permanent and temporary employment. In theory, self-employment can also be temporary or permanent, but this cannot be ascertained from the LFS data. We decided to use overlapping categories since there is some interest in knowing the position of whole groups; for example, of all temporary employees. Also, there were insufficient numbers in all of the possible subgroups, and too many of them, to carry out the intended analyses.

For a definition of 'flexible employment' we included the following:

- any part-time employment;
- any temporary employment;
- self-employment without employees.

Unless otherwise stated, all of the analyses were undertaken on the population of working age; that is women aged 16 to 59 and men aged 16 to 64.

NON-STANDARD EMPLOYMENT IN 1994

Total in Flexible Jobs

The figures in Tables 4.1 and 4.2 present the Labour Force Survey estimates of the extent of various forms of non-standard employment among men and women of working age in 1994. In this analysis 22 per cent of employed men could be defined as being employed in non-standard forms of work in 1994. Approximately 51 per cent of employed women were in flexible jobs. These figures differ from those produced in Watson (1994) because our analysis has been restricted to those of working age, and it does not include unpaid family workers or the self-employed with employees. We can confirm that flexible employment constitutes a much higher percentage of the employment of individuals above statutory retirement age. Flexible employment also characterises almost all of the jobs, 99 per cent, held by those young men and women who were in full-time education in 1994.

Separate Types of Flexible Jobs

When we examine the separate types of flexible employment it is important to remember that these are not mutually exclusive. Most of the overlaps are presented in Tables 4.1 and 4.2. Of the men who were not in full-time education, 5–7 per cent were in part-time jobs, 5 per cent were in temporary jobs, 17 per cent were self-employed and 2 per cent were on a government scheme. The self-definition and the hours definition of part-time work give slightly different results. Of the women who were not in full-time education, 41 per cent thought of themselves as working part time, 7 per cent were in temporary jobs, 7 per cent were self-employed and one per cent were on a government scheme. However, a slightly higher percentage of women, 46 per cent, were employed less than 31 hours per week (after including overtime). Relatively small proportions of women and men had two part-time jobs although this was much higher for women than for men; 3 per cent of employed women and 0.4 per cent of employed men. These figures are in broad agreement with all the other sources. They show that:

- women were far more likely to be in part-time employment than men;
- relatively few men were in part-time employment;

Table 4.1 Profile of non-standard forms of employment among men of working age in Britain in 1994: LFS

per cent*

	Employed 16–64		Employed. Not in FT education		Employed. In FT education	
Full-time permanent	**73.1**		**74.1**		**0.8**	
Part-time						
self-definition	**6.1**		**3.7**		**93.8**	
hours < 31	**7.7**		**5.3**		**93.6**	
hours <8		1.4		0.5		34.7
hours <16+<2 yrs		1.9		0.6		56.9
hours 8-15+<5yrs		1.5		0.6		43.2
More than 1 PT job		0.6		0.4		5.3
Uncovered 94	**24.2**		**22.4**		**71.4**	
Temporary						
all	**5.4**		**4.9**		**27.1**	
seasonal		0.3		0.3		2.3
casual		1.0		0.6		14.5
fixed term		3.0		3.0		5.1
other		1.1		1.0		5.2
full-time		3.9		3.9		5.3
part-time		1.5		1.0		21.8
Self-employed						
all	**16.9**		**17.3**		**1.9**	
with employees		4.4		4.2		–
without employees		12.4		13.1		1.8
full-time		15.2		15.6		0.1
part-time		1.8		1.7		1.8
Government scheme	**1.6**		**1.6**		**1.4**	
Job changers last year						
same firm/diff. occup.		3.6		3.3		1.0
same firm FT-PT		0.6		1.9		0.5
same firm employee/ self-employed		0.6		0.5		–
Any flexible	**22.4**		**20.7**		**99.1**	
N, thousands		13 577		13 258		299

* Do not add up to 100% since overlapping categories.

Table 4.2 Profile of non-standard forms of employment among women of working age in Britain in 1994: LFS

per cent*

	Employed 16–59		Not in FT education		Employed. In FT education	
Full-time permanent	**46.6**		**50.5**		**0.9**	
Part-time						
self-definition	**43.2**		**41.0**		**96.1**	
hours < 31	**46.1**		**44.4**		**96.3**	
hours <8		6.0		4.7		42.5
hours <16+<2 yrs		8.3		6.3		67.6
hours 8–15+<5yrs		8.2		7.1		40.9
More than 1 PT job		3.6		3.2		7.8
Uncovered 94	**30.9**		**29.1**		**79.6**	
Temporary						
all	**7.6**		**7.0**		**23.6**	
seasonal		0.4		0.3		2.5
casual		1.7		1.3		14.0
fixed term		4.0		4.0		4.6
other		3.4		1.4		2.5
full-time		2.8		2.8		2.9
part-time		4.8		4.8		20.7
Self-employed						
all	**6.8**		**6.9**		**1.3**	
with employees		1.7		1.8		–
without employees		5.0		5.1		1.3
full-time		3.3		3.4		0.0
part-time		3.4		3.5		1.3
Government scheme	**1.0**		**1.1**		**0.4**	
Job changers last year						
same firm/diff. occup.		3.9		3.4		1.2
same firm FT-PT		2.2		4.5		0.5
same firm employee self-employed		0.3		0.2		–
Any flexible	**51.0**		**48.9**		**99.1**	
N, thousands	10 751		10 401		334	

* Do not add up to 100% since overlapping categories.

- men were more likely to be self-employed than women;
- women were more likely than men to be in temporary jobs;
- the majority of men's self-employed jobs and temporary jobs were full-time;
- the majority of women's temporary jobs were part-time;
- approximately one-half of women's self-employed jobs were full-time and one-half were part-time jobs;
- over one-half of temporary jobs, for both women and men, were fixed-term contracts;
- larger percentages of women than men were in most of the sub-groups of temporary work, i.e. in casual, fixed-term and other temporary jobs;
- similar proportions of men and women were in seasonal employment; and
- over three-quarters of the self-employed jobs were without employees for both men and women.

Women constituted the vast majority of part-time employees and a minority of the self-employed. Of all employed men of working age in 1994 approximately between 828 and 1045 thousand were employed part time compared to between 4644 and 4956 thousand women. Also, approximately 731 thousand women and 2294 men of working age were self-employed in 1994; 539 thousand women and 1684 thousand men were self-employed without employees.

Women also comprised a majority (53 per cent) of all temporary employees, 63 per cent of casual workers, 44 per cent of seasonal workers, 51 per cent of fixed-term temporary employees and 52 per cent of other temporary employees. Casey's (1988) study of temporary workers in 1984 found that women constituted 54 per cent of all temporary workers and 64 per cent of seasonal workers. This might suggest that women's overall share of temporary work has stayed fairly constant although with some variations across the separate categories of temporary employment. In Watson (1994) approximately 728 thousand women and 650 thousand men of working age were employed in temporary jobs; 135 thousand women and 80 thousand men were in casual jobs; 416 thousand women and 398 thousand men were in jobs with fixed term contracts; and 31 thousand women and 40 thousand men were in seasonal jobs in the first quarter of 1994.

Full-time Education

Young men and young women in full-time education who also had a job were almost wholly located in the flexible workforce, as we have already noted. They were concentrated in part-time jobs but, with the exception of self-employment, their proportions in all the subgroups of flexible work were always higher than for the majority employed population who were not in full-time education. The vast majority of these part-time jobs, 71 per cent of the men's jobs and 80 per cent of the women's jobs would not have been covered by employment protection legislation in 1994. As we might expect, those employed in full-time education were found in particularly high proportions (27 per cent for men and 24 per cent for the women) in temporary jobs.

Not Covered by Employment Protection Legislation (1994)

We can assess the extent to which individuals were not covered by many of the provisions of employment protection legislation which were introduced in 1994 (although they came into force in 1995). Prior to 1994 the legislation was such that employment protection was not available for certain classes of part-time employees, dependent upon their tenure of employment. From 1995 onwards, employment protection legislation has covered all employees, irrespective of their weekly hours of work, provided they have had two or more years of tenure with their employer. Unfortunately not all employees in the 1994 LFS were asked to give full details about the date their current job started.[9] We have calculated the proportions in the various categories based on certain assumptions about those who were not asked when they had started with their current employer.[10] This means that the results should be regarded as estimates, and less reliable than most of the other values.

Twenty-two per cent of men of working age, who were not in full-time education, were not covered by employment protection legislation in 1994. However, the equivalent figure for women who were not in full-time education was 29 per cent. For those who were in full-time education, the percentages who were not covered were considerably higher; they constituted approximately three-quarters of the jobs held by women and men in full-time education; however there was still a higher percentage of women than men in full-time education who were not covered. Of all the employed of working age, 3286 thousand men and 3322 thousand women were not covered. Even though

Table 4.3 Reason for holding a temporary job, by sex and self-defined hours of work: LFS 1994

Reason	Men		Women	
	Full-time	*Part-time*	*Full-time*	*Part-time*
Contract which includes period of training	8.9	(2.2)	15.7	2.1
Could not find permanent job	58.2	33.8	47.4	33.7
Did not want permanent job	6.7	42.4	11.5	41.7
Other reason	26.2	21.5	25.3	22.4
Total	100	100	100	100
N, thousands	419	166	269	463

( ) – based on small cell sizes

the legislation has changed such that it is now less discriminatory against women who are employed part-time, there is still a higher proportion and a higher number of women than men who are not covered by employment protection legislation.

Reasons for Having a Temporary Job

The reasons that individuals gave for having temporary jobs are displayed in Table 4.3. These varied by hours of work and, to a lesser extent, by gender. Men and women with full-time jobs were more likely than those with part-time jobs to say they had a temporary job because they could not find a permanent job or because their contract included a period of training. Full-timers were far less likely than part-timers to have a temporary job because they did not want a permanent one. Fifty-eight per cent of men who were temporarily employed full-time, and 47 per cent of women in the same position could not find a permanent job compared with 34 per cent of men employed in part-time temporary jobs and 34 per cent of the equivalent women. On the other hand, only 7 per cent of men and 12 per cent of women who were temporarily employed in full-time jobs said that they did not want a permanent job. This compared with 42 per cent of men and the same percentage of women who were temporarily employed in part-time jobs. Thus women were less likely than men to say that they could not find a permanent job, and were more likely to say that they did not want a permanent job. However, as indicated in the literature review earlier in this chapter, a slightly different picture can emerge if

Table 4.4 Employment in flexible working arrangements, LFS 1994

thousands

	Total	Men Full-time	Part-time	Total	Women Full-time	Part-time
Annual hours	660	634	20	649	393	250
per cent of employed	4.9			6.0		
Term-time	227	188	34	871	362	503
per cent of employed	1.7			8.1		
Job sharing	31	15	15	189	14	171
per cent of employed	0.2			0.8		
Sunday work						
usually	1326	1187	135	1051	547	501
per cent of employed	9.8			9.8		
sometimes	3887	3746	128	2031	1278	748
per cent of employed	28.6			18.9		
Shiftwork						
any	2414	2295	111	1466	843	620
N – employed, thousands	13 577			10 751		

Data are for working age population (16–59/64).
Source: Weighted data.

individuals are allowed to give more of the reasons behind their choices of answers. Earlier studies have shown that a sizeable group of women who say they did not want a permanent job say this because of constraints they face in the home, rather than purely as a matter of their preference.

Other Types of Flexible Jobs

The Labour Force Survey also provides information about other types of flexible work. The amounts of annual hours work, term-time only work, job sharing, Sunday work and shift work in 1994 are set out in Table 4.4.

Annual hours – Approximately 649 thousand women and 660 thousand men had annual hours contracts in 1994; these covered 6 per cent of employed women and 5 per cent of employed men of working ages. Three-fifths of women on annual hours contracts worked full-time and two-fifths worked part-time, whereas almost all men on annual hours contracts worked full-time.

Term-time – Approximately 871 thousand women (8 per cent of employed women), and 227 thousand men, (2 per cent of employed men) were employed term-time only. The majority of women employed

term-time only were in part-time jobs, whereas most men on these
contracts were employed full-time.

Job sharing – There were very few women or men in job sharing
positions. Women held 86 per cent of these positions; this constituted 189 thousand women and 31 thousand men of working age.
Almost all of these jobs were part-time positions.

Sunday work – A total of 3082 thousand women and 5213 thousand
men said that they either usually or sometimes worked on Sunday
as part of their job. This constitutes 29 per cent of employed women
and 38 per cent of employed men. The majority in both cases only
worked on Sundays sometimes rather than usually.

Shift work – Approximately 1466 thousand women and 2414 thousand
men of working age in 1994 did shift work as part of their job.
Approximately one-third of the jobs which involved shift work were
held by women and two-thirds were held by men. The majority of
these jobs, for women and men, were full-time jobs.

Family workers – Approximately 35 thousand men and 78 thousand
women described themselves as family workers in 1994.

CONCLUSIONS

Sizeable proportions of men and women were employed in jobs which
had non-standard conditions in 1994. Over one-fifth of men and one-
half of women held non-standard jobs; these figures amount to 5.5
million women and over 3 million men. Some calculations put the
figures higher than this although the gap between men and women is
the same. Women were more likely to be in flexible jobs than men,
largely because they were so much more likely to be in part-time jobs.
Men were more often in self-employed jobs than women. Where women
were in self-employment, a much larger proportion than men were
working part-time. Self-employed women would be less likely than
self-employed men therefore to gain high earnings from their employment. The Meager (1994) study of the incomes of the self-employed
found that women were more likely than men to be low-earning self-
employed. As far as sex equality is concerned, women are disproportionately located in flexible jobs, and in jobs which are not covered by
protective legislation. Students constitute a small part of the flexible
workforce, and here male and female full-time students were employed
in similar types of flexible jobs.

This examination of 1994 LFS data has shown that a significant minority of men and at least one-half of women were employed in non-standard employment in 1994. Part-time jobs constituted the majority of women's flexible jobs, while self-employment constituted the majority of men's flexible jobs. Even after the 1994/95 legislative changes, being uncovered by employment protection legislation will still be the experience of large numbers of women, and it is a source of gender inequality in the labour market which can have wide-ranging implications.

Notes

1. Robinson does not give details of the definition used or alternatively of the source from which the figure is cited. However, most of his work does draw on the Labour Force Survey data.
2. These figures were cited in Hakim (1987) concerning the early to mid 1980s.
3. There has been a recent increase in women returning to work full-time after childbirth. This has been facilitated by taking maternity leave (McRae, 1991).
4. The LFS question asks people to say why they took a part-time rather than a full-time job and code the first that applies from: you were a student/you were at school; you were ill or disabled; you could not find a full-time job; you did not want a full-time job. It is not clear which option would be chosen by, for example, a woman with a young child who relied on informal child care arrangements while working part time.
5. For example see Hakim (1987), Scase and Goffee (1982) and Blanchflower and Oswald (1991).
6. See for example, Rees and Shah (1986), Dolton and Makepeace (1990) and Taylor (1994), the latter using the first wave of the BHPS data. There are some conceptual and measurement problems with the earnings data of the self-employed which need to be remembered.
7. This was a finding of Carter and Cannon (1988) and Johnson et al. (1989).
8. An analysis by Laurie and Taylor (1992) of the extent to which these categories overlapped in the British Household Panel Study found that all of those working *from* home were self-employed, and 60 per cent of those who were working at home were also self-employed. Also, 27 per cent of those who were working at home did not have permanent contracts and 46 per cent of the same group were employed part-time. An extremely small number of full-time homeworkers with permanent contracts will have been excluded from our calculations. If they were to be included, the estimates of the extent of flexible employment would increase, but by an extremely small percentage.
9. If individuals had started their job more than eight years ago they were not asked about the start date.
10. Individuals who were employed and who had missing start dates for their employment were assumed to have been in their current job for more than eight years.

5 Characteristics of Individuals in Flexible Jobs

In Chapter 4 we examined the extent to which individuals were in non-standard forms of work in Britain in 1994. In the present chapter, we wish to know also something about their characteristics. Since some of the tables have been published in Dex and McCulloch (1995) we do not reproduce them here. For the full statistics on the characteristics we discuss we refer the reader, when it is appropriate, to this other publication.

We use the Labour Force Survey for Spring 1994 and the British Household Panel Study (Wave 2) to provide a more detailed picture of some aspects of non-standard work than has been done previously.[1] All of the analyses, as previously, were undertaken on the population of working age; that is women aged 16–59 and men aged 16–64.[2]

PERSONAL CHARACTERISTICS

Age (LFS 1994 Cross-Section)

The percentages of men of different age groups in the various types of flexible employment are displayed in Table 5.1. Individuals who were full-time students, but who were also employed, have been included in the analysis. The 16–19 year olds had distinctly different types of employment from other age groups. Part of the reason for this difference is that this group contains those who are still in full-time education. Those in full-time education constituted approximately one-half of the employed men and women in this age group. Less than one half of 16–19 year old men (43 per cent) had standard jobs; nearly one-half were employed part-time; 17 per cent were in temporary jobs but very few were self-employed (3 per cent). There was a gradual decline with age of the percentage in full-time permanent jobs. The percentage who were self-employed clearly increased with age. The category of self-employed with employees increased up to the 40–49 age group, then remained the same, but the percentages of the self-employed who did not have employees grew progressively with age up to 65. The

Table 5.1 Profile of non-standard forms of employment, by age of working age men in 1994: LFS

per cent*

		Age groups				
	16–19	20–29	30–39	40–49	50–59	60–64
Full-time permanent	43.0	79.0	76.5	74.0	69.8	62.6
Part-time						
self definition	48.4	5.1	(2.7)	(2.6)	5.8	14.7
more than 1 PT	3.6	(0.3)	(0.2)	(0.4)	(0.4)	(0.7)
Uncovered 94	72.1	32.3	17.3	12.0	10.7	8.0
Temporary						
all	16.9	7.0	4.4	3.6	3.8	4.8
seasonal/casual	10.9	1.6	(0.4)	(0.5)	(0.8)	(1.7)
fixed term	3.4	3.9	3.2	2.4	2.2	2.5
Self-employed						
all	3.0	10.6	17.3	20.4	22.7	25.6
with employees	(0.1)	(1.5)	4.5	6.7	6.3	6.2
without employees	2.9	9.1	12.8	13.7	16.4	19.4
Job-change employee,						
self employed	(0.7)	(0.2)	(0.2)	(0.2)	(0.1)	(0.1)
Any flexible	53.6	17.2	17.3	18.6	22.9	35.0
N, thousands	558	3272	3558	3256	2166	597

* Do not add up to 100% since categories are not mutually exclusive.
( ) Based on small cell size

oldest men's age group to be considered, 60–64, had much in common with the youngest group; they had higher rates of part-time, and any flexible employment than any of the younger groups, except for 16–19 year olds.

Removing those in full-time education from these samples had the effect of substantially reducing the extent of flexible employment among 16–19 year old young men. Twenty-nine per cent of this group were employed in flexible jobs. This was still slightly higher than the percentages in flexible jobs in the older age groups, but it was a smaller percentage than for the 60–64 year old men. However, a higher percentage were in either part-time or temporary employment than in older age groups up to age 60.

A comparison with figures from 1992 suggests that the percentage of older men (aged 60–64) employed part-time has risen. EOC (1993) found that 11 per cent of male employees aged 60–64 worked part time compared with 15 per cent in 1994. Part-time work may be becoming a transitional stage for men, between employment and retirement. This is likely to be different for women who have entered part-time work at earlier ages and often remain in it.

The age distributions for women are displayed in Table 5.2. For women, as for men, those aged 16–19 are particularly likely to be in flexible jobs. Sixty per cent of this youngest group of women were in part-time jobs, and compared with other age groups, they had the largest proportion of jobs which were not covered by employment protection legislation (81 per cent), and the highest percentage of temporary employment (15 per cent), particularly seasonal/casual temporary employment (10 per cent). These figures, as for men, are being weighted by those who were in full-time education. However, while the percentage of total flexible employment for the youngest age group was the highest of the age groups, many groups of women had very similar experiences of flexible employment overall. The exception was the 20–29 year age group which had a much lower level of flexible employment; only 30 per cent compared with over 55 per cent in all the other age groups of women. This arose from the low levels of part-time employment and relatively low levels of self-employment of this age group: both part-time work and self-employment become more substantial at older ages. Flexible employment for women in the other age groups was at a fairly constant level, but for slightly different reasons; part-time employment remained a constant component for all age groups (except 20–29 year olds), temporary employment was lower in the older age groups but self-employment was higher, helping to make the overall amount of non-standard employment for women similar across the age groups.

Removing those in full-time education from these samples had the effect of substantially reducing the extent of flexible employment among 16–19 year old young women. The relative extent of flexible work among women also changed as a result of removing students. Young women who were not in full-time education no longer had substantially higher proportions of part-time or temporary employment than older women. In fact they had the lowest percentage of part-time employment, and a percentage in temporary employment which was closer to the experiences of other age groups. The youngest age group of women (not in full-time education) had 37 per cent in flexible jobs.

Clearly flexible employment, for the most part, is associated with joining and leaving the labour force. This is more the case for men

Table 5.2 Profile of non-standard forms of employment, by age of working age women in 1994: LFS

per cent*

			Age groups		
	16–19	*20–29*	*30–39*	*40–49*	*50–59*
Full-time permanent	35.5	67.0	44.5	45.3	41.3
Part-time					
self definition	60.2	25.0	48.2	47.2	52.3
more than 1 PT	5.5	2.0	3.7	4.1	2.9
Uncovered 94	81.0	39.9	27.8	18.1	12.4
Temporary					
all	15.2	8.8	7.5	6.8	4.7
seasonal/casual	10.4	(1.9)	(1.8)	(1.3)	(1.4)
fixed term	3.1	5.3	4.2	4.1	2.4
Self-employed					
all	(1.5)	3.3	8.6	8.5	8.2
with employees	(0.0)	(0.4)	(1.9)	2.5	2.6
without employees	1.5	2.8	6.6	5.9	5.7
Job-change employee,					
self employed	(0.4)	(0.8)	(1.3)	(0.8)	(0.5)
Any flexible	63.9	30.4	55.8	55.1	59.4
N, thousands	556	2689	2742	2858	1810

* Do not add up to 100% since categories are not mutually exclusive.
( ) Based on small cell sizes

than for women. However, there is a solid block of individuals in flexible work in the middle age ranges. These consist largely of self-employed men and women employed part-time.

Marital Status (LFS 1994 Cross-Section)

The extent of non-standard employment by marital status is displayed for men and women in Dex and McCulloch (1995, pp. 46–7, tables 3.8 and 3.9). Percentages of part-time employment were higher among single, widowed and divorced men than in the other groups. Jobs uncovered by employment protection and jobs with temporary contracts were more common among the single men, findings which overlap with the fact that single employees were also concentrated in the youngest age groups. For the same age-related reason, self-employment was lower among the single. Fixed-term temporary contracts were most common among men who were single. Self-employment was highest among the divorced and the legally married men, approximately one-fifth of whom were self-employed. The patterns were somewhat different according to whether the self-employed had or did not have employees. For those self-employed men with employees, the highest proportion could be found among those who were legally married (6 per cent). In the case of the self-employed without employees, who constituted a much larger proportion of the self-employed men in total, divorced men had the highest percentages in this position. In total, flexible jobs were most common among men who were either divorced or single, largely because of their higher self-employment rates in the case of the divorced and because of their higher temporary and part-time rates in the case of the single.

Single women shared many characteristics with single men and for the same reason, that they were younger in age. They had the highest proportions in temporary jobs, both seasonal/casual and fixed term contracts; they also had the lowest percentages in self-employment. Self-employed women were also found in higher proportions among the widowed, separated and legally married women. In the case of the legally married women, this result overlapped with the findings about men. Legally married and separated women retained the highest percentages of the self-employed without employees, although in the case of the self-employed with employees, married and widowed women had the highest percentage (2 per cent). Part-time employment was highest for women who were legally married, or widowed. The percentages of part-time employment were much lower in the other groups, but lowest among women who were single and women who were living with a partner. In total, flexible jobs were most common among women who were married or widowed. This was mainly because they had the highest rates of part-time employment; these women had 58–60 per cent of their jobs characterised by non-standard conditions. Flexible jobs were least common among those who were living together who had 29 per cent of their jobs in non-standard categories.

Ethnic Origin (LFS 1994 Cross-section)

The extent of non-standard employment by ethnic origin is displayed for men and women in Dex and McCulloch (1995, pp. 51–2, tables 3.11 and 3.12). The ethnic origin categories have been aggregated, because of their smaller size, into five groups. However this still leaves some of the individual cell breakdowns with small numbers. Thus we restrict ourselves to the broad levels of comparison only.

Flexible employment in total was more common among the group described as Black Other, the Asian group and the Chinese and Other groups. It was least common among the Black Caribbean group, with Whites lying somewhere in between. As many as 30 per cent of Asian men were in flexible jobs compared with only 17 per cent of Black Caribbean men and 20 per cent of White men. High proportions of Asian men (25 per cent), Chinese and Other men (21 per cent) were self-employed. Self-employment with employees made up a much larger share of this total in self-employment than was the case for self-employed men who were White. The high proportion who were self-employed in the Asian and Chinese groups was mainly responsible for their high total percentage in flexible employment. Although many of the ethnic minority groups also had higher proportions than Whites in part-time employment, in jobs not covered by employment protection, and in temporary employment, in most cases these differences were not large. However, the ethnic groups described as Black Other and the Chinese and other, had notably higher percentages of temporary jobs, 12–14 per cent, as compared with 5 per cent for Whites.

There were also some important differences between women according to their ethnic origin, in ways which differed from men. A much higher proportion of White than ethnic minority women worked part-time. Only 30 per cent of Black Caribbean women were employed in part-time jobs, and the highest percentage in part-time jobs among the minority groups was 35 per cent for the Black and Other group. Many of the ethnic minority women had far higher percentages of employed women working full-time. Asian and Chinese women, like their male equivalents, had much higher percentages in self-employment, and as with the men, it was largely self-employment without employees. The highest percentages of temporary jobs was among the Black and Other group, at 15 per cent; White women had the lowest percentages of jobs on temporary contracts.

In some ways these comparisons between groups of different ethnic origins were predictable. The greater degree of full-time employment among ethnic minority women, especially Black Caribbean is well known, as they are more often the sole earners in the household and are living at lower levels of income. The predominance of self-employment among Asian and Chinese ethnic minorities in the British labour markets is also well known.[3] It has probably been partly a response to facing discrimination in the labour market that ethnic minorities, with the appropriate traditions and ability to raise capital, have gone down this route, and have often made a success of their businesses. The women of the same ethnic origin appear to have followed the men. Bhavnani (1994) discusses the reasons for ethnic minority women having entered self-employment.

Ethnic minority men appear to experience more temporary work and more part-time employment than the white majority, while ethnic minority women also have more temporary jobs than white women, but far fewer part-time jobs.

Attitudes (BHPS 1992 Cross-Section)

The BHPS data asked individuals to give their responses to a series of statements some of which covered their attitudes to women working. In Table 5.3, the responses are reported to the statement 'A child suffers if the mother works'. The level of disagreement with this statement was higher among women than men. In addition, there were variations according to the status of the jobs held. Disagreement was higher among men who held permanent full or part-time jobs. Self-employed men appeared to be the most traditional of the groups of men. For women, disagreement was strongest among those in permanent full-time jobs, and as for men, the most traditional group were the self-employed. The definition of 'any flexible' in this and other analyses of BHPS data includes any part-time, temporary or self-employed work. BHPS retrospective data do not distinguish between self-employed with and without employees.

The responses to another statement, 'A family is happier if the women works' are reported in Table 5.4. Again self-employed men appeared to be the most traditional, having the highest proportion of men who disagreed with this statement and the lowest percentage who agreed. The most agreement came from men employed in permanent part-time jobs, but they also had a high degree of disagreement. For women, the most agreement for this statement came from those in permanent full-time and permanent part-time jobs. Self-employed and temporarily employed women were more traditional than these other groups, although the differences were not great.

Having a flexible job is associated with having slightly more traditional attitudes towards women's roles in the home and the labour market. The most outstanding difference is in the attitudes of the self-employed, both men and women. In some cases, there was both more agreement and more disagreement with the statements evident in the

Table 5.3 Attitudes to mother working, by job status at Wave 2 for employed men and women in BHPS sample

Question: A child suffers if mother works?

	FT permanent	PT permanent	Self-employed	Temporary	Any flexible
		Job status			
	Men – per cent				
Strongly agree	15.2	14.8	18.2	13.8	16.3
Agree	37.0	40.6	43.2	41.0	42.1
Not agree or disagree	25.3	21.1	22.8	25.2	23.2
Disagree	18.2	21.1	13.8	14.8	15.4
Strongly disagree	4.2	2.3	2.0	5.2	3.0
Total	100	100	100	100	100
N	1833	128	391	210	729
	Women – per cent				
Strongly agree	7.5	11.4	15.0	13.9	12.3
Agree	24.6	28.6	32.7	26.9	28.8
Not agree or disagree	23.6	25.3	22.4	30.0	25.8
Disagree	32.5	27.8	26.5	22.0	26.7
Strongly disagree	11.8	6.8	3.4	7.2	6.5
Total	100	100	100	100	100
N	1106	909	147	223	1279

Table 5.4 Attitudes to women working, by job status at Wave 2 for employed men and women in BHPS sample

Question: Family is happier if woman works?

Response	FT permanent	PT permanent	Self-employed	Temporary	Any flexible
		Job status			
	Men – per cent				
Strongly agree	2.1	0.8	2.0	2.4	1.9
Agree	19.4	24.2	14.0	16.1	16.4
Not agree/disagree	49.6	43.0	47.8	54.5	48.9
Disagree	25.1	28.9	33.1	21.8	29.1
Strongly disagree	3.8	3.1	3.1	5.2	3.7
Total	100	100	100	100	100
N	1832	128	393	211	732

continued on page 72

Table 5.4   continued

Response	FT permanent	Job status PT permanent	Self- employed	Temporary	Any flexible
		Women – per cent			
Strongly agree	3.4	2.3	4.1	4.1	2.8
Agree	18.0	19.8	13.7	15.3	18.3
Not agree/disagree	55.9	49.4	56.2	51.8	50.6
Disagree	21.2	26.2	24.7	26.1	26.0
Strongly disagree	1.4	2.2	1.4	2.7	2.2
Total	100	100	100	100	100
N	1104	908	146	222	1276

responses of those in flexible jobs. However, the differences are not sufficient in size to take a major part in explaining why individuals take up
flexible jobs, or why more women take up such jobs. Individuals obviously take up flexible jobs for a variety of reasons. Clearly, it is not just
because they can more easily manage a job and caring for children.

Individuals in BHPS were also asked which, of a list of items, was
the most important aspect of a job. The percentages who said that 'job
security' was either the first or the second most important aspect of
their job are displayed in Table 5.5. These figures show that the security of their own job was more important to men than to women.
However, far more of those in full-time permanent jobs thought security to be the most important aspect of a job. It is interesting that
those in seemingly the most secure jobs were most concerned about
job security, with the exception of the unemployed. It could be the
case that their position in full-time permanent jobs has been motivated
by this concern, and that those who are less concerned about job security are happier to be in less secure jobs. Alternatively, the results
may be expressing a worry by those in full-time permanent jobs, about
the risks of losing them in the general climate of uncertainty of the
1990s' labour market.

Job Satisfaction (BHPS 1992 Cross-Section)

Individuals scored their levels of satisfaction with job security and
overall job satisfaction on a 10-point scale in BHPS (10 = completely
satisfied). The mean scores are displayed in Table 5.6. Temporary

Table 5.5 Most important aspect of a job: per cent who say job security is most or second most important by economic activity status: BHPS Wave 1

Per cent saying job security

Current status Wave 1	Men		Women	
	Most important	2nd most important	Most important	2nd most important
FT permanent	37.0 (1914)	20.1 (1912)	26.7 (1261)	15.9 (1261)
PT permanent	16.7 (60)	18.3 (60)	22.1 (702)	22.1 (702)
Self-employed	20.4 (393)	14.6 (390)	13.1 (145)	11.8 (144)
Temporary	21.2 (193)	16.6 (193)	13.6 (265)	10.6 (204)
Unemployed	40.1 (274)	16.1 (274)	13.3 (120)	14.2 (120)
Inactive	27.1 (317)	16.5 (316)	17.2 (661)	8.8 (660)

( ) – sample sizes in status category in parentheses.

Table 5.6 Satisfaction scores, by status of job: BHPS Wave 2

Satisfaction with job security
Mean score

Current status Wave 2	Men	Women
FT permanent	4.91 (1796)	5.22 (1189)
PT permanent	5.56 (55)	5.61 (631)
Temporary	2.81 (88)	3.77 (149)

Satisfaction with overall job

	Men	Women
FT permanent	5.29 (1803)	5.61 (1202)
PT permanent	5.89 (56)	6.02 (635)
Temporary	5.09 (87)	5.72 (150)

workers, both men and women, were the least satisfied about their job security. Part-time permanent employees were the most satisfied, on average.

On the measure of overall job satisfaction, permanent part-timers were again the most satisfied of the men's and women's groups. Men in temporary jobs had the lowest satisfaction scores for men, whereas for women, those in full-time permanent jobs had the lowest scores.

Much has been made of the fact that women employed part time exhibit higher amounts of satisfaction than women in full-time jobs, and than men. The differences here are mostly very small, but it is worth noting that men in permanent part-time jobs have similar satisfaction scores on job security to permanent part-time employed women. Gender differences do not always persist when other factors are controlled.

General Health Questions (GHQ) (BHPS 1992 Cross-Section)

Individuals were asked about their general state of mental health, using the question 'Have you recently been feeling reasonably happy, all things considered?' The responses are displayed in Table 5.7. The majority of both men and women were likely to say that they were feeling the same as usual. Among the men, the self-employed and those with temporary jobs included slightly larger proportions who were less happy in 1992 than usual. However, men in temporary jobs also had the larger percentage (17 per cent) who were more happy than usual. Women in temporary jobs were more likely to be happier than usual, and a larger percentage of self-employed women were much less happy. In view of the discussion about the satisfaction of part-time women workers we can also compare part- and full-time employed women with respect to their GHQ replies. There is some evidence that women employed in permanent part-time jobs are slightly happier than those in permanent full-time jobs, but again, the differences are minimal.

It is possible to calculate a GHQ score from 12 questions (Goldberg, 1972). This score is a general indicator of psychological well-being. The score has a range of -12 to $+12$, and the lower the score, the better an individual's psycho-social well-being or levels of stress is thought to be. The mean scores are displayed in Table 5.8 for Wave 2.

The scores suggest that men and women in temporary jobs are exhibiting the greatest degree of stress. For women, the differences between the other jobs are relatively small. However, for men, being in a part-time permanent job is associated with the lowest levels of stress, followed by being in a full-time permanent job. Self-employed men have the highest scores and thus the lowest levels of well-being.

While temporary workers gave lower priority to job security than those in full-time permanent jobs (Table 5.5), it might have appeared that workers in temporary jobs are better able to cope than others with having an insecure job, and possible they may prefer these jobs. These scores show that temporary work does lead to deterioration in well-being for men and women, over and above having other types of jobs.

Table 5.7 General health questionnaire (GHQ score), by job status at
Wave 2 for employed men and women in BHPS sample

Question: Have you recently been feeling reasonably happy,
all things considered?

GHQ	FT permanent	PT permanent	Self-employed	Temporary	Any flexible
		Job status			
	Men – per cent				
More than usual	14.1	16.5	10.6	16.8	13.4
Same as usual	75.1	74.8	77.6	67.8	74.3
Less so	9.6	8.7	11.1	14.4	11.6
Much less	1.3	–	0.8	1.0	0.7
Total	100	100	100	100	100
N	1835	127	397	208	732
	Women – per cent				
More than usual	14.5	12.8	11.4	16.8	13.4
Same as usual	69.6	74.0	75.8	68.1	73.2
Less so	13.5	11.6	8.7	12.8	11.5
Much less	2.4	1.5	4.0	2.2	1.9
Total	100	100	100	100	100
N	1102	913	149	226	1288

Table 5.8 GHQ mean score, by type of job: BHPS 1991 Wave 2

	Full-time permanent	Part-time permanent	Self-employed	Temporary	Any flexible
		Current job			
Men	1.43	1.27	1.63	1.89	1.66
Women	1.88	1.84	1.84	2.21	1.91

QUALIFICATIONS AND WORK HISTORY

Education (BHPS 1992 Cross-Section)

The highest qualifications of employed men and women in various
jobs are displayed in Table 5.9. There is an increase in the percentage

Table 5.9 Highest educational qualifications, by job status at Wave 2 for
employed men and women in the BHPS sample

Highest education	FT permanent	PT permanent	Self-employed	Temporary	Total	Any Flexible	N
			Job status				
		Men – row per cent					
Degree	75.5	4.5	16.1	3.8	100	24.5	286
A-Level	75.7	3.0	18.1	3.2	100	24.3	835
O-Level	74.7	3.4	18.4	3.4	100	25.3	467
CSE	79.3	2.6	15.5	2.6	100	20.7	116
Vocation	70.4	3.1	24.5	2.0	100	29.6	98
None	70.1	3.5	23.7	2.7	100	29.9	71
		Women – row per cent					
Degree	60.6	19.7	8.7	11.1	100	39.4	208
A-Level	60.5	23.8	9.0	6.7	100	39.5	600
O-Level	54.3	32.8	7.6	5.3	100	45.7	606
CSE	49.3	36.6	9.9	4.2	100	50.7	71
Vocation	44.4	45.0	6.5	4.1	100	55.6	169
None	37.3	51.1	5.3	6.2	100	62.7	133

of flexible jobs as educational qualifications decline for both men and
women. The increase is more marked for women than for men. For
men, this effect is caused almost solely by a higher incidence of self-
employment at the lower levels of education, since temporary jobs and
permanent part-time jobs are experienced in similar amounts by those
with varying levels of educational qualifications. A different pattern
emerges for women. The increase in flexible jobs is caused by higher
percentages of permanent part-time jobs at the lower levels of qualifications. The percentages of self-employment and temporary jobs vary
slightly across the various qualification levels but not systematically.
However, it is worth noting the much higher level of temporary jobs
for women with degrees: 11 per cent of employed women with degrees were in temporary jobs in comparison with 4–7 per cent in the
other groups.

Training (LFS 1994 Cross-Section)

Individuals in the LFS were asked whether they had experienced any
training in their job over the past four weeks. The extent to which
individuals had had some training given in their various forms of em-

ployment was reported in Dex and McCulloch (1995, p. 79, table 5.6). Those who were in full-time education were excluded from these samples since individuals who were receiving education will also be recorded as receiving training. Overall, men and women in flexible jobs, but especially women, were less likely than those in full-time permanent jobs to have received training. For women in full-time permanent jobs, 19 per cent had received training compared with 12 per cent of women in flexible jobs. For men in permanent full-time jobs, 15 per cent had received training compared with 10 per cent of men in flexible jobs. In the case of the men, the lower overall figure for flexible jobs is due to the depressing effect of lack of training opportunities for men in self-employment.

Women in part-time employment experienced less training than those in full-time permanent jobs but this was not the case for men. Men in part-time jobs received slightly more training than men in full-time permanent jobs. Men and women in temporary jobs as a whole experienced training to a greater extent than those in full-time permanent employment. The jobs which held out the best training opportunities for women and men appeared from these figures to be the fixed-term contract jobs.

Women in full-time permanent jobs had experienced more training than men in the same jobs; 19 per cent of women said they had received training compared with 15 per cent of men. Women in part-time jobs received less training than men in part-time jobs. Women had received training to a slightly higher extent when they held temporary jobs; 21 per cent of women in temporary jobs and 18 per cent of men had received training. Women and men in fixed-term jobs were far more likely than women in seasonal/casual jobs to say that they had received training. Relatively few of the self-employed had received any training; only 6 per cent of self-employed men and 9 per cent of self-employed women.

Hourly Earnings (BHPS 1991/2 Cross-Section)

A distribution of the hourly earnings quartiles for some jobs is presented in Table 5.10. There were too few data on the earnings and hours of the self-employed to make this a worthwhile comparison. It is very striking that both men and women in permanent part-time and temporary jobs were vastly more likely to be receiving hourly earnings in the lowest quartile than individuals with full-time permanent jobs. Approximately one half of the flexible groups were receiving the

Table 5.10 Hourly earnings quartiles, by job status at Wave 2 for employed men and women in the BHPS sample

Hourly earnings quartiles	FT permanent	PT permanent	Temporary	Any flexible
		Job status		
Men – per cent				
Lowest	9.7	50.4	40.2	39.3
2	20.0	13.7	25.9	19.6
3	32.3	11.1	19.6	18.4
Highest	38.0	24.8	14.3	22.7
Total	100	100	100	100
N	1667	117	112	321
Women – per cent				
Lowest	23.3	46.4	49.5	45.6
2	30.7	29.8	23.4	28.4
3	26.8	13.8	12.8	14.4
Highest	19.3	10.0	14.4	11.5
Total	100	100	100	100
N	997	842	188	1030

lowest levels of hourly pay in comparison with 10 per cent of men and 23 per cent of women in permanent full-time jobs. At the top end of the pay scale, the differences were not always so marked, although more permanent full-timers were receiving the highest pay. Temporarily employed men were doing the worst at the top end of the pay hierarchy with only 14 per cent receiving the highest pay. Since young men are more predominant in this group of temporarily employed men, the lower levels of pay are to be expected.

The mean hourly rates of pay in 1992 for different types of jobs are displayed in Table 5.11, where reliable sample sizes were available. The figures are broken down by age since earnings are well known to be age-related. For women, those in full-time permanent jobs tended to have the highest mean hourly rates of pay across most of the age groups; an exception was women in their thirties on fixed-term contracts who had the highest mean hourly rates for women in this age group. The lowest rates of pay for women were most often in temporary casual jobs. Women in part-time permanent jobs were often on lower rates of pay than women in part-time temporary jobs. There was considerable variation in the mean hourly rates of pay being received

Table 5.11 Mean hourly gross paid of men and women, by category and age group at Wave 2 of BHPS*

	16–19	20–29	30–39	40–49	50–59	60–65
			Men			
Self-employed						
with employees	n.a	11.02	12.40	7.73	n.a	n.a
without employees		5.30	9.71	4.42	6.19	(3.46)
Full-time permanent	2.81	6.36	8.91	9.06	8.52	6.57
Part-time permanent	(3.01)	(3.20)	n.a	n.a	(8.40)	(3.16)
Part-time temporary						
Temporary–fixed term	(1.94)	4.87	10.95	7.49	8.17	
Temporary–casual	3.81	6.02	(10.91)	(3.10)	(6.26)	(2.30)
			Women			
Self-employed						
with employees		(5.56)	(7.54)	(1.80)	(9.23)	
without employees		(10.18)	3.87	4.01	(5.23)	
Full-time permanent	3.01	6.21	7.43	7.43	6.11	
Part-time permanent	(2.81)	3.36	5.13	4.43	6.11	
Part-time temporary	(2.65)	5.58	5.27	(5.00)		
Temporary–fixed term		(6.72)	8.96	5.78		
Temporary–casual	2.50	4.38	4.68	4.21	(6.45)	

* Missing earnings values have been replaced by imputed earnings values.
( ) statistic based on sample size of less than 20.

by women in self-employment, much more so than by men, although there were far fewer reliable statistics for the women, due to smaller samples.

The picture for men is more complicated than that for women. There was relatively little variation in the mean hourly rates earned by 16–19 year old men, as would be expected. In the 40s to 50s and 50s to 60s age groups, men were earning the highest mean hourly rates in full-time permanent jobs, followed by jobs with temporary fixed-term contracts and the self-employed. At younger ages, the self-employed had the highest rates. Full-time permanent jobs had the second highest mean hourly pay in the 20s age group, but in the 30s those in temporary jobs were earning more than those in permanent full-time jobs.

This brief review of pay differentials suggests that full-time permanent jobs give women the best pay, and give middle-aged and older men higher rates, on average, than other sorts of jobs. Flexible jobs, on the whole, are giving women and many men lower rates of pay.

Past Unemployment History (BHPS 1992 Cross-Section)

The experience of past periods of unemployment of men and women in various jobs are displayed in Table 5.12. The histories are based on the retrospective data recalled by BHPS individuals up to Wave 2. Men in self-employment at Wave 2 were the least likely to have had any previous experiences of unemployment; 73 per cent had not had any previous unemployment experience. Men in temporary jobs were the most likely to have had an unemployment period in the past; 60 per cent of temporarily employed men had had at least one previous period of unemployment. Men in temporary jobs were also more likely to have had three or more previous periods of unemployment than men in the other groups; 10 per cent of men in temporary jobs had had three or more unemployment spells compared with the minimum value of 5 per cent for men in permanent full-time jobs.

This relationship of past unemployment and a temporary job was also evident for women, but the differences between women in different statuses at Wave 2 were considerably smaller than they were between men; 29 per cent of women in temporary jobs, 23 per cent of women in full-time permanent jobs, and 18 per cent of women in self-employed jobs had not had any previous unemployment. The differences between women's multiple experiences of unemployment were slight.

The percentages of their past working life which individuals had spent unemployed reflect the earlier results on the periods of unemployment they had experienced. The figures are in Table 5.13. Given that individuals had been unemployed in the past, the vast majority of these individuals who were currently employed had spent less than one-third of their working lives unemployed. This was the case for both men and women, and irrespective of their current employment status. However, 6 per cent of men in temporary jobs had spent between one- and two-thirds of their working lives unemployed. This suggests that there is a small group of men who have had a career of unemployment interspersed with short-term or temporary jobs.

Lastly, on the issue of past unemployment, we examine the extent to which these employed individuals had ever had a period of long-term unemployment. Again, men (and women to a far lesser extent) in temporary jobs stand out by having a far higher proportion who ever had a past period of long-term unemployment (21 per cent of men and 8 per cent of women in temporary jobs). In the case of men, this is approximately double the experience of long-term unemployment found in the other groups.

Table 5.12 Periods of unemployment, by job status at Wave 2 for employed men and women in the BHPS sample

Past unemployment periods	FT permanent	Job status PT permanent	Self-employed	Temporary	Any flexible
		Men – row per cent			
0	65.8	61.0	72.5	40.3	67.0
1	22.6	27.3	17.1	27.8	19.8
2	7.0	5.2	5.1	21.2	7.2
3 or more	4.5	6.5	5.3	9.7	6.0
Total	100	100	100	100	100
N	1680	77	432	72	581
		Women – row per cent			
0	77.2	81.1	81.9	71.4	80.0
1	16.0	14.1	14.4	21.8	15.2
2	4.7	3.4	2.5	3.8	3.3
3 or more	2.0	1.4	1.3	3.0	1.6
Total	100	100	100	100	100
N	1097	716	160	133	1009

Table 5.13 Percentage of working life spent unemployed, by job status at Wave 2 for employed men and women in the BHPS sample

Per cent unemployed	FT permanent	Job status PT permanent	Self-employed	Temporary	Any flexible
		Men – per cent			
0	65.8	61.0	72.5	40.3	67.0
1–33	32.3	37.7	27.1	52.8	31.7
34–67	1.5	1.3	0.2	5.6	1.0
68–100	0.4	–	0.2	1.4	0.3
Total	100	100	100	100	100
N	1680	77	432	72	581
		Women – per cent			
0	77.2	81.1	81.9	71.4	80.0
1–33	21.6	17.7	18.1	27.8	19.1
34–67	1.1	0.8	–	–	0.6
68–100	0.1	0.3	–	0.8	0.3
Total	100	100	100	100	100
N	1097	716	160	133	1009

HOUSEHOLD CHARACTERISTICS

Housing Tenure (BHPS 1992 Cross-Section)

The tenure of individuals in the various job status categories are displayed in Table 5.14. Men in permanent full-time jobs were the least likely to own their house outright (11 per cent) in comparison to the other groups where approximately one-quarter of the individuals did own their own houses. In the case of the men in permanent part-time and self-employed jobs, their higher rates of outright ownership are likely to be due to their older age distribution. Men in full-time permanent jobs were far more likely to be buying a house with a mortgage than other groups; 71 per cent were doing this. When considering ownership in total (owned outright or mortgage), it was highest among the self-employed men (84 per cent). However, even among temporary workers, who had the lowest rates of ownership and the highest rates of renting, ownership was still the option of the majority (76 per cent). It is also worth noting that there is a sizeable pocket of permanently employed part-time men in Local Authority rented housing, far higher than in other groups.

The picture among women is less differentiated. Self-employed women were the most likely among the groups to be owning (outright or mortgage) their own house, but the differences are not great. The experiences of women in temporary jobs, unlike the men, are on a par with those in other job statuses. Since buying a house is a joint activity but one which will often be decided more on the basis of the (male) partner's earnings and job stability, it is perhaps not surprising to see more variation in housing tenure based on men's jobs than for women's jobs.

Dependent Children (LFS 1994 Cross-Section)

The extent to which men and women had at least one dependent child are displayed in Dex and McCulloch (1995, p. 49, table 3.10). A dependent child is defined in the LFS as being under the age of 16, or is aged 17–18 and still in full-time education. There were hardly any differences in men's employment status according to whether or not they had a dependent child. Approximately one-fifth of men who had a dependent child, and one-fifth of men who did not were in flexible jobs. Also, the types of these jobs were broadly similar for both groups. Men who did not have a dependent child were slightly more likely to be in temporary jobs.

Table 5.14 Housing tenure, by job status at Wave 2 for employed men and women in BHPS sample

Housing tenure	FT permanent	Job status PT permanent	Self-employed	Temporary	Any flexible
		Men – per cent			
Own, outright	11.3	23.4	23.8	22.2	23.6
Own, mortgage	71.1	48.1	60.6	54.2	58.2
LA rent	8.5	15.6	5.1	6.9	6.7
Other rent	9.1	13.0	10.5	16.7	11.5
Total	100	100	100	100	100
N	1679	77	432	72	581
		Women – per cent			
Own, outright	12.5	15.8	23.1	14.3	16.7
Own, mortgage	67.9	64.1	65.0	67.7	64.7
LA rent	9.4	12.6	3.8	9.0	10.7
Other rent	10.2	7.5	8.1	9.0	7.9
Total	100	100	100	100	100
N	1097	716	160	133	1009

LA = Local Authority.

However, for women, having a dependent child was associated with major differences in their types of employment. At the overall level, flexible jobs were considerably more common among women who had a dependent child than among women who did not have such a child; 71 per cent of women with a dependent child were in flexible jobs compared with only 37 per cent of those who did not. Most of this difference was accounted for by part-time employment; 62 per cent of women with a dependent child were in part-time jobs, compared with only 32 per cent of those women without a dependent child. Women with dependent children were also more likely than those without to be in jobs which were uncovered by employment protection, to have two or more part-time jobs, to be in temporary jobs, and in self-employment. However, these differences were slight compared with the difference in the extent of part-time employment.

Lone Parents (BHPS 1992 Cross-Section)

Table 5.15 shows the extent to which lone parents appear in each of these job status groups. The percentages are all very small. It is notable that there is a far higher percentage of lone parents among women in temporary jobs (8 per cent), especially compared with permanent full-timers (4 per cent) and the self-employed (3 per cent). Those men in permanent part-time jobs are more likely to be lone parents, but the numbers are very small.

Caring for the Elderly and Sick (BHPS 1992 Cross-Section)

Individuals in the BHPS sample were asked whether or not they cared for an elderly relative or a sick child in their own home. (Caring for healthy children was not included.) The extent to which individuals had such caring responsibilities within their homes is examined in Table 5.16. Men and women in permanent part-time jobs were slightly more likely to have had caring responsibilities (4 per cent) compared with other groups, but the numbers are small.

Household Income (BHPS 1991 Cross-Section)

The quartiles of household income for individuals in various job status groups are displayed in Table 5.17.[4] Men in temporary jobs were likely to have the lowest household incomes, although permanent part timers and the self-employed also had much larger percentages whose household incomes were in the lowest quartile at Wave 1, in comparison with full-time permanently employed men. Hardly any of the permanent full-time employed men had incomes in the lowest quartile in contrast to 8 per cent of temporarily employed men. Women exhibit a similar ranking. Women in temporary jobs were those with the highest proportions with the lowest incomes, and permanent full-time women employees were those with the lowest proportions in the lowest income group. But self-employed women did better than their male counterparts and had equal levels of household income to women in full-time permanent jobs.

At the top end of the income distribution, men in permanent part-time jobs had the highest proportions in top household income quartile (49 per cent) and self-employed men have the lowest (38 per cent). However, it should be remembered that the incomes of the self-employed are more difficult to assess. For women, permanent full-timers had the

Table 5.15 Lone parent status by job status at Wave 2 for employed men and women in BHPS sample

	FT permanent	PT permanent	Self-employed	Temporary	Any flexible
		Job status per cent			
		Men – per cent			
Lone	0.7	2.6	0.9	1.4	1.2
Rest	99.3	97.4	99.1	98.6	98.8
Total	100	100	100	100	100
N	1680	77	432	72	581
		Women – per cent			
Lone	4.4	5.0	2.5	8.3	5.1
Rest	95.6	95.0	97.5	91.7	94.9
Total	100	100	100	100	100
N	1097	716	160	133	1009

Table 5.16 Whether individual is a carer for someone inside the household, by job status at Wave 2 for employed men and women in BHPS sample

Carer	FT permanent	PT permanent	Self-employed	Temporary	Any flexible
		Job status			
		Men – per cent			
Yes	2.6	3.9	2.1	1.4	2.2
No	97.4	96.1	97.9	98.6	97.8
Total	100	100	100	100	100
N	1680	77	432	72	581
		Women – per cent			
Yes	2.2	4.1	1.3	1.5	3.3
No	97.8	95.9	98.8	98.5	96.7
Total	100	100	100	100	100
N	1097	716	160	133	1009

Table 5.17 Household income quartiles, by job status at Wave 2 for
employed men and women in BHPS sample

Household income quartiles	FT permanent	PT permanent	Self-employed	Temporary	Any flexible
		Job status			
Men – per cent					
Lowest	0.5	7.3	6.5	8.1	7.2
2	16.3	19.5	25.5	23.2	23.9
3	39.6	24.4	30.1	27.3	28.3
Highest	43.5	48.8	37.9	41.4	40.6
Total	100	100	100	100	100
N	1091	41	153	99	293
Women – per cent					
Lowest	2.3	7.5	2.2	8.5	7.3
2	15.0	22.7	34.8	26.3	24.4
3	35.8	34.5	23.9	27.1	32.1
Highest	46.9	35.4	39.1	38.1	36.3
Total	100	100	100	100	100
N	618	415	46	118	579

highest proportion in the top income quartile, and permanent part-
timers had the lowest percentage in this top category.

Individuals were asked how they felt about their financial situation
and their replies are in Table 5.18. These replies largely overlap with
the income distribution figures. Men in permanent part-time jobs were
more likely to think that they were living comfortably (35 per cent),
the most satisfied category. Men in temporary jobs were the least likely
to feel they were living comfortably (23 per cent). Men in temporary
jobs were the most likely to be finding it quite or very difficult to
manage (17 per cent in total). Self-employed men were the next most
likely to be finding it difficult to manage.

Among women, permanent part-timers were the least likely (23 per
cent) and self-employed women the most likely (32 per cent) to say
they were living comfortably. Women in temporary jobs were the most
likely (15 per cent) and permanent full timers the least likely (6 per
cent) to say that they were either finding it quite or very difficult to
manage.

Table 5.18 Financial situation, by job status at Wave 2 for employed men and women in BHPS sample

Financial situation	Job status			Temporary	Any flexible
	FT permanent	PT permanent	Self-employed		
Men – per cent					
Living comfortably	28.3	34.9	28.6	22.7	28.1
Doing all right	35.5	31.0	25.2	26.5	26.6
Just about getting by	29.5	25.6	33.8	33.6	32.3
Finding it quite difficult	5.3	6.2	7.4	13.3	8.9
Finding it very difficult	1.4	2.3	4.9	3.8	4.2
Total	100	100	100	100	100
N	1857	129	405	211	745
Women – per cent					
Living comfortably	29.8	23.2	32.0	26.5	24.8
Doing all right	36.8	33.3	31.3	31.4	32.7
Just about getting by	27.1	32.6	28.7	27.0	31.2
Finding it quite difficult	4.2	7.4	6.0	10.2	7.7
Finding it very difficult	2.1	3.6	2.0	4.9	3.6
Total	100	100	100	100	100
N	1118	920	150	226	1296

CONCLUSIONS

This examination of 1994 LFS and BHPS data has revealed that flexible work is not evenly distributed in the British economy. It is disproportionately experienced by individuals with certain characteristics. Part-time jobs constituted the majority of women's flexible jobs, while self-employment constituted the majority of men's flexible jobs. However, the predominant types of flexible jobs, as well as their extent, were found to vary across age groups, marital status groups, by family circumstances (in the case of women only), and by ethnic origin. Women's predominance in part-time work is largely a reflection of their family circumstances.

Men and women who were either at the beginning of their labour market careers or at its end experienced a much wider range of flexible jobs, as well as a higher incidence of them, than those in the middle age ranges. Those in flexible jobs were also more likely than those in standard jobs to be married, and to have dependent children. Young women who were employed and not in full-time education seemed less likely than similar young men to be in temporary jobs, but more likely to be in part-time jobs. Those young men and women who were employed as well as being in full-time education were almost wholly in flexible jobs.

This analysis has suggested that flexible jobs do appear to be related to a range of personal characteristics, human capital, job related characteristics, household and labour market characteristics. The characteristics examined in this section are often quite different for the self-employed, part-time and temporary employees, and different between the gender groups also. This makes summaries difficult to carry out. However, we can note some of the main findings for each type of flexible work separately below.

Self-employed men in this analysis were likely to be among the lower educated although this is not the case for self-employed women. The findings of earlier studies, that the self-employed were more likely to have A-level qualifications, may not necessarily conflict with these results. The earlier results may be the average of both self-employed men's and women's levels of educational qualifications.

The self-employed were also likely to own or be buying their own houses, to have a dependent child, to be older and have more traditional attitudes. They were also more likely to have found themselves with lower levels of mental health and well-being, and having financial difficulties.

Permanent part-time jobs were primarily women's jobs, occupied more extensively by women with low levels of educational qualifications. Such jobs were among those with the lowest earnings for men and women and they offered women little training. Women holding permanent part-time jobs were the least likely to say that they were living comfortably.

Temporary jobs were more common among the very young and the old. They had strong links with past unemployment, and past long term unemployment, for a sizeable minority of men. They produced low levels of hourly earnings and were associated with low household incomes. Temporary jobs offered little training. They were also more likely to be occupied by lone parents. Individuals holding temporary jobs were also more likely than those in other jobs to say that they were experiencing financial difficulties, and had lower levels of mental health. Individuals taking temporary jobs were far less likely to join a workplace union, even when unions were recognised. Temporary jobs were clearly the most obviously disadvantageous of the alternative flexible types of work. This applies both to men and women, but the disadvantages may be worse for men.

While some individuals in flexible jobs, particularly men in temporary jobs, were also in low income households, it was not the case that all men and women with flexible jobs were in low income households.

Notes

1. The base for the jobs which are compared in this section is the employed sample of men and women at Wave 2 (1992) of the BHPS who had full interviews; that is approximately 2270 men and 2110 women. It is the current (Wave 2) jobs of these individuals that are analysed.
2. There are some differences between the versions of the LFS which are available through the Data Archive and those which are published in the *Employment Gazette*. The *Employment Gazette* figures are often revised but a new version of the data is not sent to the Data Archive until some time later, if at all.
3. Owen (1994) and Bhavnani (1994) document and discuss these characteristics of ethnic minority women.
4. In contrast to the other analyses contained in this section, we have carried out this cross tabulation using Wave 1 figures. This has been done to make use of the imputed income data which had been constructed for Wave 1. It was not available when some of these analyses were being carried out for Wave 2 BHPS household incomes. Using Wave 1 household income figures therefore allows us to increase the sample size for the analysis substantially.

6 Changes in Flexible Work in Britain during the 1980s

In this chapter we wish to examine the extent to which non-standard forms of employment changed during the 1980s. Unfortunately, this task is not as straightforward as it might appear, largely because the sources of data changed over the period. Flexible employment is a relatively recent area of interest in British labour market studies and the data which are now available on this subject reflect this new interest. The same data were not always collected in the past, partly because there was less interest in the topic, and partly because the newest forms of non-standard work were not of a sufficient size to make it worth examining.

PROBLEMS OF CONSTRUCTING A SERIES OVER TIME

Some estimates have already been made of the extent of the changes in non-standard flexible forms of work in Britain. All attempts to quantify these changes are hindered by the lack of systematic data. The Labour Force Survey is the most obvious source to use for such calculations, but the questions, some of the coding categories, and the sample populations who have been asked certain questions have all changed over time. In addition, the government warns users not to trust the data from the early surveys in the 1970s. Questions about temporary work are only available from 1984.[1] The coding categories for the types of temporary jobs are more extensive in the 1990s than they were in the 1980s. Given these problems, we should be careful in our interpretation of trends from series of LFS data, particularly with respect to temporary employment and employer tenure.

It would be interesting to have a complete record of the changes in all of the categories over the whole of the 1980s, but this is not possible from the available data. We have therefore pieced together the best picture that can be assembled from the data which are available, supplementing it in places with the analyses of other researchers.

EXISTING ESTIMATES OF THE CHANGES DURING THE 1980s

There have been a number of attempts to estimate the extent to which non-standard forms of employment grew over the 1980s. Naylor (1994) has analysed the changes in part-time work. Part-time employment has increased steadily. Women comprise the vast majority (86 per cent in 1993) of the part-time workforce. Part-time work's share of total employment was 28 per cent in 1994 compared with 21 per cent in 1985 and the trend has a considerably longer history. The proportion of jobs that are part time increased at a faster rate between 1990 and 1993 than in previous years (ibid.). Part-time employment was also an increasing share of women's employment from the 1950s to the 1980s when a plateau was reached at around 44 per cent of women's employment. However it is important to recognise that men's part-time work has increased substantially from 3 per cent of men's employment in 1971 to 5 per cent in 1994 (ibid.). The bulk of part-time work is voluntary and those who say that they work part-time involuntarily because they cannot find full-time work are a minority. This proportion does vary cyclically; 10 per cent of all part-timers were working part-time involuntarily in 1987, 6 per cent in 1990 and 13 per cent in 1993. Involuntary part-timers were a much lower percentage of all those in employment although there has been an increase in the early 1990s; 2 per cent in 1984 and 3 per cent in 1993 (Robinson, 1994). However, as we noted in Chapter 4, the concepts of voluntary and involuntary part-timers, as derived from Labour Force Survey questions, are problematic for women.

Self-employment was in long-term decline up to the late 1960s but then began to increase in most, but not all, industries. Since the 1970s, self-employment has increased markedly in Britain, from 7 per cent of the employed in 1979 to 12 per cent in 1993 (17 per cent of men's but only 7.1 per cent of women's employment in 1993). Approximately two-thirds of those classified as self-employed work alone. However, in the early 1990s, the growth of self-employment faltered, and the numbers of self-employed declined. Over half of the decline came in construction, hotels and distribution.

Temporary work, on the other hand, remained fairly stable between 1985 and 1993, at 5–6 per cent of all employees. Women constitute the majority of temporary workers: 54 per cent of all temporary workers, 64 per cent of seasonal workers, and 63 per cent of agency workers in 1984 were women (Casey, 1988). Casey suggested that in 1984 two-thirds of temporary workers were in seasonal/casual work and one-third on fixed-term contracts. By 1993 Robinson (1994) suggested that by 1993 approximately one-half of those in temporary employment were on fixed term contracts. Agency temporary work made up a very small minority (3 per cent) of the total workforce in 1984 (Casey, 1988). Involuntary temporary employment has displayed cyclical variations. In 1993, 43 per cent of temporary workers said they held such jobs because they could not find a permanent job. This was almost double the percentage from 1990 (Robinson, 1994).

Hakim (1987) calculated that flexible work's share of total employment increased from 30 to 35 per cent between 1981 and 1986, an increase of over one million individuals. A similar calculation by Watson (1994) showed that the number of flexible workers increased by 1.25 million between 1986 and 1993, when flexible work accounted for 38 per cent of the workforce.[2]

It is far more difficult to gain evidence about some of the other more minor categories which comprise flexible work. Brannen et al. (1994) have reviewed the sources of flexible work and flexible family friendly practices. There are some limited data on home working, shiftworking and telework, but there is currently no large-scale statistical evidence on the extent of zero-hours contracts.

Estimates from the 1993 Labour Force Survey (LFS) suggest that approximately 10 per cent of the employed were homeworkers, that is, there were 2.4 million homeworkers in Britain. A comparison with earlier surveys suggests that these figures represent an increase in homeworking. Over half worked from home as a base and these were mainly men; one quarter worked in their own home and were mainly women; and less than one quarter worked in the same grounds or buildings as their own home and were mainly men. The majority of those working at home would also be classed as self-employed; mostly, therefore, the at-home workers are not a separate category of flexible workers. The increase in homeworking has already been reflected in the increase in self-employment reported earlier. The most recent estimates from the Census (Felstead and Jewson, 1995) suggest that homeworking has increased considerably since 1981.

Another overlapping flexible category is telework. The majority of teleworkers are homeworkers. One source of increased homework has probably come from the increase in telework. The extent of telework is also very difficult to assess, although a recent survey for the Employment Department by Huws (1994) has improved our knowledge of this form of work. This study found that in 1992 one in ten employers were using some form of home-based work, and that approximately one-half of these were using teleworkers. A further 8 per cent of employers expected to introduce teleworking at some point in the future. Teleworking would seem to be increasing and is likely to increase further. The existing teleworkers overlapped with other forms of flexible workers since some of them were also temporary, subcontractees, freelance, self-employed or had other non-standard forms of contract. Telework was described as being very much a 'made-to-measure' form of work to meet particular requirements. Currently, it is not a category which is distinguished in the LFS data.

Brannen et al. (1994) review the evidence on shift work and note that some sources suggest it has increased, while others suggest there was no change over the 1980s. However, the evidence on the time of day working patterns of employees suggests that these have changed (ibid.).

We turn now to our own analysis of the Labour Force Survey data during the 1980s. We are able to add further detail to the picture which has been assembled by others, although we restrict ourselves to a narrower definition of what counts as flexible employment.

CHANGES IN THE TYPES OF NON-STANDARD EMPLOYMENT

We set out in Tables 6.1 and 6.2 a profile of some of the changes in non-standard forms of work during the 1980s for men and women. For both sexes, the extent of individuals in flexible jobs increased between 1986 and 1994. Our calculations for the population of working age suggest that the proportion of men in flexible jobs increased from 15 per cent in 1986 to 22 per cent in 1994; for women the percentage remained the same at 50–51 per cent at the two dates. We are unable to calculate the same statistic for the earlier years because of the lack of information about temporary work. However, we can calculate statistics based on part-time and self-employment (without employees) alone since the mid-1970s. Using this more partial definition of flexible employment 8 per cent of men were in flexible jobs in 1975. This rose to 13 per cent in 1986 and 19 per cent in 1994. For women, 41 per cent were in flexible jobs in 1975; this had risen to 48 per cent in 1986; in 1994 it was at the same level as in 1986. Part-time employment and self-employment increased over the 1980s, but temporary work fluctuated more, as other commentators have noted.

These changes represent a growth of 834 thousand men's flexible jobs between 1986 and 1994. The figures are based on the percentages

Table 6.1 Changes in non-standard forms of work over time for men as per cent of employed men of working age, LFS

	per cent			
	1975	*1981*	*1986*	*1994*
Full-time permanent	n.a	n.a	**79.3**	**73.1**
Part-time				
self-definition	**2.4**	**1.7**	**3.5**	**6.1**
hours < 31	**6.1**	**2.6**	**5.7**	**7.7**
hours < 8	3.6		0.8	1.4
hours < 16 + < 2 yrs	0.6		1.4	1.9
hours 8–15 + < 5 yrs	0.2		1.0	1.5
More than 1 PT job	0.2	0.2	0.4	0.6
Temporary				
all			**4.4**	**5.4**
seasonal/casual			2.4	0.3
casual			–	1.0
fixed term			2.0	3.0
other			–	1.1
full-time			2.6	3.9
part-time			1.8	1.5
Self-employed				
all	**10.9**	**11.9**	**14.6**	**16.9**
with employees	5.1	7.2	5.6	4.4
without employees	5.8	4.7	9.0	12.4
full-time			13.7	15.2
part-time			0.9	1.8
Government scheme	–	**0.3**	**0.0**	**1.6**
Job changers				
same firm/diff. occup.			1.5	3.6
same firm, FT to PT			2.4	0.6
same firm employee/ self employed			0.3	0.4
Flexible				
self-employed + PT	**8.2**	**6.4**	**12.5**	**18.5**
Any flexible			15.1	22.4
N thousands	**13 276**	**13 654**	**13 423**	**13 577**

* Do not add up to 100% since categories overlap.
  FT to PT : hours change, full to part time.
  n.a. not available – lack of 'permanent' classification.

of men of working age only. We estimate that the growth in part-time and self-employed men's flexible jobs was approximately 1952 thousand men's jobs between 1975 and 1994. The number of women's flexible jobs increased from 4780 thousand to 5483 thousand between 1986 and 1994. The number of women's part-time and self-employed jobs increased by 2152 thousand jobs between 1975 and 1994.

Robinson (1994) has plotted the rates of involuntary part-time employment between 1984 and 1993. Individuals are deemed to be invol-

Table 6.2 Changes in non-standard forms of work over time for women as per cent of employed women of working age, LFS

	1975	per cent 1981	1986		1994	
Full-time permanent	n.a	n.a	**47.7**		**46.6**	
Part-time						
self-definition	**39.0**	**40.6**	**43.8**		**43.2**	
hours < 31	**42.2**	**41.3**	**47.1**		**46.1**	
hours < 8		5.6		5.4		6.0
hours < 16 + < 2 yrs		6.1		9.8		8.3
hours 8–15 + < 5yrs		6.9		9.7		8.2
More than 1 PT job		0.8	1.2	2.5		3.6
Temporary						
all			**8.2**		**6.2**	
seasonal				6.3		0.4
casual				1.7		1.7
fixed term				1.8		4.0
other				–		1.4
full-time				1.9		2.8
part-time				6.3		4.8
Self-employed						
all	**3.9**	**4.5**	**6.6**		**6.8**	
with employees		1.7	2.9	2.1		5.0
without employees		2.2	1.5	4.5		5.0
full-time				3.4		3.3
part-time				3.2		3.4
Government scheme		**0.4**	**0.0**		**1.0**	
Job changers						
same firm/diff. occup.				1.3		3.9
same firm FT to PT				1.7		2.2
same firm employee self-employed				0.1		0.3
Flexible (self-empl. + PT)	**41.2**	**42.1**	**48.3**		**48.2**	
Any flexible			**50.2**		**51.0**	
N thousands	**8086**	**8818**	**9522**		**10 751**	

* Do not add up to 100% since overlapping categories.
  n.a: not available – lack of 'permanent' classification.
  FT to PT : hours change, full to part time.

untarily employed in part-time jobs if they say that they are working part-time because they are unable to find a full-time job. However, we need to remember that some of these women, who are classified therefore as voluntarily part-time, have been shown to experience constraints on their choices, as described in Chapter 4. The proportions of involuntary to all part-time jobs are systematically higher for men than for women, and in both cases, they follow the business cycle; the rates rise and fall as unemployment rates increase and decline respectively (see Appendix Figure A1.1). Moreover, there has been a very large increase, especially for men, in the rates of involuntary part-time employment since 1992.

We can also examine some of the subcomponents of these overall changes.

Short Hours Part-Time

If we examine the various states of very short hours part-time work we find a similar pattern for both women and men. Between 1975 and 1994 the percentages of the employed who worked under 8 hours per week fell for men but stayed approximately the same for women. However, the proportions were in most cases very small. In the cases of the other part-time categories, working less than 16 hours per week with short durations, these percentages increased from 1975 to 1986 and from 1986 to 1994 for men. For women the percentages in these categories increased up to 1986 but fell slightly from 1986 to 1994, probably because of the recession. The extent to which men were holding more than one part-time job was also small but it too increased between 1975 and 1994.

Temporary Jobs

The percentage of women's temporary jobs declined slightly between 1986 and 1994, although these temporary jobs increased in number from approximately 780 thousand to 817 thousand. The percentage of men's temporary jobs increased slightly between 1986 and 1994. There was a fall in seasonal/casual (and part-time) jobs among men and especially women between 1986 and 1994, and this was the main component of the change in the level of temporary work between these dates for women. Over this period the LFS changed from being a yearly to a quarterly survey. Seasonal/casual work is likely to be considerably more volatile on a quarterly basis, and since we are using the spring 1994 survey, we have arguably the lowest levels of seasonal/casual jobs in 1994 in this survey. Fixed-term temporary jobs slightly increased in proportion among employed men and women between 1986 and 1994.

Robinson (1994) also plotted the rates of temporary job holding as a proportion of all employment for men and women from 1984 to 1993 (see Appendix Figure A1.2). He showed that for most of the period, men's rates of temporary employment were little changed while women's rates were on a downward trend. Women's percentages of temporary employment were always clearly above men's, although again a narrowing of the gap is visible by 1993. A very large dip in both men's and women's percentages of temporary employment took place from 1991 to 1992 and some recovery had occurred by 1992. Robinson does not consider whether the change to a quarterly survey may have been responsible for some of the change.

Robinson further calculated the percentages of men and women who were in temporary employment involuntarily between 1984 and 1993 (Appendix Figure A1.3). Men consistently had higher rates of involuntary temporary employment than women. These fluctuated with the business cycle; rates of involuntary temporary employment rose with increases in unemployment and declined with improvements in the cycle. Again, a very large increase in involuntary temporary employment was visible for both men and women from 1990. Approximately 50 per cent of men and 35 per cent of women in temporary jobs in 1993 were seemingly involuntarily employed part-time.

Self-employment

Female self-employment increased from 1975 to 1994, particularly in the 1980s, from 3 per cent of employed women in 1975, 5 per cent in 1981, to 7 per cent in 1994. Most of the growth was for self-employment without employees; women's self-employment with employees fluctuated and was the same in 1994 as it had been in 1975. Male self-employment increased from 11 per cent of employed men in 1975 to 17 per cent in 1994. Self-employed men without employees increased in proportion throughout the 1980s from 5 per cent in 1981 to 12 per cent in 1994. Men's self-employment with employees fluctuated over the decade and there was a lower percentage of employed men in this category in 1994 than there had been in the 1980s.

CHANGES BY AGE

We examine the changes over time in the total amount of flexibility by age in Table 6.3. We are only able to make this comparison for 1986 and 1994, since these are the two years of our data which contain classifications of all of the flexible categories. The percentage of employed men who were in flexible jobs increased in every age group between 1986 and 1994. However, the increase was least in the middle

Table 6.3 Total extent of flexible work by age for men and women not in full-time education over time: LFS

| | Men – per cent of age groups in year | | | | | |
	16–19	20–29	30–39	40–49	50–59	60–64
1986	13.4	8.2	6.0	5.5	6.4	10.9
1994	28.7	18.7	19.4	19.8	24.1	32.0
	Women – per cent of age group in year					
1986	17.5	27.0	62.2	58.4	57.1	
1994	37.0	32.5	56.1	56.0	59.6	

age groups, and greatest in the oldest two groups, followed by the youngest groups. Eleven per cent of employed men aged 60–64 had flexible jobs in 1986 and 32 per cent had these jobs in 1994; this represents 191 thousand men aged 60–64 who were in flexible jobs in 1994. Thirteen per cent of 16–19 year old men (not in full-time education) had flexible jobs in 1986 and 29 per cent in 1994; this represents 160 thousand young men who were in flexible jobs in 1994. Women across most of the age groups experienced an increase in their percentage of flexible jobs between 1986 and 1994; the exceptions were women aged 30–39 and 40–49 whose percentage of flexible jobs was the largest, and it fell slightly in 1994 from the 1986 value. There were very large increases in the percentage of flexible to total jobs for women aged 16–19 who were not in full-time education; the percentages of young women in flexible jobs more than doubled between 1986 and 1994 from 18 per cent in 1986 to 37 per cent in 1994; this represents 206 thousand young women who were in flexible jobs in 1994. At the older end of the age spectrum, 1079 thousand women aged 50–59 were in flexible jobs in 1994.

Since the rise of women employed in part-time jobs, often linked to family circumstances, we have come to expect a high proportion of women in flexible jobs in the middle age ranges, and to a greater extent than is the case for men. What these figures show is that even at the youngest ages, where family responsibilities play a relatively minor role in women's lives, young women are still far more likely than young men to be in flexible jobs.

A further breakdown by age for some of the disaggregated categories of non-standard employment was carried out. We concentrated on the youngest and the oldest groups in the labour market to see whether the experiences of these groups have changed significantly over the

1980s. The youngest and oldest age groups are arguably the most vulnerable to changes in the labour market, since it is probably easier for employers to alter their policies with respect to the employment of these two groups than it is for employees in the middle age ranges. However, we excluded those in full-time education.

Overall the extent to which the youngest and oldest age groups of men and women experienced flexible work increased over the 1980s and in larger proportions than the changes experienced by other groups. We could argue that this is an increase in the vulnerability of the oldest and youngest groups in the labour market. This change in their position came mainly from increases in part-time employment for young and older men and women, and from increases in self-employment, especially among the oldest groups of men. The groups who experienced the greatest increase in the extent of flexible jobs were men over 60 years old and women aged 16–19.

SECOND JOB HOLDING

We have already noted the extent to which men and women have been holding two part-time jobs. We can also examine the extent to which they hold two jobs of any sort, either full or part-time. In practice, most of those who held two jobs had one full-time job and one part-time job. It is possible to argue that second job holding is an element of flexible job holding even where both of the jobs are not part-time. The extent of any second job holding is displayed for men and women in Table 6.4.

The holding of a second job increased from less than 2 per cent of employed men in 1975 to 3 per cent in 1994, and from 1 per cent of employed women in 1975 to 5 per cent in 1994.[3] In 1975 226 thousand men and 105 thousand women held a second as well as a first job. In 1994 the figures had risen to 461 thousand men and 559 thousand women.

Second job holding appears to have become more common among women than it is among men. The differences between men and women have not been great, although the gap may now be increasing.

TENURE WITH CURRENT EMPLOYER

Jobs of short duration do not allow individuals to gain access to employment protection or eligibility to state benefits. We might expect

Table 6.4   Whether or not individual has a second job, LFS

| | per cent of employed with second job | | | |
	1975*	1981	1986**	1994
Men	1.7	2.0	2.3	3.4
N, thousands	(13 276)	(13 654)	(13 423)	(13 577)
Women	1.6	4.3	3.7	5.2
N, thousands	(8086)	(8818)	(9522)	(10 751)

* Codes include usually has two jobs plus occasionally, has two jobs.
** 'Had second job last week.'

that deregulation would lead to an increase in the number and proportion of jobs with short durations. Here we can examine the overall picture of the durations tenure with the current employer. We are dealing with data which are censored, since all of the jobs in question are uncompleted. However, this problem is common to all years so that the comparisons over time of these uncompleted job spells should still give some idea of whether employer tenure durations have been changing over time. However, we are not controlling for changes in the business cycle which are known to affect the tenure durations.

One other point about the data should be noted; the 1994 LFS data only asked individuals the date at which they started their current job if they had started it within the past eight years. We have assumed that if someone is employed and has missing data on the date at which they started their current job, they have been in it for more than 5 years. In practice, a small minority of the missing cases will be genuine missing cases and our procedure will then be categorising their tenure wrongly. We are likely to be over-emphasising long tenure in 1994 by this method and must take care to remember this in drawing conclusions from this comparison.

Tenure Changes Over Time

The distribution of current employer tenures for men and women are displayed in Table 6.5 for selected years where the data were available in the LFS. Women were likely to have spent shorter durations with their current employers than men overall in every year examined. However, in 1994 the tenure gap between men and women appeared to have got much narrower. For both men's jobs, the proportion of short tenure jobs increased during the 1980s; 5 per cent of men's jobs had lasted less than 6 months in 1975 compared with 8 per cent in

1994; 63 per cent of men's jobs had lasted more than 5 years in 1975 compared to 57 per cent in 1994. For women job tenure at the bottom end fell between 1975 and 1986 but at the top end tenure increased from 1975 to 1986 and again from 1986 to 1994; 9 per cent of women's jobs had lasted less than 6 months in 1975 compared with 10 per cent in 1994; 40 per cent of women's jobs in 1975 lasted more than five years compared with 45 per cent in 1994.

We were concerned that the assumptions we had to make about the data in order to construct these distributions may have overemphasised longer jobs. We do not need to worry that the declining trend in longer jobs evident in men's employment tenures is genuine. We should probably be concerned about the women's trend which shows a slight increase in longer jobs. This could be an artefact of the calculations.

The OECD (1993) has charted the enterprise tenure profiles of men and women by age in 1983 and 1991. The UK profiles show that men's shorter tenure in 1991, as compared with 1983, only applies at ages below 30 and above 50. In the middle age ranges, average tenure had not changed over time. Women's average tenure profiles by age had changed less than those for men between 1983 and 1991, but again there was a slight reduction in women's average tenure in 1991 compared with 1983, for those aged up to 30 and over 60. Since these figures do not control for changes in the business cycle we cannot be sure that tenure has changed over time.

Uncovered by Employment Protection Legislation

The figures in Table 6.5 allow us to estimate the percentages of men and women who were uncovered by employment protection legislation. Since 1995, coverage by the legislation has relied upon having worked for an employer for two years or more. It is instructive to see whether this group has been changing over time even though this is not the criterion which was operating up to 1994. Up to 1994, having at least two years' tenure was only one of the qualifying conditions in order to be covered by employment protection legislation. The figures in Tables 6.1 and 6.2 display some of the specific hours and duration combinations which limited individuals' access to employment protection up to 1993.

Women are more likely not to have been covered than men (using the 1995 criterion) in every year. In addition, for both women and men, the proportions and the numbers of individuals in this uncovered category increased between 1975 and 1986 from 19 per cent to 24 per

Table 6.5 Tenure durations with current employer over time: LFS

Duration months	Men			Women		
	1975	1986	1994	1975	1986	1994
< 6	5.4	8.0	8.2	9.2	12.1	9.8
6–11	7.1	7.3	7.3	12.0	10.7	9.7
12–23	6.6	8.9	8.7	10.9	13.0	11.4
24–59	18.0	18.1	19.3	27.7	22.7	23.9
60+	62.9	57.7	56.5	40.1	41.5	45.3
Total	100	100	100	100	100	100
N, thousands	13 910	13 403	13 507	8196	9509	10 675

cent for men, and from 31 to 36 per cent for women. In 1986 and 1994, the men's rates stayed the same at 24 per cent; the women's rates fell from 36 per cent to 31 per cent. Changes in the business cycle will be part of the explanation for these changes.

CONCLUSIONS

Non-standard forms of work appear to have increased in Britain over the past two decades. The structure of employment looks very different in the early 1990s from its appearance in the 1970s. Over the 1980s there was a growth, for both men and women, in self-employment, part-time employment, fixed-term contract jobs, the holding of second jobs, and short duration jobs. An assessment about changes in temporary employment is hampered by the lack of data and by changes in the way the LFS data have been collected. The major growth in percentage terms of flexible jobs which took place over the 1980s occurred over the early half of the decade. The falling back of some of the percentage increases in the late 1980s and early 1990s was probably due to the recession. If the decline in the share of flexible jobs in all employment was due to the recession, it would support the view that employers were exploiting the vulnerability of these non-standard jobs.

Many of the changes are bound up with women's increased participation in the labour force. The size of the women's labour force increased during the 1980s, so that percentage increases also represent an increase in the numbers of women with the experience in question. The structure of men's employment altered less than women's, although the overall picture also changed considerably. While elements of men's employment often changed less than the components of women's employment, the men's workforce was also declining in the 1980s. Despite this, the percentage increases in men's experiences of flexible work were sufficiently large to represent increases in the numbers of men employed in these jobs. The youngest and oldest groups in the labour market have probably experienced the greatest amount of change in their labour market status. At the older end, this may represent the increased use of part-time employment for men as a transition from employment to retirement.

The rate of growth in self-employment and part-time employment had slowed down by the 1990s. Whether these forms of work will start to increase as the recession has eased remains to be seen. There is other evidence that women's part-time employment may have stabilised, especially that experienced over the family formation phase of women's lives. There is considerable scope and some institutional pressures for men's part-time employment to continue to increase. Men's part-time employment may well continue to increase therefore. Temporary employment is also likely to continue to fluctuate, as it always has. The fixed-term component of temporary employment has been increasing, and may well continue to do so, given the changes which have been occurring in the public sector.

In many ways the restructuring of employment which has been taking place in Britain is not unique and there is evidence that some of the changes are being duplicated in many other industrialised countries. We consider changes in other countries more fully in Chapter 9.

Notes

1. A question about temporary contracts was asked in some earlier surveys but the data are unreliable and only a small sample of individuals responded.
2. These figures are quoted in Watson (1994).
3. The question used by the LFS changed in 1986 to one about 'holding a second job last week'.

7 Flexible Jobs over the Lifetime

In this chapter we examine the extent to which individuals in the BHPS data experienced flexible employment over their working lives. We draw upon the details recorded in the retrospective accounts of their past working lives between leaving full-time education and 1990. This is supplemented by further details about jobs from the panel wave interviews. We should remember that the retrospective data are subject to recall biases. Studies of recall reliability show that short periods of employment, which were not particularly significant to the individual, will be more likely to have been forgotten than longer more salient periods (Dex, 1995). With this proviso, we can examine the extent to which individuals recalled having experienced any self-employment, part-time permanent and any temporary employment (either part or full-time) over their lifetime. Individuals were allowed to define all of the states used to classify their jobs for themselves. In addition, a category of 'any flexible' has been constructed. This includes any self-employed, part-time or temporary job.[1]

The literature review in Chapter 4 pointed to some of the reasons individuals have given when studied for wanting to have self-employed, part-time or temporary jobs. These reasons were diverse and very different for each kind of flexible work. Individuals were found to have entered self-employment often in order to gain independence, fulfilment or autonomy at work, although it could be in response to having been made redundant or unemployed. Entry into part-time work was often linked, for women, to a certain point in their lifecycle, as they became responsible for child care. Entry into temporary jobs sometimes followed unemployment and was thought to be a way of getting training. Taking a temporary job could also be because the individuals could not get a permanent one. However, in some cases the individuals did not want permanent jobs.

In addition, there have been some multivariate analyses of the flows into self-employment. Evans and Leighton (1989) found that flow of US workers into self-employment was not related to age, but it did increase as the assets of workers increased, if they had had a previous experience of self-employment, and if they were low wage workers with a previous history of instability. They found that flows into self-employment declined as the job tenure of workers increased.

Individuals in BHPS were not asked why they had taken up particular sorts of work. The aim of this analysis is to fill in more of the characteristics of individuals at the time they took up flexible jobs, as far as our data permit.[2]

FLEXIBLE JOBS IN THE PAST

It is clear from these figures that having experience of a flexible job is very common. But it was relatively uncommon for both men and women to have had more than one kind of flexible job. This suggests that the different kinds of flexible jobs are not interchangeable in individuals' experiences. The frequency with which individuals experienced flexible jobs is set out in Table 7.1. This shows that 74 per cent of women and 47 per cent of men had experienced flexible employment at some point in their working life.

More than half of all women (59 per cent) had held a part-time job during their working life. Just under a third had been in temporary employment and 9 per cent had been self-employed. Six per cent of women had had both self-employment and a part-time job, 3 per cent of women had had self-employment and a temporary job, and 20 per cent of women had both a part-time and a temporary job.

One quarter of the sample of men had been self-employed at some time in their working life; 11 per cent had been in permanent part-time employment, and a fifth had held a temporary job. We also examined the extent to which men and women had experienced more than one type of flexible job during their working lives. These figures were much smaller: 3 per cent of men and 6 per cent of women had both been self-employed and worked part-time at some point in their working life. Approximately 7 per cent of men and 3 per cent of women had both been self-employed and employed in a temporary job; and 5 per cent of men and 20 per cent of women had held both a part-time and a temporary job. It was very uncommon for men or women to have experienced all three types of flexible employment.

Table 7.1 Experience of flexible jobs in entire working life of men and women in BHPS sample

Jobs	percentage of individuals ever held job/s	
	Men	Women
Self-employed	26.8	9.1
Part-time **	11.2	59.0
Temporary *	20.5	30.2
Self-employed + part time	2.7	6.4
Self-employed + temporary	7.4	2.9
Part-time + temporary	5.2	19.5
Any flexible time	46.5	74.0
N	3343	3914

* Temporary here does not include self-employed temporary jobs.
** Part-time here means permanent part-time.

NUMBERS OF FLEXIBLE JOBS

The number of flexible jobs of varying kinds which these individuals had experienced over their working lives is displayed in Table 7.2. The patterns for self-employment and temporary employment appear similar whereas the experience of permanent part-time employment contrasts with the other types of employment.

Where men had been self-employed, they were most likely to have had only one spell of self-employment; 17 per cent of men had had one spell of self-employment and 3 per cent had had two spells. Similarly, 16 per cent of men had had one temporary job, 6 per cent had had two temporary jobs and 4 per cent had had three or more temporary jobs over their working lifetime. However, men were more likely to have had multiple part-time jobs than they were to have had multiple jobs in other flexible categories; 10 per cent of men had experienced one part-time job, 4 per cent had two, and 8 per cent had three or more part-time jobs. Altogether, 21 per cent of men had experienced one period of flexible employment; 9 per cent had experienced two and 17 per cent had experienced three or more flexible jobs. Multiple flexible jobs were more common for women than men; 19 per cent had held two flexible jobs and as many as 30 per cent had held three or more. This was due to the much greater likelihood that women had held multiple part-time jobs, since women had held multiple self-employed or temporary jobs in approximately the same proportions as

Table 7.2 Number of flexible jobs of varying kinds held by BHPS sample of men and women up to Wave 3

Number of jobs	Part-time permanent	Self-employed	Temporary	Any flexible
		Men, per cent		
0	77.3	78.7	75.0	52.5
1	10.3	17.4	15.8	21.0
2	4.2	3.0	5.6	9.2
3 or more	8.2	0.9	3.7	17.4
Total	100	100	100	100
N	3314	3314	3314	3314
		Women, per cent		
0	41.0	90.9	69.8	26.0
1	23.6	7.7	19.8	24.6
2	16.1	1.1	5.9	19.2
3 or more	19.2	0.4	4.5	30.2
Total	100	100	100	100
N	3941	3941	3941	3941

men. Indeed, women seemed almost as likely to have had three or more part-time jobs as they were to have had one or two part-time jobs.

In Table 7.3 we show the number of flexible jobs according to the ages of these individuals when interviewed. For both men and women, the likelihood of having held a flexible job of any kind increased with age. However, the trend was much more pronounced for women than for men; 83 per cent of women aged 46–59 had held a flexible job, compared to only 48 per cent of those aged 16–29. Forty-seven per cent of men aged 46–65 had been flexibly employed at some point, compared to 37 per cent of those aged 16–29.

At all ages, men were more likely than women to have had a spell of self-employment and the probability of having had a self-employed job clearly increased with age. Also, the likelihood of having multiple flexible jobs increased with age for men and women. Whereas 14 per cent of men and 6 per cent of women under 30 had had at least one period of self-employment, 34 per cent of men and 15 per cent of women over the age of 45 had had at least one spell of it. These results are consistent with other findings showing that individuals in the middle age groups are more likely than younger individuals to be in self-employment at a cross-sectional point.

Table 7.3 Numbers of flexible jobs over working life by age group at Wave 3: BHPS

	Men			Women		
	16–29	30–45	46–64	16–29	30–45	46–59
Self-employed jobs						
0	85.6	70.5	66.5	94.2	86.8	85.3
1	11.7	21.8	23.6	5.2	10.2	11.7
2	2.4	4.8	7.3	0.4	2.4	2.0
3+	0.4	2.9	2.6	0.1	0.7	1.0
Total	100	100	100	100	100	100
Part-time permanent jobs						
0	85.0	91.0	91.8	64.7	38.6	25.6
1	12.9	7.1	6.7	23.6	31.6	31.0
2	1.4	1.0	1.3	7.1	14.5	20.3
3+	0.7	0.9	0.2	4.7	15.3	23.1
Total	100	100	100	100	100	100
Temporary jobs						
0	80.1	77.9	80.6	75.4	69.7	73.7
1	15.4	13.6	13.7	18.5	19.9	17.4
2	3.5	5.0	3.8	4.6	5.5	5.0
3+	1.0	3.5	2.0	1.6	4.9	3.9
Total	100	100	100	100	100	100
Any flexible jobs						
0	62.8	54.6	52.6	51.6	25.4	17.4
1	22.2	24.6	26.3	23.7	29.1	27.7
2	9.9	10.1	11.6	13.9	16.7	20.6
3+	5.2	10.8	9.6	10.9	28.7	34.2
Total	100	100	100	100	100	100
N	720	1116	974	764	1306	862

Women were much more likely than men in every age group to have worked part-time. However, whereas men aged 16–29 were most likely to have worked part-time, women in this age group were least likely to have been in part-time employment. Fifteen per cent of men under 30 had worked part-time compared to 8 per cent of men over 45. In contrast, 35 per cent of women under the age of 30 had had a part-time job, whereas 74 per cent of women over 45 had worked part-time. Moreover, the probability of having multiple part-time jobs increased with age for women, but not for men. These results suggest that women, but not men, worked part-time when their children were small. In contrast, that men were most likely to work part-time in the youngest age group suggests that part-time work may be becoming more common for men, but that this trend has yet to affect older age groups.

Women were more likely than men to have experienced temporary employment in every age group. For example, 25 per cent of young women had held a temporary job compared with 20 per cent of men; 19 per cent of men aged over 45 had had at least one temporary job compared with 26 per cent of women. Those aged 30–45 were most likely to have held a temporary job, but the variations between the age groups were small.

TIME SPENT IN FLEXIBLE JOBS

In Table 7.4 we show the percentage of their working lives which individuals had spent in flexible jobs, since leaving full-time education. If an individual had been self-employed, the amount of time she/he had been in this state was expressed as a percentage of their potential working life. The same approach was adopted for individuals who had experienced permanent part-time or temporary work. Two thirds of men who had been self-employed had spent one-third or less of their working lives in self-employment; a further quarter had spent between one- and two-thirds in self-employment, and one-tenth had spent almost all of their working life in self-employment. Very few men had ever worked part-time; for three-quarters of these this time amounted to less than one-third of their working lives. Nearly 90 per cent of men who had held a temporary job had done so for no more than a third of their working life.

Table 7.4 also shows that most men (70 per cent) who had ever held a flexible job had done so for no more than a third of their working lives. One in five had spent between a third and two-thirds of their working lives in flexible jobs and only 9 per cent had spent two-thirds or more of their working lives in such jobs. An analysis by age of the amounts of time spent in flexible work by those who had some experience of it revealed no significant difference between the age groups (table not presented).

Table 7.4 shows that 70 per cent of women who had some experience of a flexible job had spent no more than a third of their working lives in flexible employment; this was exactly the same proportion as for men. Men who had worked part-time were more likely than women who had worked part-time to have spent two-thirds or more of their working lives in part-time employment. These experiences were evenly

Table 7.4 Percentage of working life spent in various flexible states for
men and women with at least one flexible job, BHPS

Percentage of working life in state	Self-employed*	Part-time* permanent	Temporary*	Any flexible**
	Men, per cent			
1–33	66.9	78.0	88.6	69.8
34–67	23.8	11.0	8.7	20.9
68–100	9.3	11.0	2.7	9.3
Total	100	100	100	100
N	593	173	439	944
	Women, per cent			
1–33	78.6	70.6	91.8	69.8
34–67	15.9	23.7	6.6	23.5
68–100	5.4	5.7	1.6	6.7
Total	100	100	100	100
N	276	1373	619	1671

* Of those with an experience of self-employment/part-time/temporary, percentage of working life they have spent self-employed, part-time or temporary respectively.
** Of those with any flexible job, percentage of working life they have spent
in any flexible job.

divided across the age groups, as they had been for men. These overall similarities do mask some differences, however. Men were more
likely than women to have spent longer periods in self-employment or
temporary jobs. Overall, women were more likely to have had a flexible job than men, but they were slightly less likely to have spent
almost all of their working lives in flexible jobs. Some of this difference is likely to be because women spent more of their working lives
than men working in the home.

  We can examine whether individuals who spent a large proportion
of their working lives in flexible work did so by having a lot of flexible jobs. One might expect that this relationship would hold for temporary work, since these were the jobs of shortest duration, and this
was in fact the case. Thirty-nine per cent of men who had spent more
than two-thirds of their working lives in temporary jobs had had three
or more temporary jobs, compared to only 8 per cent of those who
had spent no more than a third of their time in such jobs. Similarly,
30 per cent of women who had spent more than two-thirds of their
working lives in temporary jobs had had three or more temporary jobs,

Table 7.5 Percentage of time spent in flexible jobs, by numbers of flexible jobs held for BHPS sample of men and women up to Wave 3

Percentage of working life in flexible jobs	number of flexible jobs ever held				
	1	*2*	*3 or more*	*Total*	*N*
Men – row per cent					
0	5.7	24.4	69.8	100	1587
1–33	0.3	9.2	90.6	100	794
34–67	1.2	17.5	81.3	100	252
68–100	5.6	33.7	60.7	100	89
Women – row per cent					
0	13.6	30.9	55.5	100	1021
1–33	0.9	12.9	86.3	100	1593
35–67	0.9	12.3	86.8	100	570
68–100	1.0	13.9	85.1	100	101

compared to only 2 per cent of those who had spent no more than a third of their time in such jobs.

Those who had worked in flexible employment tended to have had more jobs. However Table 7.5 shows that it was not the case that those who had spent a larger amount of their working lives in flexible employment did so by having more flexible jobs. This is a result we might have expected from examining the durations of flexible jobs, since these, with the exception of temporary ones, were not always shorter than full-time permanent jobs. For example, 91 per cent of men who had spent up to one-third of their working lives in flexible work had had three or more jobs, compared to only 61 per cent of men who had spent over two-thirds of their working lives in flexible work. For men, the number of jobs decreased as the percentage of time spent in flexible jobs increased. For women, there was no relationship between the number of jobs held and the amount of time spent in flexible jobs.

AGE AND COHORT EFFECTS

Our earlier analyses have suggested that there are age and life-cycle effects in individuals' experiences of flexible work. Temporary work and part-time men's work were more often experienced by young people,

whereas self-employment and part-time women's work were more often the experience of those in the middle age groups. What we have
been unable to see is whether flexible employment has become more
widespread for successive cohorts of men and women, and whether
this increase has been occurring at the same age or life-cycle stage for
all cohorts. We consider these issues below.

The separation of age and cohort effects can be achieved by plotting
out the experiences of successive cohorts on a graph. This approach
follows that of Gershuny and Brice (1994) in drawing these figures,
and is based on a modified version of Gershuny's programme. The
experiences which are plotted out count up the individuals with any
experience in that year of the job in question. The job may not have
occupied them for the whole year. However, even with this liberal
definition, for some states we do not have sufficient observations to be
able to plot out the experiences of separate cohorts; in particular, this
cannot be done for men in part-time jobs, men in temporary jobs, or
women in self-employment. For this reason we only present in this
chapter the data for men and women in permanent and permanent full-
time jobs, men in self-employment, women in part-time jobs, all temporary jobs and women's temporary jobs.

Permanent Jobs

Men's permanent jobs have been decreasing as we examine successive
cohorts in Figure 7.1, and at all ages. There were some fluctuations in
cohorts' experiences at certain points which were probably due to the
period effects of the business cycle fluctuations. The most recent cohort, born in the 1970s, were far less likely to be in permanent jobs at
the start of their employment history than were earlier generations of
men. Part of this reduction in men's permanent jobs is undoubtedly
due to the tendency to stay on longer in education. However, the reduction in permanent jobs is still evident when men had reached their
mid and late twenties. While we cannot consider men's temporary jobs
because of insufficient sample sizes, it is likely that part of the explanation for this drop is an increase in men's temporary jobs when they
first entered the labour market, as well as an increase in unemployment and longer stays in education at this entry point. The figures on
temporary work experiences support these conclusions. The experiences
of full-time permanent jobs by successive cohorts of men were essen-
tially the same as those of permanent jobs in total.

Women's experiences of permanent jobs are displayed in Figure 7.2.

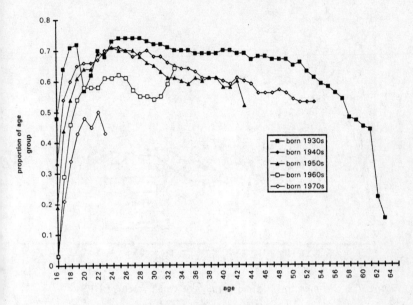

Figure 7.1 Men in permanent employment, BHPS

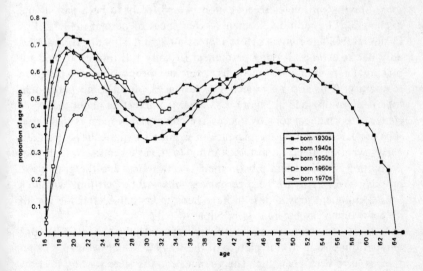

Figure 7.2 Women in permanent employment, BHPS

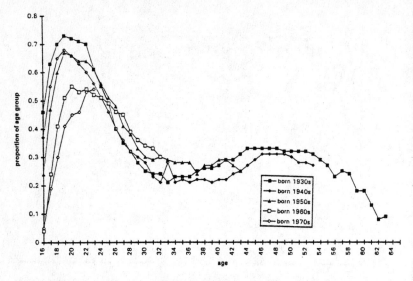

Figure 7.3 Women in full-time permanent employment, BHPS

The same downward trend in successive cohorts of women's experiences of permanent jobs was apparent, as it was in men's permanent jobs. Staying on longer in education is also likely to be a part of the explanation. In addition, women's experiences of permanent jobs dips in the middle age ranges before increasing again. This dip is undoubtedly due to women leaving permanent (usually full-time) jobs and replacing them with part-time jobs, a greater proportion of which are temporary. This dip in women's experiences of full-time permanent jobs is more obvious in Figure 7.3. What is interesting about the experience of permanent jobs by successive cohorts of women is that these jobs appeared to be on the increase in women's experiences after their early twenties. Each cohort is starting to have a successively higher proportion of permanent jobs in their late twenties, and the graphs are crossing over. Many of these permanent jobs will be part-time women's jobs. Permanent jobs appear to have been more stable after the age of 40 for women, as far as it is possible to tell.

Women's experiences of full-time permanent jobs (Figure 7.3) adds another dimension to this picture of the ways in which women's experiences have been changing. The younger cohorts were starting to show increases in full-time permanent jobs when they were in their late twenties, and less of a falling off of full-time jobs in the thirties than was apparent in earlier older cohorts. This fits in with other evidence

showing that some women are delaying their first childbirth and continuing to work full-time to a greater extent, even when they have
children, by taking advantage of maternity leave provisions.

Self-employment

The picture of men's self-employment is displayed in Figure 7.4. There
we can see an increase in men's self-employment starting from the
earliest ages and increasing at all ages as they were reached by successive cohorts. The predominance of this experience in middle age is
also obvious in the diagram, although the younger cohorts did not appear
to have the same falling off in self-employment at older ages that older
cohorts were displaying. Again, it is probably too early to be sure
about this latter point.

Women's Part-time Jobs

The changes in women's part-time employment experiences are displayed in Figure 7.5. This shows an increase in women's experiences
of part-time employment over successive cohorts. The increase may
be slowing down and stabilising since women born in the 1960s were
displaying a very similar set of experiences to those born in the 1950s
after they reached the age of 30. There appears to have been a large
increase in young women's experience of part-time work by the most
recent cohort born in the 1970s. This could be linked to a greater
propensity for women to have a part-time job while staying on longer
in education. Thus the increases over time in women's part-time employment in the childbearing age ranges, linked to family formation,
appear to have reached their peak and there is some evidence of a new
growth of part-time work among younger women.

Temporary Jobs

The experiences plotted out in Figure 7.6 represent both men's and
women's experiences of temporary jobs. Temporary work displays far
more fluctuations over individuals' lives than is apparent for some of
the other types of flexible jobs. Some of the variations are likely to be
due to period effects like fluctuations in the business cycle. However,
some patterns are evident. A much greater incidence of temporary jobs
at younger ages is the experience of the most recent cohorts, born
since the 1960s. Temporary jobs were less common at the start of

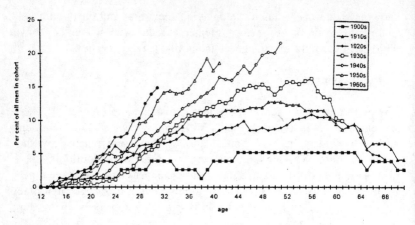

Figure 7.4   Men self-employed throughout the year, BHPS

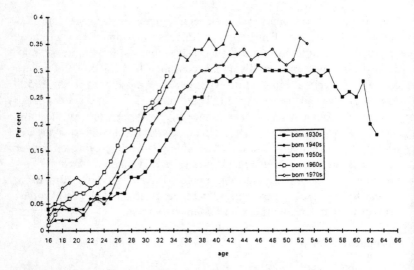

Figure 7.5   Women in part-time employment, BHPS

individuals' entries into the labour market in the past. Women's experiences of temporary jobs (Figure 7.7) display similar patterns. It is likely therefore that for both men and women, the youngest cohorts have seen a large increase in their experiences of temporary jobs at the beginning of their working lives.

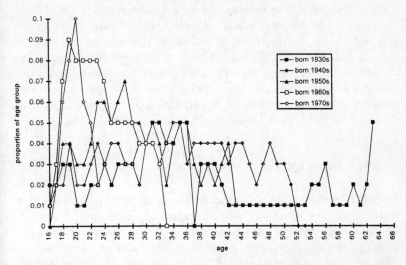

Figure 7.6 Temporary employment (men and women), BHPS

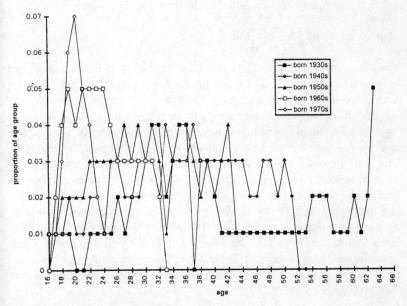

Figure 7.7 Women's temporary employment, BHPS

Our conclusion to examining the separate cohorts over time is that the experience of flexible work has been found to have become more common in the working lives of individual men and women. This is the case even for temporary jobs which have increased in the experiences of men and women born since the 1960s. There is some evidence that full-time permanent jobs are starting to increase in women's experiences to begin to reverse the increase in part-time work which has been the dominant trend in women's employment over recent decades.

ROUTES INTO AND OUT OF FLEXIBLE JOBS

Since BHPS data covers the complete job histories of individuals after leaving full-time education, we can describe the positions of these individuals prior to their entry into flexible jobs. We have had to aggregate the flexible categories in order to have reasonable samples to examine; even then, the sample of men's part-time jobs was very small. It is important to remember that these are not necessarily mutually exclusive categories since 'temporary' includes some part-time temporary, and 'part-time' includes some temporary part-time.

Age at Start of Flexible Job

The ages of individuals when they started their first flexible jobs are displayed in Table 7.6. These age distributions reflect what we already know about the characteristics of workers who are in these sorts of jobs. Men and women in temporary jobs were likely to be in the youngest age groups; the self-employed were more likely to be in the middle age ranges, as were part-time women workers. However, in comparison with a cross-sectional distribution of men and women by age, part-time men were over-represented in the two youngest age bands, 16–19 and 20–29, but not at the older ages; and self-employed men and women are over-represented in the 20–29 age group only and under-represented in the age groups above 40; men and women in temporary jobs were over-represented by age in the 16–19 and 20–29 year age groups, and under-represented in the rest. The difference between men's and women's ages at the start of their part-time jobs is the most notable difference between the two sexes.

Table 7.6 Age of individuals at first entry into flexible jobs and leaving all flexible jobs, by type of job – BHPS samples of men and women at Wave 3

Age when left	Self-employed		Part-time		Temporary	
	Men	Women	Men	Women	Men	Women
First entries, per cent						
16–19	8.1	33.3	30.2	8.5	9.8	28.4
20–29	46.1	32.5	49.0	43.5	42.4	42.6
30–39	27.1	10.3	10.9	28.6	34.3	19.6
40–49	10.1	6.8	5.6	13.4	9.1	5.3
50–59/64	8.5	17.1	4.4	6.0	4.4	4.2
Total	100	100	100	100	100	100
N	542	117	341	283	1032	571
After leaving flexible jobs						
16–19	4.4	4.8	32.7	8.4	27.0	24.4
20–29	33.4	32.6	39.2	37.0	48.9	44.8
30–39	26.3	29.3	10.5	32.4	13.4	20.1
40–49	20.1	18.5	15.3	14.2	5.7	6.7
50–59/64	15.7	14.5	12.3	7.9	5.0	4.0
Total	100	100	100	100	100	100
N	452	270	171	1615	544	835

Ages at Leaving Flexible Jobs

The ages at which individuals left their flexible jobs are also set out in Table 7.6, given that they had been in one or other of these categories of jobs. The distributions are not unlike those for the ages at entry into the various types of flexible work, with a slight ageing effect added in, although a larger proportion were in the 20–29 year group at the end of their temporary jobs than had been these ages at the beginning.

Marital Status at Start of Flexible Job

The marital status of men and women when they entered flexible jobs overlaps to a large extent with their age and what we know about the life-cycle links with an entry into some flexible jobs (Table 7.7). Those men entering temporary jobs were the least likely to be married at the outset – not surprising if they were the youngest group; only one quarter were married when they first started a temporary job. Women going into temporary jobs were far more likely than men to be married; 43 per cent

Table 7.7 Marital status of first entry into flexible jobs, by type of job – BHPS samples of men and women

	Self-employed		Part-time		Temporary	
	Men	Women	Men	Women	Men	Women
First entries, per cent						
Per cent married	50.2	56.7	30.4	68.9	24.0	42.6
N	612	330	148	1176	405	653
After leaving flexible jobs						
Per cent married	40.4	45.3	26.7	59.4	26.6	44.0
N	773	419	288	2220	606	945

were married when they first started a temporary job. Those most likely to be married at the start of their flexible jobs were women entering part-time jobs, a result we would expect from their entry into part-time work after having children. Men entering part-time work were far less likely to be married, coinciding with their younger age in many cases, and possibly their higher frequencies of broken or widowed marriages at the older ages. There were fewer differences between men's and women's marital status at entry into self-employment, and they are in the middle age ranges; approximately one half of those entering self-employment were married when they did so. In all cases, the differences between marital status at the first entry and all entries to flexible jobs were small.

However, compared with the percentage of all employed men who were married, 68 per cent at Wave 2 of BHPS, married men were under-represented in all of the flexible jobs. Of all employed women, 66 per cent were married. Married women were under-represented in self-employment and temporary work, therefore, but were slightly over-represented in part-time work.

Marital Status at Leaving Flexible Jobs

The marital status of individuals at the ends of their flexible jobs are also displayed in Table 7.7. Self-employed and part-time men and women were less likely to be married at the end of their self-employment than they had been at the beginning. Men and women in temporary jobs were more likely to have been married at the end than at the begin-

Table 7.8 Economic activity status prior to first occurrence of flexible job of men and women in BHPS at Wave 3

Economic activity	Self-employed		Part-time		Temporary	
	Men	Women	Men	Women	Men	Women
First entries, per cent						
Self-employed	–	–	7.6	0.8	4.3	0.8
Full-time permanent	77.8	47.8	39.2	16.3	50.2	33.1
Part-time permanent	1.0	13.6	–	–	2.6	5.9
Temporary	4.6	1.8	5.1	1.3	–	–
Unemployed	10.7	5.3	29.1	5.4	27.0	12.4
FT education	1.5	1.8	3.8	0.5	4.3	3.1
Looking after family	–	25.9	–	71.7	0.4	39.8
Other inactive	4.0	3.9	15.2	3.8	11.2	4.9
Total	100	100	100	100	100	100
N	478	228	79	841	233	387
After leaving flexible jobs, per cent						
Self-employed	9.6	12.1	3.5	1.7	2.4	0.9
Full-time permanent	67.9	41.4	49.4	26.0	45.6	37.8
Part-time permanent	1.1	11.1	7.1	22.9	1.2	9.8
Temporary	4.8	6.1	15.3	6.2	15.6	12.5
Unemployed	11.8	6.1	12.9	4.2	18.6	11.8
FT education	–	1.0	8.2	2.0	9.0	4.1
Looking after family	–	16.2	–	35.5	–	19.1
Other inactive	4.8	6.1	3.5	1.5	7.5	3.9
Total	100	100	100	100	100	100
N	187	99	85	647	333	439

ning of their temporary jobs. These differences are probably the result of ageing. Temporary workers, who were the youngest were likely to have got married as their ages increased. The groups which contain older workers appear to have been more likely to have ended their marriages as their age increased.

Economic Activity Preceding a Flexible Job

The economic activity statuses at the start of individuals' flexible jobs are displayed in Table 7.8. The picture varies considerably for the different types of flexible jobs and the genders.

Three-quarters of men's entries into self-employment were preceded by a full-time permanent job and 11 per cent were entries from

unemployment. It was relatively rare for men to enter self-employment from any of the other states of economic activity. Nearly 50 per
cent of women's entries into self-employment were from full-time
permanent employment, a much lower figure than for men. However,
there were sizeable groups of women entering self-employment from
permanent part-time jobs (14 per cent of the entry), and from looking
after the family (approximately a quarter of entries). Of those women
leaving their last job to look after the family 40 per cent said they
were leaving to have a baby.

Two out of five men entering part-time employment had previously
been in full-time permanent jobs. Just under a third had been unemployed and 15 per cent had been inactive. Thus men were equally
likely to enter part-time work from non-employment as from full-time
or part-time permanent work. In contrast, most women (72 per cent)
entering part-time work had previously been looking after their fami-
lies. Of these women one-third (22 per cent of the total) were leaving
their last job to have a baby. A smaller proportion (16 per cent) had
previously been in full-time permanent employment.

Most women entered part-time work after having a baby or looking
after the home. This constituted approximately 70 per cent of women's
entries into part-time work. Flows from full-time permanent jobs
constituted 16–17 per cent of entries.

One half of men entering temporary work had previously been in
full-time permanent jobs. This figure was lower than the equivalent
one for self-employment, but higher than that for part-time work. Just
over a quarter of male temporary workers had previously been unemployed and 11 per cent had been inactive. Thus unemployment was a
much more important source of entry into temporary and part-time
work than for self-employment. This gives credence to the view that
part-time and temporary work is a means by which unemployed men
can re-enter the labour market.

Women entering temporary jobs were likely to have come from full-
time permanent jobs (one-third), looking after the family (40 per cent),
or from having been unemployed (11–12 per cent). Of those leaving
their last job to look after the family, approximately 40 per cent
(16 per cent of the total) left to have a baby. Their flow into temporary
work from unemployment was much smaller than it was for men, but
it represented the largest of women's flows into flexible work from
unemployment. Unemployed women may therefore be able to re-enter
the labour market via temporary work.

Economic Activity After Leaving Flexible Jobs

The status of individuals after leaving flexible jobs is also set out in Table 7.8. Approximately one-tenth of the self-employed spells were followed by a further spell of self-employment. The majority of self-employment spells ended in a full-time permanent job; this was the case for two-thirds of men's spells although only 41 per cent of women's spells; going to look after the family made up the difference for the women. Full-time permanent jobs were less likely to follow part-time or temporary jobs than they were to follow self-employment, for both men and women. Just under a half of men's part-time and temporary jobs were followed by a full-time permanent job; the proportions for women were 26 per cent of part-time jobs and 38 per cent of temporary jobs were followed by full-time permanent jobs. We could consider these as the successful moves. A further temporary job followed a temporary job in the case of 16 per cent of men's and 13 per cent of women's current temporary jobs. Looking after the family was a major destination of women's moves out of part-time work (36 per cent of moves) but much less from self-employment or temporary work.

Twelve per cent of men's self-employment spells were followed by unemployment. This was a similar proportion to the unemployment following part-time men's spells but it was less than the unemployment following temporary jobs where 19 per cent of temporary jobs were followed by a period of unemployment. These same rankings of flexible jobs, according to the frequency with which they were followed by unemployment, can be seen in women's experiences, except they are at lower levels than was the case for men. However, 12 per cent of women's temporary jobs ended in a period of unemployment.

Past Unemployment History at Start of Flexible Job[3]

We can also examine how many individuals entering flexible jobs had some prior unemployment experience in their working lives (Tables 7.8 and 7.9).[4] Past unemployment experiences were greatest among men who entered part-time or temporary jobs; 33 per cent entering part-time, and 30 per cent entering temporary jobs had at least one period of unemployment before these jobs, compared to 24 per cent of those entering self-employment. Multiple past periods of unemployment were most common among men who entered part-time jobs; 11 per cent of the men entering part-time jobs had already had two or

Table 7.9 Number of unemployment periods before first entry into flexible jobs by type of job – BHPS samples of men and women at Wave 3

Number of unemployment periods	Self-employed		Part-time		Temporary	
	Men	Women	Men	Women	Men	Women
First entries, per cent						
0	76.3	85.8	68.2	88.3	69.1	83.8
1	15.7	11.5	18.9	9.5	23.7	13.6
2	4.7	2.1	8.1	2.0	5.9	2.5
3+	3.3	0.6	4.7	0.3	1.2	0.2
Total	100	100	100	100	100	100
N	612	330	148	1176	405	653
After leaving flexible jobs						
0	88.1	95.4	81.5	92.9	72.3	84.7
1	7.9	3.9	13.3	5.7	17.5	11.3
2	2.6	0.7	3.0	1.0	6.1	3.0
3+	11.3	–	2.2	0.3	4.2	1.0
Total	100	100	100	100	100	100
N	759	410	270	2182	606	945

more periods of unemployment compared with 9 per cent of men who entered temporary work and 8 per cent of those who entered self-employment.

Women were less likely than men to have been unemployed before entering flexible jobs. Thirteen per cent of the women who entered self-employment, 12 per cent of those who went into part-time, and 15 per cent of those who entered temporary jobs had had at least one period of unemployment at some point before this entry. While unemployment was most common before women's first entries into temporary jobs, the differences between these groups of women were very small. Multiple experiences of unemployment prior to entering flexible jobs were relatively rare; only 2–3 per cent of women who entered any of these flexible jobs had previously had two or more periods of unemployment.

Unemployment Periods After Leaving Flexible Jobs

As well as the status immediately following flexible jobs, we have the complete record of spells of unemployment up to the interview waves. The unemployment periods which followed these flexible jobs, up to

Table 7.10 Reasons why left last job, before first entry into flexible jobs by type of job – BHPS samples of men and women

per cent

Reason left last job	Men			Women		
	Self-employment	Part-time	Temp.	Self-employment	Part-time	Temp.
Better job	14.8	3.2	13.4	6.2	1.4	6.8
Different job	51.3	28.0	39.9	39.9	10.1	20.9
Redundant	13.7	21.5	21.8	3.9	2.1	5.9
Dismissed	2.7	1.1	2.9	–	0.3	0.9
Temporary job ended	2.7	4.3	–	2.3	1.4	–
Retired	1.6	17.2	2.5	0.6	1.0	1.1
Health reasons	2.5	8.6	2.1	3.2	2.5	3.4
Family care	0.7	–	0.8	31.8	72.4	44.0
Other	5.9	9.7	8.8	5.2	2.6	4.8
War service	0.9	1.1	2.5	0.6	1.2	0.9
Moved house	2.1	3.2	2.9	4.2	5.0	7.7
FT education	1.1	2.2	1.7	1.9	5.0	3.2
Total	100	100	100	100	100	100
N	561	93	238	308	1035	441

the end of the work history record are displayed in Table 7.9. Those in self-employment had the least, and those in temporary jobs had the most experience of unemployment following their flexible jobs; 12 per cent of men's self-employed jobs which ended were followed by at least one period of unemployment compared with 18 per cent for the part-time jobs, and 27 per cent for men's temporary jobs. Unemployment periods following temporary work were also more common following women's temporary jobs compared with self-employment and part-time; 15 per cent of women's temporary jobs were followed by at least one period of unemployment. Multiple experiences of unemployment were also far more common following temporary jobs, for men and, to a lesser extent, for women; 10 per cent of men's temporary jobs were followed by recurrent spells in these records. Since short unemployment spells were thought to be probably under-recorded in our data, this may be an underestimate of the extent of recurrent spells.

Reasons for Leaving Last Job Before Entry to Flexible Jobs

The reasons for leaving the last job before entering a flexible job are displayed in Table 7.10. Compared with the 20 per cent of leaving reasons for all jobs (table not shown) which were to go to a better job, entries into the first flexible job were under-represented in this reason for leaving; men's entry into part-time jobs was rarely for this reason. Compared with the 30 per cent of reasons men gave for changing all jobs to go to a 'different job', those entering self-employment were more likely, those entering part-time were less likely, and those entering temporary jobs were equally likely to give this as their reason for leaving their last job. Redundancies were more common preceding entries into part-time or temporary jobs. Retirement was extremely common as the reason given for leaving a last job before entering a part-time job; retirement constituted 5 per cent of men's reasons for leaving all jobs and 17–18 per cent of reasons for leaving the jobs prior to taking up a part-time job. There is a similar over-representation of health reasons preceding men's entries into part-time jobs.

For women, their reasons for leaving the last job preceding their entry into a flexible job also varied according to the type of flexible job. Compared with leaving all jobs, women's first entries to flexible jobs were much less likely to have followed leaving a last job to go to a better one; 13 per cent of all job leaving reasons were to go to a better job compared with 6–7 per cent of the moves into self-employment or temporary work, and only 1–2 per cent of moves into women's part-time jobs. Women's entries into part-time and temporary jobs were preceded by moves to a different job and because of redundancy far less than all job moves. However, moves into self-employment were more likely than all jobs to have followed being made redundant. Women who entered flexible jobs rarely did so following on from retirement from an earlier job. Having a baby or looking after the family were far more likely to have been the reasons for leaving the last job preceding these entries into self-employment, part-time or temporary jobs; entries into part-time jobs by women were dominated by this reason. Compared with 25 per cent of all women's job moves for these reasons, 32 per cent of job moves into self-employment were preceded by women having left their last job to look after their family, 72 per cent of moves into part-time work and 44 per cent of moves into temporary jobs were all preceded by this reason. This is merely confirming the well-established link between flexible jobs and family formation for women. The link is less apparent in the case of women's self-employment.

Individual men and women who moved into flexible jobs were less likely than those who made other moves to perceive it as an improvement in their job. A certain proportion of men moved into flexible work involuntarily because of redundancy, dismissal and possibly retirement and ill health, but there are some men who saw their move into self-employment and temporary jobs as on a par with their earlier job, but different. These constitute the majority of moves into self-employment and 40 per cent of moves into temporary jobs. Women's moves into self-employment were also dominated by this reason which constituted 40 per cent of all the reasons for leaving their last job. Women left their previous job before getting a part-time job and, to a lesser extent before they got a temporary job, mainly for domestic and caring reasons.

Successful or Unsuccessful Moves from Temporary Jobs

We were particularly interested in pursuing the question of whether some individuals leave flexible jobs to go to other more secure jobs. However, the literature indicates that some of those in part-time and self-employed jobs in some sense prefer a flexible job. The same is true of those in temporary jobs, but to a lesser extent than is the case for the other types of flexible work. We have therefore only considered routes out of temporary jobs, in order to see how far they are 'successful' in leading to full-time permanent jobs. In the rest of this section, we consider one set of transitions: those from temporary jobs to full-time permanent jobs. We call these the 'successful' moves and examine some of the characteristics associated with these moves out of temporary jobs, as compared with the transitions out of temporary work to any other state, which we call 'unsuccessful'. We are interested in examining whether we can identify any of the reasons why some individuals make successful transitions out of temporary jobs.

Duration of temporary jobs
The durations of temporary jobs were examined according to whether they were followed by a successful or an unsuccessful transition to a full-time permanent job (table not included). For men, there were few differences in the durations of their temporary jobs, although the successful transitions had slightly longer durations in their temporary jobs, based on the five years and over category. For women the successful moves were associated with shorter durations of time spent in the temporary job.

Number of flexible jobs held
Prior to having a temporary job, very few individuals had any other experience of flexible work. However, more of those men and women

who were unsuccessful at leaving temporary jobs had experienced either self-employment or part-time work before their temporary job; 10 per cent of unsuccessful, compared with 3 per cent of successful men had a flexible job before having a temporary job. For women, 11 per cent of the successful and 18 per cent of the unsuccessful had had a previous flexible job (table not included).

Past unemployment experiences
The past unemployment experiences of those who moved out of temporary jobs are presented in Table 7.11. Far fewer of the successful men had any past experience of unemployment than was the case for the unsuccessful men; 20 per cent of the successful but 36 per cent of the unsuccessful had a prior experience of unemployment. There was also a greater incidence of multiple past spells of unemployment among the unsuccessful. However, there were no differences between successful and unsuccessful women's experiences.

Age at start of temporary job
For men, we get no indication from their ages of why some made successful transitions out of temporary work while others did not (table not included). For women, the successful movers tended to be younger, with far more being in the 16-19 year age band.

Highest educational qualifications
The highest educational qualifications of those moving out of temporary jobs are displayed in Table 7.12. For men, there were few differences between the highest education of the successful and unsuccessful; slightly more unsuccessful men had a degree than was the case for the successful. This higher frequency of degrees among the unsuccessful was repeated for the women. In addition, unsuccessful women were in higher proportions in the 'no qualifications' category. There is a little evidence, therefore, that the lack of success in moving out of temporary jobs for women was associated with their having no educational qualifications, but this was not the case for men.

Occupations of successful jobs
The occupations of the successful full-time permanent jobs which individuals took up at the end of their temporary jobs were examined, using the Registrar General's Social Class classification (table not included). Successful men were in skilled manual (37 per cent), skilled non-manual (18 per cent) and managerial jobs (15 per cent). Successful women were in skilled non-manual (50 per cent), managerial (21

Table 7.11 Whether had previous unemployment experience before temporary job, by whether a successful move made at the end of temporary job – BHPS samples of men and women at Wave 3

per cent

Number of prior unemployment periods	Men		Women	
	Successful*	Unsuccessful**	Successful*	Unsuccessful**
0	79.8	63.5	84.3	84.6
1	16.5	24.5	15.3	11.8
2 or more	3.7	12.1	0.4	3.5
Total	100	100	100	100
N	242	364	268	677

* successful means moved to full-time permanent job at end of temporary job.
** unsuccessful means did not move to full-time permanent job at end of temporary job.

Table 7.12 Highest educational qualification according to whether individual makes a successful transition out of temporary work – BHPS sample of men and women at Wave 3

per cent

Education	Men		Women	
	Successful*	Unsuccessful**	Successful*	Unsuccessful**
Degree	17.1	20.9	9.3	12.7
A-level	31.7	31.0	33.2	25.8
O-level	15.4	15.9	25.4	23.3
CSE	3.8	4.1	4.1	2.4
Vocational	7.9	5.2	9.7	8.7
None	24.2	22.5	18.3	27.0
Total	100	100	100	100
N	240	364	268	677

* successful means moved to full-time permanent job at end of temporary job.
** unsuccessful means did not move to full-time permanent job at end of temporary job.

per cent) and partly skilled (17 per cent). The majority of these jobs involved some level of skill, more so for men than for women. This suggests that the successful job transitions out of temporary jobs may have been partly because the temporary job was in some way a training for the skilled job which followed.

Table 7.13   Duration of full-time job for those
who successfully left temporary jobs, BHPS

per cent

Duration of full-time job in months	Men	Women
1–6	15.3	16.9
7–12	15.7	13.4
13–24	22.5	23.0
25–60	28.0	29.5
61+	18.6	17.2
Total	100	100
N	236	261

Durations of successful full-time jobs
The durations of time individuals spent in the full-time permanent jobs
following their temporary jobs are set out in Table 7.13. These durations
are distributed across the range of duration categories; some of them
will be uncompleted and censored spells. Many of men's and wom-
en's successful moves out of temporary jobs became reasonably long-
lasting jobs; 47 per cent of both men's and women's jobs had lasted
over two years by the end of their work history record, and approaching one-fifth of these jobs had lasted more than five years. This suggests
that many of these transitions out of temporary jobs were truly successful and not particularly short-lived.

CONCLUSIONS

The experience of flexible work has been found to have become more
common in the working lives of individual men and women. This is
the case even for temporary jobs which have increased in the experiences of men and women born since the 1960s. There is some evidence that the dominant trend in women's employment over the past
decades, the increase in part-time employment over the family formation period, has probably slowed down.
    In this chapter we have also examined some of the characteristics of
individuals at the point at which they left their flexible jobs, and we

have examined their destinations. There were wide varieties of experiences which followed flexible jobs. Some of this variation was linked to the type of flexible job held, and some to the gender of the individuals. If we consider successful moves as those transitions from flexible jobs into full-time permanent jobs, having held a self-employed job gave one the best chance of making this transition. However, it is likely that some of the self-employed who made this transition back into being an employee may have seen this as an unsuccessful move brought on by the failure of their business. However, in an analysis which we have not reported, a sizeable group of the self-employed, both men and women, became managers after leaving self-employment and these individuals may have had a more positive view of their exits from self-employment.

Our analysis found a link between unemployment and temporary work, since a disproportionate percentage of moves into temporary jobs were preceded by a spell of unemployment for men, and to a lesser extent, for women. However, men entering part-time jobs had also often been unemployed. The examination of individuals' past experiences of unemployment up to entering flexible jobs found a similar relationship. Full-time permanent jobs were under-represented in the states preceding men's and women's entries into flexible jobs, even for those moves into self-employment, although the gap was much less in this latter case. Multiple spells of unemployment were also more likely to follow on from temporary jobs than from any of the other flexible states. However, some men and women made successful transitions out of temporary jobs to full-time permanent positions, and many of them were still in these jobs over two years later.

Our examination of what helped some temporary workers to move successfully to permanent jobs found that for men success was linked to never having had a spell of unemployment or a flexible job before their temporary job. For women, success was linked to having spent shorter time periods in the temporary job, being younger, having some as opposed to no educational qualifications, and having never had a flexible job before their temporary job. Previous spells of unemployment, unlike for men, did not distinguish successful from unsuccessful women.

Notes

1. It is important to note that the definition of self-employment contained in this chapter does not restrict itself to those without employees. It is not

possible to distinguish between these two groups of self-employed in the BHPS retrospective employment histories.

2. Some of the characteristics which we describe in this chapter relied upon a matching between the work history data collected at Wave 2 of BHPS which contained the unemployment spells, and the job history data collected at Wave 3. There is a less than perfect match of these, as we have indicated already, and this leads to lower sample sizes for some of our investigations.

3. Individuals were asked to define for themselves whether or not they had had any past periods of unemployment.

4. In some cases, as we saw above (Table 6.8) the unemployment experience immediately preceded the entry. However, the unemployment periods recorded in Table 6.9 could have occurred at any time prior to the first and subsequent flexible jobs. Unemployment was left for the individual to define for him/herself and does not necessarily coincide with official definitions.

Part III
Households

8 Flexible Jobs and Households

In this chapter we examine the experiences of flexible jobs within households. The employment status of all adult household members (aged 16 or more) was recorded in the BHPS at each wave, as well as their past job histories. We will examine the cross-sectional picture of households' flexible employment and also summarise past experiences of flexible working of household members. For the cross-sectional picture there are now several waves of data which could be used. In some cases more than one cross-sectional picture is provided, in order to show that it does not matter particularly which one is chosen.

A profile of households' experiences of flexible work is provided first, followed by a breakdown by household type. The relationships between the economic statuses and mental health of husbands and wives are then compared. Lastly, some household characteristics are related to experiences of flexible jobs.

CURRENT EXPERIENCES OF FLEXIBLE WORK

In Table 8.1 the number of household members currently in self employment, permanent part-time or temporary jobs is displayed. Approximately 13 per cent of households contained an individual who was self-employed. Less than 2 per cent of households contained two individuals who were self-employed. Having three individuals in self-employment was extremely uncommon. More households contained an individual who had a permanent part-time job: 21 per cent of households in 1991, and 22 per cent in 1993. Two per cent of households contained two members with permanent part-time jobs, and three or more was extremely uncommon. Approximately 10 per cent of households contained at least one person with a temporary job and less than one per cent of households contained two individuals with temporary jobs.

When we consider having any flexible job, the percentage of households which contain at least one member in a flexible job increases, over the consideration of the separate types of flexible jobs, to 32 per

135

Table 8.1 Current experiences of flexible work in BHPS households at Waves 1 and 3

per cent

Number of individuals	Self-employed	Part-time	Temporary	Any flexible	Any flexible or unemployed
		Wave 1			
0	87.2	78.6	89.2	67.7	60.4
1	11.0	19.6	10.0	25.4	30.5
2	1.7	1.8	0.7	6.4	8.0
3 or more	0.0	0.1	0.1	0.6	1.0
Total	100	100	100	100	100
N	4852	4852	4852	4852	4852
		Wave 3			
0	87.2	77.6	89.3	67.1	60.0
1	11.2	20.1	9.8	25.5	30.5
2	1.6	2.2	0.8	6.5	8.1
3 or more	0.1	0.2	0.1	0.9	1.4
Total	100	100	100	100	100
N	4354	4354	4354	4354	4354

cent. Also, the percentage of households where two individuals were in flexible jobs increases to 6–7 per cent. Having three individuals in flexible jobs was still very uncommon, less than one per cent of households. Approximately one-third of British households in the 1990s had some experience of flexible work.

Also, in the far right column of Table 8.1, we have considered the extent to which BHPS households experienced either flexible work or unemployment. Forty per cent of BHPS households in 1991 or 1993 had at least one member either in a flexible job, or unemployed at the interview wave.

PAST EXPERIENCES OF FLEXIBLE WORK

In Table 8.2 the past job history experiences of individual household members have been used to calculate the extent to which households have ever experienced flexible work. In practice, we cannot know that these individuals were in these very same households when they ex-

Table 8.2 BHPS households' past experiences of flexible work up to Wave 3 BHPS

	per cent of households
Ever having had self-employed spell	21.4
Ever having had part-time spell	56.1
Ever having had temporary spell	39.1
Ever having had any flexible spell	75.1
N	3781

Table 8.3 Number of flexible jobs ever experienced in BHPS households up to Wave 3

	per cent of households
0	24.9
1	22.3
2	16.2
3	11.6
4 or more	25.0
Range	0–17
N	3781

perienced the past periods of flexible work. The figures give us only a suggestion of the extent to which households might be affected by flexible work therefore. The extent of flexible work by households grows considerably when past experiences are taken into consideration.

Twenty-one per cent of households may have had some experience of self-employment. Fifty-six per cent of households may have had some experience of permanent part-time employment, and 39 per cent of households may have experienced a spell of temporary employment. Taken all together, 75 per cent of these households may have had some past experience of flexible work.

The numbers of flexible jobs which this represents are displayed in Table 8.3. A quarter of households had not had any experience of flexible jobs in the present or in the past. Just over one-fifth of households had experienced one flexible job; 16 per cent of households had experienced two flexible jobs; 12 per cent of households had experienced 3 flexible jobs. One quarter of BHPS households had experienced 4 or more flexible jobs in the past and present.

FLEXIBLE JOBS BY HOUSEHOLD TYPE

In Table 8.4, the numbers employed in flexible jobs are displayed according to the type of household. The classification of household type used here has given priority to a couple, and to the youngest child's age in the classification produced. Thus, a couple with dependent children may also contain non-dependent children. As the overview figures from Table 8.1 illustrated, the vast majority of households contained either zero individuals in a flexible job, or one. A small minority of households contained two individuals in flexible jobs. However, these distributions varied considerably across the different types of households. Single elderly households have been included, for completeness, but very few of such households contained anyone in flexible employment; 5 per cent had an individual with some sort of flexible job. The majority of these were in part-time employment.

Couple households had more experience of self-employment than households containing only single people. Lone parents with dependent children were the least likely of the working age households to contain anyone who was self-employed. Couples with dependent children and couples with non-dependent children were the households which were most likely to contain someone who was self-employed. In the case of couples with non-dependent children, this type of household was the one most likely to contain two self-employed adults; 6 per cent of such households contained at least two self-employed adults.

Earlier studies had suggested that there were considerable intergenerational transfers of self-employed status; also that self-employed husbands and wives can often be working in the same family businesses. While self-employed parents may be influencing their children to become self-employed, these results suggest that it is rarely while they are living in the same household that this transfer takes place. Otherwise we might expect to see greater proportions of two-person self-employed households than are evident in these figures. We can argue, similarly, that the concurrence of husbands and wives both working in the same self-employed business is also not large, although we have some more direct figures on this topic to be presented later in this chapter.

Part-time work was also more common in couple households than in households with only single people. Couples with dependent children were the most likely to contain a part-timer (42.5 per cent) followed by couple households with non-dependent children (37 per cent). These two types of household were also those where it was most likely

Table 8.4 Number of individuals with current flexible jobs, by type of household at Wave 1 BHPS

	Single non-elderly	Single elderly	Couple no children	Couple + dependent child	Couple + non-dependent child	Lone parent + dependent child	Lone parent + non-dependent child	Two unrelated adults	Other households
Number of self-employed									
0	90.2	98.6	86.9	79.0	79.0	96.5	87.9	81.8	88.2
1	9.8	1.4	10.9	18.4	15.2	3.5	10.6	15.6	9.8
2 or more	–	–	2.2	2.6	5.8*	–	1.5	2.6	2.0
Total	100	100	100	100	100	100	100	100	100
N	599	314	1330	1256	310	283	132	77	51

* contains one household with 3 self-employed.

	Single non-elderly	Single elderly	Couple no children	Couple + dependent child	Couple + non-dependent child	Lone parent + dependent child	Lone parent + non-dependent child	Two unrelated adults	Other households
Number of part-time employed									
0	94.5	96.1	83.1	57.5	62.6	78.4	83.3	84.4	90.2
1	5.5	3.9	16.0	37.7	32.6	20.5	15.9	15.6	9.8
2 or more	–	–	0.9*	4.8*	4.8	1.1	0.8	–	–
Total	100	100	100	100	100	100	100	100	100
N	599	814	1330	1256	310	283	132	77	51

* contains 1, 2 households with 3 part-timers.

	Single non-elderly	Single elderly	Couple no children	Couple + dependent child	Couple + non-dependent child	Lone parent + dependent child	Lone parent + non-dependent child	Two unrelated adults	Other households
Number of temporary employed									
0	93.2	98.2	90.8	82.0	80.0	91.5	90.2	76.6	89.0
1	6.8	1.8	8.4	16.6	17.4	8.5	9.8	23.4	2.0
2 or more	–	–	0.8	1.4*	2.6*	–	–	–	–
Total	100	100	100	100	100	100	100	100	100
N	599	814	1330	1256	310	283	132	77	51

* Contains 1, 2 households with 3 in temporary jobs.

that two or more individuals with part-time jobs could be found (5 per cent of such households).

Households containing an individual working in a temporary job were most common in the two-unrelated adult households; approximately a quarter of such households contained one temporarily employed individual, although the sample of such households is small. Temporary jobs were also common amongst the members of couples with dependent children, and couples with non-dependent children where 18 and 20 per cent of such households, respectively, contained someone with a temporary job. Across the range of flexible jobs, lone parents were less likely to be in such jobs than members of couple households who were the most likely to experience flexible jobs. However, the position of lone parents reflects the fact that they were less likely to be employed than many of the other groups.

The experiences of any type of flexible job by household type is presented in Table 8.5, in which either flexible jobs or unemployment experiences are also considered across household types.

The rankings across households were similar when all flexible jobs were considered together, as they were for each type of flexible work separately. Couple households were the most likely to have any experience of flexible work, especially couples with children. Households of single people were the least likely to contain someone with a flexible job. It is still the case that the majority of households, where they contain someone with a flexible job, only contain one such person. However, as many as a fifth of couple households with non-dependent children, and 15 per cent of couples with dependent children contained two or more members with flexible jobs.

HUSBANDS AND WIVES COMPARED

Economic activity

We can directly compare the status of husbands and wives at a cross-section point. We have chosen to present the comparison using BHPS Wave 2 figures in Table 8.6, but it is similar at other cross-sections. There is a tendency for husbands who were in flexible jobs to be more likely also to have wives who were in flexible jobs. Husbands who were in full-time permanent jobs were those who were most likely to have wives who were also employed in permanent full-time jobs (36 per cent of husbands with wives in a similar state). The next most

Table 8.5 Number of adults in household with a flexible job at Wave 1 BHPS

Number of adults in household	Single non-elderly	Single elderly	Couple no children	Couple + dependent child	Couple + non-dependent child	Lone parent + dependent child	Lone parent + non-dependent child	Two unrelated adults	Other households
				Any flexible job (self-employed, part-time or temporary)					
0	83.1	95.0	71.9	42.2	44.5	73.5	70.5	59.7	82.4
1	16.9	5.0	22.6	43.1	36.5	24.7	23.5	32.5	13.7
2 or more	–	–	5.5*	14.7*	19.0*	1.8	6.1*	7.8	3.9
Total	100	100	100	100	100	100	100	100	100
N	599	814	1330	1256	310	283	132	77	51
				Any flexible job or unemployment					
0	72.6	95.0	66.5	32.4	34.5	65.0	51.5	48.1	68.6
1	27.4	5.0	26.7	49.8	41.6	31.1	34.8	35.1	19.6
2 or more	–	–	6.9*	17.7*	23.9*	3.9*	13.7*	16.9*	11.8
Total	100	100	100	100	100	100	100	100	100
N	599	814	1330	1256	310	283	132	77	51

* contains households with three adults with a flexible job.

Table 8.6 Husbands' and wives' detailed job status at Wave 2 BHPS

row per cent

Husband's status				Wife's status				
	FT Perm	PT Perm	Self-employed	Temporary	Unemployed	Inactive*	Total	N
FT permanent	36.1	28.8	3.5	4.1	2.2	25.4	100	1184
PT permanent	17.6	25.5	3.9	3.9	2.0	47.1	100	51
Self employed	21.8	26.2	15.9	4.4	1.6	30.2	100	321
Temporary	(29.7)	(24.3)	(2.7)	(5.4)	(2.7)	(35.1)	100	37
Unemployed	19.2	14.4	0.8	5.6	4.8	55.2	100	125
Inactive	9.0	9.2	1.8	0.1	1.0	78.1	100	498

* Inactive includes full-time education and government scheme.

common status for husbands in permanent full-time jobs was to have wives in permanent part-time jobs (29 per cent). Where husbands were in permanent part-time jobs, the most common status for their wives was to be inactive (47 per cent), followed by permanent part-time (26 per cent). Where husbands were self-employed, their wives were either inactive (30 per cent), in permanent part-time jobs (26 per cent), in permanent full-time jobs (22 per cent) or self-employed (16 per cent). While self-employment was not the largest group among wives of self-employed men, the wives of such men were clearly considerably more likely to have been self-employed than wives in general. Temporary jobs for husbands went along with full-time permanent jobs for their wives in 30 per cent of cases, permanent part-time jobs in 24 per cent of cases and temporary jobs for wives in 5 per cent of cases. However, the number of temporarily employed husbands was quite small. Unemployed and inactive husbands were most likely to have inactive wives, overlaps which are well known in the literature.

The figures in Table 8.7 display the overlaps between flexible work for employed husbands and employed wives taking all types of flexible work together. Where husbands were in flexible jobs, 66 per cent of their wives were also in flexible jobs in comparison with 50 per cent of wives of husbands who were employed in full-time permanent jobs.

The figures in Table 8.8 display the extent to which husbands and wives have overlaps in the status of their past jobs. In comparison with the cross-sectional overlaps in status of husbands and wives, the overlaps of past statuses were much greater. However, these overlaps in status were not necessarily also overlaps in calendar time. While 15 per cent of husbands who were currently self-employed had wives who were self-employed (Table 8.6), 22 per cent of husbands who had ever been self-employed had a wife who had at some point had a spell of self-employment. Where husbands had never been self-employed, only 5 per cent of their wives had ever been self-employed.

Seventy per cent of husbands who had at some time had a permanent part-time job also had a wife who had a similar job (Table 8.8). This figure was higher than the percentage of wives with part-time jobs among husbands who had not had a part-time job (64 per cent). In the cross-sectional comparisons, 26 per cent of such husbands had a wife who had a permanent part-time job.

Forty per cent of husbands who had at some point had a temporary job had a wife who had also had held a temporary job in the past, compared with 28 per cent of husbands who had never had a temporary

Table 8.7 Employed husbands' and wives' summary job status at Wave 2 BHPS

row per cent

Husband's status	Not flexible	Wife's status Flexible*	Total	N
Not flexible	49.9	50.1	100	858
Flexible*	33.6	66.4	100	268

* Includes self-employed, part-time or temporary.

Table 8.8 Husbands' and wives' past statuses, BHPS up to Wave 2
row per cent

Husband ever self-employed?	Wife ever self-employed? Yes	No	Total	N
Yes	22.0	78.0	100	509
No	5.0	95.0	100	1611
Ever employed part-time?				
Yes	69.8	30.2	100	500
No	64.2	35.8	100	1620
Ever temporary?				
Yes	39.6	60.4	100	510
No	28.4	71.6	100	1610

job. Also, only 5 per cent of husbands in temporary jobs at the cross-section had wives in temporary jobs.

There are some overlaps in the status of husbands and wives, both at the cross-section, and in terms of their past experiences. Husbands who were either employed in flexible jobs, or who had held a flexible job in the past, were often more likely to have a wife who had a similar job. This association was particularly notable in the case of self-employment, and less evident in the case of temporary jobs. This relationship was least evident for husbands with permanent part-time jobs, especially in the cross-sectional comparisons.

Mental health and well-being

The mean GHQ scores are displayed in Table 8.9 by the combined status of husbands and wives where at least one partner has a job. Wives' scores are in the top panel of Table 8.9, and husbands' scores are in the bottom panel. The lowest stress among wives is found where wives had a flexible job while their husbands had a full-time permanent job. The highest stress is experienced by wives who were not working when their husbands had a temporary job. There are a few further generalisations which can be drawn out of wives' scores.

Not working, for a wife, always has higher stress levels than being employed in a flexible job. Having a husband with a temporary job always created higher stress scores for wives, irrespective of their own status. Having a husband who is self-employed also created higher stress values for wives in comparison with having a husband with a full-time permanent job.

Husbands' stress scores are lowest when they were self-employed or in full-time permanent jobs and their wives were in full-time permanent jobs. Husbands' stress scores were probably at their highest when they were self-employed and had a non-working wife. In general, husbands stress scores increased when they had a non-working wife, irrespective of their own status. It is not the case that men in temporary jobs or in other sorts of flexible jobs, always had lower well-being than men in full-time permanent jobs. The picture for men varies considerably according to their own, combined with their wives' status. In many cases, having a wife who was working full-time appeared to reduce the stress associated with the man's own status, as did having a wife who had a flexible job, if by a lesser amount.

These results show that the well-being of couples is very much influenced by their joint economic activity and job status. Wives suffer more from their husbands' holding of flexible jobs, especially temporary jobs, than husbands appear to suffer from having such a job themselves. Similarly wives suffer more from their husband holding a flexible job than the wives suffer themselves from holding a flexible job. Clearly, the strategy of many couples in Britain in the 1990s, of having two wages coming into the household, is one which minimises the stress scores and maximises their mental well-being. Husbands appear to get a greater sense of well-being from their wives being employed full-time than when they work full-time themselves. In contrast, wives get a greater sense of well-being by having a flexible job while their husband is employed full-time in a permanent job. The mental well-being

Table 8.9 GHQ mean scores of husbands and wives, by economic activity status: BHPS Wave 1

Husband's status	Wives' GHQ scores given wife is		
	FT permanent	Flexible**	Not working
FT permanent	1.56	1.43	1.92
PT permanent	*	(1.40)	(2.75)
Self-employed	1.83	1.66	2.00
Temporary	1.94	2.33	2.81

Husband's status	Husband's GHQ scores given wife is		
	FT permanent	Flexible**	Not working
FT permanent	1.01	1.52	2.97
PT permanent	1.41	1.30	2.37
Self-employed	0.97	1.26	(3.10)
Temporary	1.22	2.00	(2.24)

( ) based on less than 30 cases
* under 10 cases and not reported
** part-time, self-employed or temporary

of men is higher than that of their wives in almost all of the combinations of statuses.

FLEXIBLE WORK AND HOUSEHOLD CHARACTERISTICS

Housing tenure

In Table 8.10 is displayed the extent to which households with different housing tenure contain individuals with a flexible job. Households which have Local Authority rented accommodation were the least likely to contain an individual with a flexible job; only 19 per cent of such households contained an individual with a flexible job. Of households which owned their houses outright, 24 per cent contained someone with a flexible job. This was the same figure as the one which applied to households with Housing Association accommodation. The highest incidence of flexible jobs occurred in households who were buying their houses with a mortgage; 45 per cent of such households con-

Table 8.10   Housing tenure of household according to
whether household contains any individuals with a
flexible job: Wave 1 BHPS

Housing tenure	Percentage containing individual(s) with a flexible job	N
Owned outright	24.0	1120
Owned mortgage	44.9	2083
LA rent	19.0	1005
Housing association	23.4	184
Other rent	28.2	461
All	32.3	4849

tained a person with a flexible job. Many of these individuals are likely
to be women employed part-time.

Household income

The distributions of household income quartiles for different household types and according to whether the household contained anyone
in a flexible job, are displayed in Table 8.11. In the case of most
household types, households where there is at least one person employed in a flexible job had higher household incomes than those where
there was no one with a flexible job. The exception was lone parents
with a non-dependent child, where having a flexible job made hardly
any difference to the distribution of household income, but the sample
sizes are too small for us to be confident about the results in this case.
In all other household types, there were lower percentages of households in the lowest household income quartile when the household had
at least one flexible job, and higher proportions in the highest income
quartile. It is not possible to attribute the cause of the higher household income to having flexible jobs, since there were many other characteristics which varied between these households. For example, the number
of adults in each household varies in some cases. It is an interesting
result nonetheless, that where flexible jobs in general occur in households, they are not associated with lower household incomes. However, the results described in Chapter 5 demonstrated that some individuals
holding certain sorts of flexible jobs, especially temporary jobs, sometimes did have lower household incomes than those who held full-time
permanent jobs.

Table 8.11 Household income quartiles by household type, by whether household contains any individuals with a flexible job: BHPS Wave 1

Household income quartiles	Single non-elderly		Single elderly		Couple no children		Couple + dependent child		Couple + non-dependent child		Lone parent + dependent child		Lone parent + non-dependent child	
	No flex	Flex	No flex	Flex	No flex	Flex	No flex	Flex	No flex	Flex	No flex	Flex	No flex	Flex
Per cent														
lowest	29.7	27.5	74.4	(32.0)	7.6	2.7	2.7	1.1	1.3	1.7	34.4	9.1	8.5	(12.5)
2	23.4	27.5	23.2	(40.0)	35.4	16.5	19.3	8.0	8.9	1.7	45.4	61.4	26.8	(31.3)
3	35.9	23.5	2.1	(16.0)	36.1	37.8	35.4	36.0	26.6	21.7	15.8	11.4	39.4	(31.3)
highest	11.0	21.5	0.3	(12.0)	26.9	43.1	42.6	54.9	63.3	75.0	4.4	18.2	25.4	(25.0)
Total	100	100	100	100	100	100	100	100	100	100	100	100	100	100
N	401	51	767	25	777	188	404	350	79	60	183	44	71	16

No flex – no one with a current flexible job in household.
Flex – at least one person in household with a current flexible job.
Flexible job – self-employed, permanent part-time or temporary.

CONCLUSIONS

This analysis of flexible jobs in households has shown that the experience of flexible work is not a small minority experience of British households in the 1990s. Furthermore, if we take past experience into account, we can say that the vast majority of British households have probably had some experience of flexible work. Where households were experiencing flexible work, in the majority of cases, it was only likely to be one person who had a flexible job.

Certain sorts of households were more likely than others to contain someone with a flexible job. Couples with dependent children and couples with non-dependent children were the most likely types of households to have contained someone with a flexible job. To some extent this link is likely to be because a large percentage of flexible work consists of women's part-time jobs, and part-time work is often done by women at a certain point in their lifecycle: when they have dependent children.

Evidence was found that self-employed husbands were more likely than husbands with other types of jobs to have a self-employed wife. However, in the distribution of all households, having two self-employed people within one household was a relatively rare occurrence at any one point in time. Wives' flexible jobs were also more common when the husband's job was flexible.

Households which contained an individual in a flexible job were found to be prevalent in households with certain sorts of housing tenure; in particular, flexible jobs were highest in households which had a mortgage to buy their houses. Flexible jobs were not found to be associated with households which had the lowest incomes.

Part IV
Britain's Jobs in the World Economy

9 How does Britain Compare with Other Industrialised Countries?

We can place the changes which are occurring in Britain in the context of developments in a selection of other industrialised countries. The Organisation of Economic Cooperation and Development (OECD) examined the extent of deregulation in industrialised countries over the 1980s. We could conclude from its interest in this topic that deregulation is a widespread phenomenon, but further examination suggests that this is not an accurate representation of what is a very complex picture.

In this chapter we are able to examine the extent of union membership and union coverage across a selection of OECD countries. We also have data on the extent of different forms of non-standard employment in a range of countries, and on how these have been changing. Unfortunately, we are not in a position to carry out a full-scale comparative study where each country's regulative framework and social policies are placed alongside its use of various forms of flexible work. This would make it possible to analyse whether the regulations and social policies explained most of the differences between countries. Marullo (1995) has started to assemble some of the necessary information on national systems of regulations and social policies in European Union countries which would be necessary for such an analysis. In this chapter we present a picture of the use by OECD countries of various types of non-standard forms of employment.

SOURCES

On the whole, the statistics for these comparisons come from two main sources. One is the OECD regular reviews of employment matters in their Employment Outlook. These figures have the benefit of being based on large-scale nationally representative data but not on harmonised definitions. The other main source is a European survey of human resources management practices carried out by Price Waterhouse and

Cranfield School of Management (PWCM survey) and reported in Brewster et al. (1992) and Brewster and Hegeswich (1993) and collected in 1991–2. This study, across all sectors and sizes of organisations, is based on much smaller sized samples, but has more harmonised definitions and covers a wider range of types of non-standard forms of employment, from the employer's perspective. We are able to consider part-time, temporary, short duration employment, self-employment, shiftworking, weekend work, annual hours, homeworking and sub-contracting.[1]

It is vitally important to remember when drawing conclusions from these statistics that they rest on differing definitions, and in many cases the dates at which statistics are available for comparison vary by country, sometimes very significantly. In addition, the regulations and conditions which attach to the various forms of non-standard employment vary across countries. This is the case for all of the major forms of non-standard employment which we have considered in this report. Part-time, temporary and self-employment have very different legal statuses and conditions of employment across countries. We cannot automatically assume that part-time employment or temporary contracts represent the same degree of disadvantage in each country, or the same disadvantage as they do in Britain. Meulders and Plasman (1994) attempt to document the enormous complexities of the statuses of non-standard forms of work across European countries, and the OECD (1991, 1992) has added some further comparisons of the conditions and status of self-employed individuals across industrialised countries. The complexities of these comparisons go beyond the scope of this chapter but this is not to say they are unimportant. Our consideration restricts itself to setting out how the UK fits into the patterns and structures of employment which occur in a selection of other industrialised countries.

TRADE UNION MEMBERSHIP AND COVERAGE

The OECD in 1994 analysed collective workers' representation in industrialised countries. Their aim was to examine whether there had been a generalised long-term trend towards decentralisation and disorganisation in labour relations and collective bargaining. That this trend has been occurring in some countries, notably in Great Britain and the USA, is not disputed. The OECD considered the trends under two headings. First, they examined whether or not the process of deregulation, by which they meant the substitution of collective agreements by mar-

Table 9.1 Changes in trade union membership as a percentage of wage and salary earners in selected countries over time: 1970–90

	1970	*1980*	*1990*	*Whether reduced coverage rates 1980–90*
Australia	50.2i	48.0j	40.4	Yes
Belgium	45.5	55.9	51.2	n.a
Canada	31.0	36.1	35.8	No
Denmark	60.0	76.0	71.4	n.a
Finland	51.4	69.8	72.0	No
France	22.3	17.5	9.8	No
Germany	33.0	35.6	32.9	No
Greece	35.8a	36.7e	34.1	n.a
Ireland	53.1	57.0	49.7	n.a
Italy	36.3	49.3	38.8	n.a
Japan	35.1	31.1	25.4h	Yes
Luxembourg	46.8	52.2f	49.7	n.a
Netherlands	38.0	35.3	25.5	Yes
Norway	51.4b	56.9	56.0	n.a
Portugal	60.8c	60.7g	31.8	No
Spain	27.4	25.0	11.0	No
Sweden	67.7	79.7	82.5	n.a
UK	44.8	50.4	39.1	Yes
USA	23.2d	22.3	15.6	Yes

Source: OECD *Employment Outlook* 1994: Table 5.7 and Table 5.8, p. 184.
n.a = not available.
a 1977; b 1972; c 1978; d 1977; e 1986; f 1981;
g 1984; h 1987; i 1976; j 1982.

ket competition, is widespread. Secondly they assessed whether decentralisation, notably a shift in the bargaining process from higher to lower levels has been occurring in a large number of countries. We review some of their conclusions below.

A selection of trade union density rates are displayed in Table 9.1. These cover a period of 20 years for a selection of European and some other OECD countries. In the UK, the rate of union membership in total (for both men and women) grew from 1970 to 1980 and then declined from 1980 to 1990 to below its 1970 level. The majority of countries shown in Table 9.1 exhibited a similar pattern, although their 1990 membership rate was not always lower than the 1970 value. In most other countries the trend over the whole 20 year period was for union membership rates to decline. Only in Finland and Sweden was there a systematic increase over the whole two decades. By 1990, the

UK had a membership rate of 39 per cent which was around the average level for OECD countries. The highest membership rates were in four Scandinavian countries and the lowest were in France and Spain.

The fact that union density rates have declined does not necessarily indicate that collective bargaining coverage rates have declined. Unfortunately, data on the coverage rates across countries are more difficult to obtain. Table 9.1 summarises the data which were presented in the OECD (1994) discussion. During the 1980s, five countries with declining membership rates, including the UK, also had declining rates of collective bargaining coverage of the workforce. Five countries with declining membership rates did not have declining coverage rates.[2] For the rest we have no data. On the basis of these figures it is not possible to tell whether the UK is part of a majority or minority experience. Of the countries for which coverage rates were reported by the OECD, the UK had one of the lowest rates at 47 per cent of the workforce in 1990. The decline in coverage in the 1980s was also larger in the UK than elsewhere.

The data are also incomplete on the issue of pay-setting, and whether it has become more decentralised. In Britain, as in Sweden and the USA, there has undoubtedly been a reduction in institutional pay-setting in the 1980s. However, in the majority of OECD countries, the sectoral level remained the main arena for wage determination, and hardly any significant changes took place. Britain has therefore been unusual, but not alone, in moving towards a decentralised system of wage determination in the 1980s.

The general trend in union membership rates has thus been that density rates increased before 1980 and decreased after 1980. Britain conformed to this pattern. The OECD does not discuss why the decline has been occurring, but in Britain, and possibly in other countries, it is undoubtedly linked to the fall in male manufacturing jobs and full-time employment in the recession of the 1980s. Bird and Corcoran (1994) show that most of the decline in trade union membership in Britain occurred in the first half of the 1980s. Britain's collective bargaining coverage also declined and there was a move towards more decentralised pay bargaining. A few other countries also experienced these changes but they were not typical. The OECD concluded that a sweeping generalisation, of the kind that the processes of deregulation and decentralisation were widespread, could not be justified.

Table 9.2 Part-time employment in selected OECD countries: 1979–92

	Part time as per cent of total employment			Women's share in part-time employment		
	1979	*1983*	*1992*	*1979*	*1983*	*1992*
Australia	15.9	17.5	24.5	78.7	78.0	75.0
Belgium	6.0	8.1	12.4	88.9	84.0	89.7
Canada	12.5	15.4	16.8	72.1	71.3	70.0
Denmark	22.7	23.8	22.5	86.9	84.7	75.8
Finland	6.7	8.3	7.9	74.7	71.7	64.3
France	8.2	9.7	12.7	82.2	84.4	83.7
Germany	11.4	12.6	14.1	91.6	91.9	91.0
Greece	n.a	6.5	4.8	n.a	61.2	61.3
Ireland	5.1	6.6	8.4[1]	71.2	71.6	71.6*
Italy	5.3	4.6	5.9	61.4	64.8	68.5
Japan	15.4	16.2	20.5	70.1	72.9	69.3
Luxembourg	5.8	6.3	6.9	87.5	88.9	88.5
Netherlands	16.6	21.4	32.8	76.4	77.3	75.0
Norway	25.3	29.0	26.9	83.0	83.7	80.1
Portugal	7.8	n.a	7.2	80.4	n.a	67.4
Spain	n.a	n.a	5.9	n.a	n.a	76.8
Sweden	23.6	24.8	23.5	92.8	89.8	85.2
UK	16.4	19.4	23.5	92.8	89.8	85.2
USA	16.4	18.4	17.5	68.0	66.8	66.4

* 1991
n.a = not available.
Source: OECD: *Employment Outlook* 1994, page 198, table D.

PART-TIME EMPLOYMENT

Trends in part-time employment in OECD countries are presented in Table 9.2. One problem with these figures is that they are not necessarily using the same definitions of part-time hours of work. Countries can be divided into whether they had increasing or stable proportions of part-time to total employment between 1979 and 1992. The UK along with Germany, France, Belgium, Ireland, Luxembourg and the Netherlands had an increasing proportion of part-time employment.[3] A study by the European Industrial Relations Review (1990) suggested that Spain and Denmark also increased their share of part-time employment. Except in the UK and Australia, this increasing proportion of part-time employment went alongside a stable percentage share for women's part-time employment of the total part-time employment. However, in the UK, the female share of such work declined. Clearly

Table 9.3   Women's share of part-time employment 1979–92

| | Women's % share of PT employment | | Women in PT as % of all women | |
	1992	*Change 1979–92*	*1992*	*Change 1979–92*
Australia	75.0	−3.7	43.3	+8.1
Belgium	89.7	+0.8	28.1	+11.6
Canada	70.0	−2.1	25.9	+2.6
Denmark	75.8	−11.1	36.7	−9.0
Finland	64.3	−10.4	10.4	−0.2
France	83.7	+1.5	24.5	+7.6
Germany	91.0	−0.6	30.7	+3.1
Greece	61.3	n.a	8.4	n.a
Ireland	71.6[1]	+0.4	17.8[1]	+4.7
Italy	68.5	+7.1	11.5	+0.9
Japan	69.3	−0.8	34.8	+7.0
Luxembourg	88.5	+1.0	16.5	−0.6
Netherlands	75.0	−1.4	62.9	+18.9
Norway	80.1	−2.9	47.1	−3.8
Portugal	67.4	−13.0	11.0	−5.5
Spain	76.8	n.a	13.7	n.a
Sweden	82.3	−5.2	41.3	−4.7
UK	85.2	−7.6	45.0	+6.0
USA	66.4	−1.6	25.3	−1.3

Source: OECD: *Employment Outlook*, 1994, p. 198, table D.
[1] 1991.

men's share was increasing in Britain alongside a growth in part-time employment as a whole, and at a faster rate than the growth in the part-time share in women's employment. The other countries with a declining female share of part-time work, Denmark, Portugal, the USA, Norway and Sweden, all had stable rates of part-time to total employment. In these countries during the 1980s, the proportion of part-time to total employment was increasing in the case of men's but not in the case of women's employment. The UK experienced a 6 per cent addition to the percentage of part-time to all employed women between 1979 and 1992 (Table 9.3), alongside similar increases in Belgium, France, Germany, Ireland, and Italy.

By 1992 Britain, with Sweden, had one of the highest rates of part-time to total employment at 24 per cent of the countries analysed by the OECD. Only Norway, Australia and possibly the Netherlands had higher proportions. However, differences in the definitions of part-time hours need to remembered here. Compared with 30 hours in the UK, in Norway part-time is less than 37 hours, and in Australia, Sweden and the Netherlands it is less than 35 hours. If the UK took these higher weekly hours values as a basis for defining part-time work, the amount of part-time would rise and the UK would be among the countries with the largest proportions of part-time work. The UK was also among the countries where women's share of part-time employment, while falling, was still in the top range at 85 per cent; Germany had the highest share, 91 per cent, and Greece the lowest at 61 per cent.

Data on average weekly hours of part-timers in OECD countries are displayed in Table 9.4. The UK had part-time hours in the bottom range in 1983 and in 1988 for both male and female part-timers. This point reinforces the problems caused by the definitions of part-time hours varying across these countries. The public sector in most countries has been found to make more use of part-time employees than the private sector (Bruegel and Hegewisch, 1994).

One other topic which is discussed in the cross-national context is the extent of involuntary part-time employment. In 1991, there were just over 9 million involuntary part-time employees in the OECD labour force or 2.5 per cent of the OECD labour force. In most countries, the involuntary proportion of all part-timers ranges between 20 and 30 per cent, and, in most cases, a higher proportion of women than men state that they work part-time because they cannot find a full-time job, (OECD, 1993, p.18).

The UK has one of the highest proportions of part-time employment and women's part-time employment. Moreover, the part-time share of total employment has been rising more rapidly in the UK than in many other OECD countries. Given that the UK's part-time hours are less than in many other countries, the UK position would be likely to move higher up the rankings of percentages of part-time employment, although not to contest the top position of the Netherlands, whose average part-time hours are also low.

The PWCM survey of employers found, not surprisingly, that the UK had one of the highest percentages of organisations using part-timers in 1992. The UK, along with Sweden, Denmark, Norway, Germany and the Netherlands had well over 80 per cent of employers using part-timers in 1992. Turkey had the minimum percentage at 22 per cent. The UK was in the middle band of countries with 18 per cent of its organisations being high users of part-time employees, where high use of part-time was defined as having at least 20 per cent of the workforce as part-timers. Sweden had the highest proportion of high

Table 9.4   Average hours worked in reference week by part-timers in selected OECD countries

| | Men | | Women | |
	1983	1988	1983	1988
Australia	17.5	16.0	16.1	16.5
Belgium	22.0	20.0	19.8	19.8
Canada	14.5	15.1	15.7	16.4
Denmark	16.9	14.4	22.4	21.5
Finland	n.a	17.0	n.a	17.8
France	24.3	22.3	20.9	21.4
Germany	21.4	20.7	20.7	21.0
Greece	23.5	21.6	23.1	21.2
Ireland	26.2	20.6	20.9	17.9
Italy	24.6	28.0	22.5	22.4
Luxembourg	28.7	33.3	21.0	20.3
Netherlands	21.3	19.5	17.4	16.6
Norway	20.3	18.5	18.8	18.8
Portugal	n.a	23.9	n.a	19.3
Spain	n.a	19.2	n.a	17.8
Sweden	19.6	22.4	21.9	24.7
UK	17.1	15.8	17.3	17.1
USA	18.6	19.4	19.4	19.9

n.a = not available; no data for Japan.
Source: OECD: *Employment Outlook*, 1990, table 1.6.

part-time organisations at 28 per cent and Spain, Portugal, Turkey and France had fewer than 5 per cent of organisations as high users of part-time labour. The percentage of manufacturing organisations which employed more than 1 per cent of its workforce part time followed the same rankings, with the UK being in the middle band. Increases in an organisation's employment of part-time workers over the previous three years were greatest in Italy, the Netherlands, West Germany and the UK. In the case of the Netherlands, West Germany and the UK, the highest increased usage came from public sector organisations. These three countries were also those which had the highest proportions of organisations, between 50 and 60 per cent, saying that they had been offering part-time employment as an aid to recruitment.

TEMPORARY EMPLOYMENT

One more aspect of non-standard working time is temporary employment. An attempt to assess developments in a number of countries meets the usual problem when making cross-national comparisons, that definitions and conditions of employment in temporary work across countries vary. There was a general presumption that temporary employment was increasing in industrialised countries through the 1980s, but an examination by the OECD (1993) concluded that it had been relatively stable in most countries.

Data on temporary employment in selected OECD countries are displayed in Table 9.5. The OECD concluded that whilst many countries had experienced a relatively stable proportion of temporary employment, it had increased sharply in France and Spain and more modestly in the Netherlands and Ireland. Temporary employment had remained stable in the UK.

Table 9.5 also shows that in 1991 the UK had one of the lowest proportions of temporary employment at 5 per cent. Belgium, Italy and Luxembourg had similar proportions. The countries with the highest proportions of temporary employment were Spain, Australia, Portugal and Greece. In all countries, temporary employment constituted a larger proportion of part-time than of full-time employment. Again the UK had one of the lowest proportions of both full-time and part-time temporary employment at 2 per cent of full-timers and 15 per cent of part-timers. The percentage for full-time employment was the lowest of the OECD countries examined, except for Luxembourg.

Women constituted the majority of temporary employees in 10 of the 15 countries for which data were reported by the OECD (1993). Japan had the highest female share in temporary employment; the UK had the third largest share. Spain and Greece, with their very large proportions of temporary employment in all employment, had the lowest shares of women in temporary jobs at 38 per cent for Spain and 34 per cent for Greece (Table 9.6). This suggests that where temporary jobs constituted a larger proportion of all jobs, men were likely to occupy a larger share of those jobs. Conversely, in the UK (and elsewhere) where temporary jobs were a small percentage of all jobs, women were likely to occupy a larger share. However, compared with the share of women to men in the labour force as a whole, women were overrepresented in temporary jobs in all countries except Greece, although to varying degrees.

We can also examine the extent of involuntary temporary employment. Individuals are employed in these jobs because they cannot find a permanent job. The European Labour Force Surveys (ELFS) investigate this issue and some figures for 1987 are presented in Table 9.7. The UK had a slightly below average amount of men's involuntary

Table 9.5   Temporary workers as a percentage of total employment 1983–91

	1983	1987	% all employment	1991 % of full-time	% of part-time
Australia	n.a	21.2	19.7	6.7	47.1
Belgium	5.4	5.1	5.1	3.7	13.9
Denmark	n.a	11.1	11.9	11.5	13.4
Finland	11.1	11.2	13.1	12.0	38.0
France	3.3	7.1	10.2	8.7	21.1
Germany	n.a	11.6	9.5	9.5	9.4
Greece	16.3	16.6	14.7	13.2	68.8
Ireland	6.2	8.6	8.3	4.6	45.1
Italy	6.6	5.4	5.4	2.9	50.0
Japan	10.3	10.5	10.5	n.a	n.a
Luxembourg	3.2	3.5	3.3	1.8	22.3
Netherlands	5.8	9.4	7.7	5.2	12.9
Portugal	n.a	16.9	16.5	15.8	36.4
Spain	n.a	15.6	32.2	31.1	57.2
UK	5.5	6.0	5.3	2.4	15.0

n.a. = not available.
Source: OECD: *Employment Outlook* 1993 tables 1.10 and 1.11.

Table 9.6   Demographic composition of employees in temporary jobs in 1991

row per cent

	Men	Women	Total	Whether women over or under represented in temporary jobs
Belgium	35.9	64.1	100	+
Denmark	47.9	52.1	100	+
Finland	40.3	59.7	100	+
France	47.4	52.6	100	+
Germany	54.9	45.1	100	+
Greece	65.6	34.4	100	−
Ireland	44.8	55.2	100	+
Italy	47.1	52.9	100	+
Japan	28.1	72.0	100	+
Luxembourg	46.8	53.2	100	+
Netherlands	46.9	53.1	100	+
Portugal	52.4	47.6	100	+
Spain	61.7	38.3	100	+
UK	37.5	62.5	100	+

Source: OECD: *Employment Outlook*, 1993, table 1.12.
+ over-represented.
− under-represented.

Table 9.7 Share of persons having a temporary contract because they could not find a permanent job, 1987

	Men	*Women*
Belgium	34.6	36.8
Denmark	27.0	38.6
Greece	85.9	83.3
Ireland	67.8	52.6
Italy	65.9	56.2
Luxembourg	15.2	23.5
Netherlands	72.7	63.7
Portugal	70.4	70.4
Spain	85.9	77.5
UK	52.7	25.2
Mean	68.9	50.6

Source: Meulders and Plasman (1989) based on Eurostat Labour Force Survey Data.

temporary employment and a well below average amount of women's involuntary temporary employment. In a comparison of men's involuntary temporary employment, Luxembourg, Denmark, and Belgium all had much lower proportions of involuntary temporary employment than the UK, and Greece, Spain, Portugal, Ireland, the Netherlands and Italy had much higher amounts in 1987. For women, the UK (25 per cent), along with Luxembourg (24 per cent) had the lowest proportion of women's involuntary temporary work. The range extended at the top end to Spain (78 per cent) and Portugal (70 per cent).

Temporary contracts can also cover a period of training and be specifically related to training periods. This has also been examined in the ELFS. The extent to which training was a part of a temporary contract in 1987 is displayed in Table 9.8. The UK, at 6 per cent for men and 3 per cent for women, had one of the lowest percentages of temporary jobs specifically linked to training in 1987. Portugal, Spain and Greece were the other countries with low percentages of training in temporary jobs. Germany, France and Luxembourg were the countries with the largest proportions of training in temporary jobs among European countries in 1987.

The PWCM survey investigated the numbers of organisations in European countries using non-permanent employment (Brewster et al, 1992). The UK has one of the lowest rates of organisational usage of fixed-term contracts at approximately 60 per cent. Only Denmark and Turkey have lower rates. The UK is among the countries with the largest rates of using other temporary employees, although from the

Table 9.8   Percentage of temporary contracts covering a period of training, 1987

	Men	Women
Belgium	32.1	18.4
Denmark	46.9	31.4
France	34.2	28.5
Germany	49.8	53.5
Greece	3.9	3.8
Ireland	22.3	20.5
Italy	15.6	12.5
Luxembourg	52.0	31.7
Netherlands	11.1	10.8
Portugal	0.6	0.7
Spain	4.3	5.7
UK	5.6	2.9

Source: Meulders and Plasman (1989 Table 16)

UK's employee rates of temporary employment, it is clear that UK firms must be employing far fewer temporary workers per firm than many other countries. In fact the PWCM survey confirms this deduction in its plot of the percentages of organisations who were high (more than 10 per cent of the workforce) users of fixed term and temporary workers. The UK was among the countries with the smallest proportions of high temporary usage organisations. However, on the percentages of organisations increasing their use of any temporary employment over the three years preceding 1991, the UK along with the Netherlands had the highest values approaching 40 per cent of organisations.

In the context of other European countries, the UK has a small amount of temporary employment among both its full- and part-time employees. Women have a disproportionate share of these jobs, as they do in most other countries. Relatively few of the UK temporary jobs are involuntary and relatively few are linked to training. Clearly some countries (France, Germany and Luxembourg) use temporary jobs as a part of their training programmes for their workforce and that is why they have more of such jobs. Other countries (Spain, Portugal and Greece) may have such high proportions of temporary jobs because of the sectoral structures and nature of their economies, and possibly also because of the levels of protection and regulation which apply to full-time permanent positions and not to temporary ones. In Britain the level of regulation about full-time permanent jobs is low relative to other European countries, and the extent of temporary work in Britain is low relative to those countries partly for this reason; it is low, in addition, because Britain does not use temporary employment as part of its workforce training programmes.

The 1980s saw certain changes which may gradually be altering this picture. A large percentage of UK organisations were increasing their use of temporary employment in the late 1980s. Other countries were also relaxing some of their restrictions on the use of fixed-term contracts. The PWCM survey pointed out that a number of countries had been encouraging temporary employment in the early 1980s as a response to unemployment. Spain, Belgium, France, Germany and the Netherlands all made fixed term employment easier to create in the 1980s. Also many countries feeling the pressure of public sector deficits in the 1980s were using temporary employment to a greater extent in their public sector employment.

SELF-EMPLOYMENT AND SUBCONTRACTING

The extent of self-employment varies across countries, as does the statutory position of the self-employed. Table 9.9 displays the proportions of the self-employed in total employment over the 1980s for women and men in a selection of countries. In 1979, the UK was at the bottom end of the ranking of countries according to their percentages of self-employed men and women. At 9 per cent of employed men in 1979, the UK had larger amounts of men's self-employment than Sweden and Finland; it was on a par with the USA and Norway, but considerably below Greece, Italy and Spain. By 1990, the UK's percentage of men's self-employment had risen to be more akin to that of Portugal and Spain although still below that of Italy and Greece. A number of other countries also experienced a growth in self-employment over this period; but the increase was not so dramatic as in the UK.

In 1979, the self-employment share of female employment in the UK at 3 per cent was on a par with Norway and Sweden, and considerably below the very large values for Greece (15 per cent) and Italy (15 per cent). However, by 1990 this proportion had doubled to 7 per cent. No other country experienced as large an increase in the proportion of employed women who were self-employed during this period.

Why Britain should have had such a large proportionate increase in self-employment in the 1980s has been the subject of some discussion, although not one which is conclusive. Meager et al. (1994) note

Table 9.9 Self-employment's share of total employment in selected OECD countries: 1979–90

	Men			Women		
	1979	1983	1990	1979	1983	1990
Australia	13.9	13.6	14.4	10.0	9.7	9.6
Belgium	12.6	14.1	16.7	8.8	9.2	10.3
Canada	7.2	7.8	8.3	6.0	6.2	6.4
Denmark	n.a	n.a	10.4	n.a	n.a	2.8
Finland	7.9	9.1	11.5	4.2	4.9	5.6
France	n.a	n.a	11.9	n.a	n.a	5.5
Germany	9.4	n.a	9.7	4.8	n.a	5.4
Greece	34.0	32.8	32.7	25.7	15.2	15.4
Ireland	n.a	n.a	16.8	n.a	n.a	6.1
Italy	21.7	24.1	25.8	12.8	13.5	15.1
Japan	14.6	13.7	12.1	12.9	12.6	9.3
Luxembourg	n.a	n.a	7.9	n.a	n.a	5.8
Netherlands	n.a	n.a	9.6	n.a	n.a	7.3
Norway	8.7	9.6	8.8	3.4	3.2	3.5
Portugal	n.a	n.a	18.3	n.a	n.a	12.3
Spain	17.1	18.2	19.2	12.5	14.1	13.9
Sweden	6.2	6.5	10.1	2.5	2.9	3.9
UK	9.0	11.1	16.6	3.2	5.1	7.0
USA	8.7	9.5	8.7	4.9	5.6	5.9

n.a. = not available.
Source: OECD *Employment Outlook*, 1994, table 2.12; (1994b) table 4.5.

that the UK has had much higher rates of inflow and outflow into self-employment and has had a higher entry into self-employment from unemployment, compared with other European Union countries; these UK rates also grew strongly in the 1980s. The incentives from policy interventions to promote small business and self-employment which operated in the UK over the decade have been suggested as having played some part in singling out the UK from other industrialised countries (OECD, 1991, 1994a).

The PWCM survey (Brewster et al., 1992) asked organisations about their use of subcontracting. Subcontracting was at its lowest use in Sweden and the Netherlands where 44 per cent of organisations do not use this form of employment neither were they increasing their usage to any greater extent. The survey found that there had been a steady increase in the use of subcontracting by European countries over the three year period leading up to 1992. Between 35 and 41 per cent of organisations in Germany, Ireland and Spain had increased their use of subcontracting at the top end and 10–15 per cent of organisations in Sweden and Norway at the bottom end had increased their use of subcontracting. The UK is towards the top end of this range with approximately 30 per cent of organisations having increased their use of subcontracting at this time. Larger organisations made more active use of subcontracting in the UK. More than 90 per cent of organisations which employed between 500 and 1500 people reported using subcontractors. However, in other European countries, there was no relationship between the use of subcontracting and employee size. The conclusion of this survey was that subcontracting had not increased as much as might have been expected according to the flexible firm models.

HOMEWORK

Comparable estimates of homeworking across European countries are notoriously difficult to obtain. Brewster et al. (1992) provide some out-of-date estimates for the early 1980s although they are heavily qualified and not subject to harmonised definitions. Among Italy, France, Portugal, Spain and Greece, the UK is in the middle range in its numbers of homeworkers.[4] The vast majority of these workers in every country were women. Homeworking in Europe, as in the UK, is concentrated in certain regions, in urban areas associated with textiles and in peripheral less industrialised regions (*Employment in Europe*, 1992).

The PWCM study did ask organisations about their usage of homeworkers by which they meant the more traditional homeworkers and teleworkers. Homeworking involved less than one per cent of the workforce of the organisations surveyed. Small increases in the use of homeworking were found in Scandinavian countries, but other than that, there was little evidence that it was increasing. The public sector organisations were slightly more likely than private sector organisations to have increased their use of homeworkers. Since homeworking is regionally concentrated, it is possible that a relatively small survey of this kind is not large enough to pick up changes in fairly small sectors of economies. This survey may be underestimating the changes in homeworking which have taken place.

WEEKEND WORK

The *Bulletin on Women and Employment in the EU* (1995, no. 7) investigated the extent of weekend working in the EU using the European

Labour Force Survey data for 1991. Women were found to be more likely than men to work Saturdays on a regular basis in every country except the UK, Portugal and Greece. Men were more likely than women to work Saturdays on an irregular basis in every EU country. Men's weekend work was often overtime, whereas women's was part of their regular working-time schedule. Among EU countries in 1991, the UK had the highest percentage of employees working either usually or sometimes on Saturday, although the UK was among countries with average proportions of male employees usually working on Saturday. The UK had approximately average proportions of women working usually on Saturday and working at all on Saturday. The UK had the highest precentages of male employees in 1991 working usually or sometimes on Sunday, and the second highest, after Denmark, of women employees working at all on Sunday.

The PWCM survey asked their sample of European organisations about their use of weekend work. Weekend working was more commonly used in Britain than in most of its major European competitors (Brewster el al., 1992). Only 6 per cent of UK organisations in the PWCM survey did not use some form of weekend working. In contrast, in France and the Netherlands, up to a third of employers did not use weekend work. There was evidence of a modest increase in the use of weekend work across Europe in the three years preceding 1992, ranging from 19 per cent or organisations having increased their usage in Germany, Norway and Portugal to 5 per cent in Turkey. The UK had 17 per cent of its organisations having increased their use of weekend work which is at the top end of the spectrum. Much of this increase came from organisations in the private services sector. This sectoral bias was evident for only some of the countries which had increasing use of weekend work. In the UK it presumably reflects the growth in retail distribution and increased Sunday opening. The Brewster el al. (1993) report suggests that this increase in weekend work in Britain is another indicator of Britain's greater deregulation of working hours.

ANNUAL HOURS

The use of annual hours contracts was found to affect around 6 per cent of employees in Britain in the early 1990s (Wareing, 1992) and to be on the increase (Hutchinson, 1993), particularly in the services and private sectors. The PWCM survey found that 7 per cent of UK employers in 1990 reported that they had increased their use of annual hours contracts during the previous three years, and 2 per cent had decreased their use of such contracts. The bulk of the increased occurred in the public sector and in larger organisations (5000+ employees) (Brewster et al., 1992).

In the rest of Europe, Denmark and the Netherlands have the largest proportions of employment as annual hours contracts but Denmark also showed one of the largest declines in organisations using these contracts in the three years up to 1992. France and Ireland have few organisations using annual hours contracts. Increases in organisations using these contracts over the three years up to 1992 were greatest in the Netherlands (25 per cent) and Portugal and Spain (20 per cent) and least in Sweden, Finland and Turkey. The UK was in the middle band of increased usage of annual hours contracts at approximately 10 per cent of organisations having increased their use. The PWCM survey concluded that these forms of contracts were not as widespread as might have been expected, nor was their use spreading very fast in most cases. They suggest that this is because such contracts, while matching work effort more precisely to work requirements also take away flexibility from employers which they would wish to retain.

TENURE OF JOBS

Deregulation has been thought to be associated with more short-term jobs, some of which would also be temporary. On the other hand, Japan is also a model of a flexible economy where job tenure is obviously much longer than in other countries, but functional flexibility within organisations is at a high level. The OECD (1993) contains a review of enterprise tenure and labour turnover in the context of discussing flexibility and efficiency in labour markets of industrialised countries. We can summarise the conclusions reached. It is important to remember in making these comparisons, as was noted in Chapter 3, that average tenure varies with business cycle fluctuations. Comparisons between countries, at a point in time when these countries are at different parts of their business cycle, will tend to produce different conclusions if the comparisons are repeated over time. It is important to remember that the OECD comparisons have not tried to control for differences in the business cycle. The conclusions should therefore be viewed as provisional.

The percentages of jobs lasting less than a year in a selection of OECD countries are displayed in Table 9.10. The OECD describes

Table 9.10 Percentage of short enterprise tenure employment in selected countries 1985–91

| | Tenure < 1 year, per cent of employed | | |
	1985	1989	1991
Australia	22.9	27.9	21.4
Finland	18.4	22.2	11.9
France	13.1[1]	n.a	15.7
Japan	9.4	9.4	9.8[3]
Germany	8.5[2]	18.2	12.8[3]
Netherlands	11.7	n.a	24.0[3]
Spain	15.2[4]	n.a	23.9[5]
UK	18.0[1]	21.5	18.6
USA	28.9[6]	29.7[4]	28.8

[1] 1986   [4] 1987
[2] 1984   [5] 1992
[3] 1990   [6] 1983

n.a = not available.
Source: OECD *Employment Outlook*, 1993, table 4.2.

Japan, Germany and France as being at one end of a spectrum and having relatively long job tenures. At the other end are the USA, Australia, and Canada with relatively short tenures. The UK lies somewhere in between, but more towards the short-tenure end. There are also differences in the age tenure profiles between countries, although in some cases these have been changing over time. The age tenure profiles of the USA, France, Spain and the Netherlands have declined somewhat, representing an increase in shorter tenure jobs at every age over time. Japan, in contrast, has seen a strengthening of its enterprise attachments at ages over 30. In comparison with Germany, Japan, France and Spain, the UK age-tenure profile of men and women in 1991 were higher at the younger ages, but considerably lower at ages above 50. The tenure profiles of the USA lie below those for the UK indicating that the USA had shorter job tenures at every age, on average. Women's profiles dropped below those of women in other countries at a much younger age than that of men, at 35 years old. The UK has seen less change in its age-tenure profiles between 1983 and 1991 than some of the other countries considered. The small amount of movement has been to reduce the tenure durations at the youngest and oldest age groups, more so for men than for women. However, as noted above, it is necessary to control for the state of the business cycle in making comparisons in tenure across time, before being able to draw conclusions about whether deregulation was associated with shorter job tenures or not.

The OECD draws a number of conclusions about the significance of job tenure for economic performance, drawing on empirical findings from different countries. One relevant point is that less educated workers have been found to have lower tenure than more educated ones at any given level of labour market experience. There is also evidence that there is a positive relationship between tenure and training across industries. However, rather than seeing either training or tenure as a cause of the other, the OECD report suggests that they should both be seen as the result of a broader institutional framework which affects both. Finally it is difficult to assess or accurately measure the effects of legislative regulations about employment protection which might affect tenure within countries. The evidence which exists does not support a close relationship between employment protection regulations and tenure, although such a relationship may still exist. The OECD suggests that levels of regulation may play some part in a very complex set of determinants which also include labour market and social institutions. Because of these links, they warn against drawing simple policy conclusions since countries are unlikely to be able to change single elements in this complex equation and expect to change their overall position.

Against this background the UK appears to be towards the middle range of the tenure profiles although with considerably lower than average tenures at the beginning and end of individuals' labour market careers. The low tenures for young workers may well be linked to relatively poor training opportunities, and lower levels of education than are common in many otherwise comparable industrialised countries.

CONCLUSIONS

This examination of other industrialised countries has shown how the UK fits into the broader picture. The trend of falling union membership was seen to be relatively common over the 1980s, but an examination of the wider context suggested that deregulation was not as widespread as had been thought. Britain had experienced some of the largest increases in part-time work for women and men, and large growth in self-employment.

As in Britain, there is little evidence in the rest of Europe that increasing use of non-standard forms of employment is associated with a narrowly defined human resources strategy within organisations (Brewster et al., 1992). However, it is also possible to read some of the changes as part of a response to a more competitive business environment and to increased financial pressures. Thus if a broader meaning is given to 'strategy' it is possible to find some evidence that organisational strategies are being increasingly adopted across Europe which involve an increased use in non-standard forms of work. Changes in part-time work cannot be put down to labour supply or to a new desire for flexibility. The growth of part-time employment across Europe appears to be most closely related to recruitment problems rather than to a desire for flexibility (Bruegel and Hegewisch, 1994). Certainly, the growth in part-time employment in Britain preceded the more recent trend towards deregulation.

The UK has one of the lowest proportions of temporary employment of industrialised countries, although in the middle ranges for short duration jobs. These temporary and short term jobs may be less likely than in some other countries to be linked to training posts and for this reason they may be more likely to be low quality flexible jobs. The UK appears to be unusual in having a strong growth of flexible employment alongside deregulation. Its lack of regulation about part-time work is probably not so responsible for the UK's relatively unique position. Commentators have suggested that fiscal incentives, industrial structures, and public sector policies have had the most effects on part-time and temporary employment (Rubery, 1989; Bruegel and Hegewisch, 1994).

Notes

1. There is of course a range of other much smaller components of non-standard employment; notably family workers, those on government schemes, informal economy workers and others noted by Meulders and Plasman (1994). The data on these more minor types of non-standard employment forms are extremely limited.
2. In the case of France there are no figures for 1990 but the OECD believes that coverage in France is increasing. The data for the Netherlands are not entirely consistent.
3. The OECD (1994, p. 199) notes that the statistics for the Netherlands were based on a different survey from 1987 onwards which made statistics before and after this date strictly not comparable. This means that calculations of changes which span this date will be subject to some error because of the survey differences. This note affects a number of the results cited in this chapter.
4. The figures quoted, the accuracy of which is heavily qualified are as follows: Italy in 1985 had 700 000; France in 1985 had 59 600; Portugal in 1993 had 50 000; Spain in 1986 had 490 000; Greece in 1986 had 225 000; and the UK in 1981 had 229 000.

10 The Future of Britain's Jobs

In this chapter we begin to draw out the main conclusions about flexible employment from our review of other studies and from our own analyses of individuals' and households' experiences. We also return to answer the questions we raised at the outset (Chapter 1): namely whether flexible jobs are inferior; how they are distributed between individuals and households; whether they generate 'feel-bad' factors, and what the implications of flexible employment are for the British economy.

WHAT HAS BEEN HAPPENING TO NON-STANDARD FORMS OF EMPLOYMENT?

At least one quarter of men and one half of women of working age held non-standard jobs in 1994; these figures amount to over 5.5 million women and over 3.4 million men. Some calculations may put the figures higher than this, although the gap between men and women is the same. Overall, women were more likely to be in such flexible jobs than men, largely because women were so much more likely than men to be in part-time jobs. The experience of non-standard forms of employment in 1994 has been shown to have been a minority, if a sizeable minority experience for men, but characterising at least half of women's jobs.

The structure of employment in the early 1990s looks very different from its appearance at the end of the 1970s, with the most change having taken place in the first half of the 1980s. More individuals have been experiencing non-standard forms of employment. Over the 1980s there was a growth in men's and women's self-employment, in men's and women's part-time employment, in men's and women's fixed-term contract jobs, in men's and women's holding second jobs, and possibly in men's and women's short duration jobs. The trends in temporary employment are unclear because of the lack of data and changes in the way the data were collected. The falling back of some of the percentage increases in the late 1980s and early 1990s was probably due to the recession.

Many of the changes are bound up with women's increased participation in the labour force. The structure of men's participation in flexible employment has changed less than that of women's participation.
However, the overall picture, which includes the decline in men's full-
time permanent jobs and in men's employment in total, represents a
major shift in the structure of men's employment. The shift has been
occurring over a longer period than the decade of the eighties.

Overall the vulnerability in the labour market of the youngest and
oldest age groups of men and women appeared, on balance, to increase over the 1980s. This change in their position came mainly from
increases in part-time employment for young and older men and women,
and from increases in self-employment, especially among the oldest
groups. Young men have been particularly affected by the changes.
Given that unemployment has also been falling disproportionately on
this group, they are probably now the most disadvantaged group in the
labour force.

When individuals' past experiences are also taken into consideration, the experience of flexible work was something which one-half of
men and three-quarters of women have had at some point in their lives.
These figures should be regarded as being the minimum statistics for
ever having experienced a flexible job, since they rely on the individuals' recalled experiences, and it is possible that some jobs may have
been forgotten; shorter jobs in particular may have been under-reported
in these figures. This means that temporary jobs may have been more
likely to have been forgotten than other types of jobs. The experience
of flexible work would be extended by a further 8 per cent of men and
a similar percentage of women if individuals whose main job was a
standard job, but who also held a second job, were included in the
measure of flexible work.

Having had one flexible job was by far the most common experience and it was relatively rare, although less so for women than for
men, to have had three or more flexible jobs over their working life,
irrespective of the ages of individuals. For women, it was the experience of multiple part-time jobs which increased their numbers of flexible jobs to the point at which 30 per cent of women had experienced
3 or more flexible jobs. The proportions of individuals' working lives
which they had spent in flexible work was, for the majority, less than
one-third, again, irrespective of their age, and for both men and women.
Having spent larger proportions of working life in flexible work was
associated with having had more flexible jobs.

WHICH PEOPLE ARE IN FLEXIBLE JOBS?

Flexible jobs are not distributed equally across the working population or between households. There are certain points in the lifecycle when flexible jobs are more likely to occur than at other times. This means that over a lifetime, in a small minority of households, a very small minority of women but a majority of men will not have held a flexible job. The predominant types of flexible jobs, as well as their extent, were found to vary across age groups, marital status groups, by family circumstances for women only, and by ethnic origin. As we anticipated, flexible employment is associated with joining and leaving the labour force, more so for men than for women. Young women who were employed and not in full-time education seemed less likely than similar young men to be in temporary jobs, but more likely than the young men to be in part-time jobs. Those young men and women who were employed alongside being in full-time education were almost wholly in flexible jobs.

There was a greater degree of full-time employment among women from ethnic minorities. Self-employment was more common among Asian and Chinese than among White men and, to a lesser extent, White women. Men from ethnic minorities experienced more temporary and more part-time employment than White men. Women from ethnic minorities also had a greater proportion of their employment than White women in temporary jobs.

How far does flexible work affect households? Our analysis of flexible jobs in households revealed that it is not just a small minority of British households who were experiencing flexible work in the early 1990s. Furthermore, if we take past experiences into account, we can say that the vast majority of British households have probably had some experience of flexible work. Where households were experiencing flexible work, in the majority of cases, it was only likely to be one person who had a flexible job.

Certain sorts of household were more likely than others to contain someone with a flexible job. Couples with dependent children and couples with non-dependent children were the most likely types of household to have contained someone with a flexible job. To some extent this link is likely to be because a large percentage of flexible work is women's part-time jobs, and part-time work is often done by women at a certain point in their lifecycle: when they have dependent children.

Evidence was found that self-employed husbands were more likely than husbands with other types of job to have a self-employed wife.

However, in the distribution of all households, having two self-employed people within one household was a relatively rare occurrence, at any one point in time. Wives' flexible jobs were also more common when the husband's job was flexible.

ARE ALL FLEXIBLE JOBS THE SAME?

Our analysis supports the conclusions of earlier studies that it is not usually possible to add all the flexible jobs together. The characteristics examined in this section are often quite different for the self-employed, part-time and temporary employees, and also different between the gender groups. Also, the consequences of a man experiencing self-employment as compared with part-time or temporary work were often quite different, and the consequences for women can be different again.

Experiences of self-employment were associated with the lowest amounts of disadvantageous consequences, although financial and mental stress were found to be severe among small groups of the self-employed. Fewer spells of unemployment were likely to follow self-employment, and some of the men and women who left self-employment may have used their experience as a stepping-stone to a manager's job. Men's part-time work was often used as a stepping-stone to retirement, or as a way of coping with ill-health. It shared with temporary work, for both men and women, a higher risk of unemployment. Temporary jobs were clearly the most obviously disadvantageous of the alternative flexible types of work. This applies to both men and women, but the disadvantages may be worse for men. Individuals holding temporary jobs were more likely than those in other jobs to say that they were experiencing financial difficulties, and had lower levels of mental health. Women's part-time work appeared to be a very stable category but women holding permanent part-time jobs were the least likely to say that they were living comfortably. All types of flexible work had in common that they had some disadvantages compared with permanent full-time jobs, for both men and women, although in many cases there were also some advantages.

Many commentators have noted that while flexible jobs have positive as well as negative qualities to both employees and employers, the balance of advantages of these forms of non-standard contract are reaped by employers, and the balance of disadvantages are shouldered by employees. The disadvantages of flexible work were their lower levels of fringe benefits and pensions entitlements and, in some cases, lower pay, lower training opportunities, and the feelings of insecurity and stress engendered. In terms of a ranking of disadvantages, temporary work appeared to have the most disadvantages compared with full-time permanent contracts, followed by part-time employment and self-employment. One category, which we were not able to investigate in detail because of the absence of large-scale data zero-hours contracts, looks like being the most disadvantageous to employees of all types of job.

GENDER EQUALITY

It is undoubtedly the case that far more women than men are experiencing flexible jobs, at any one time, and over their lifetime of employment. Women have also been found to be disproportionately located in jobs which in 1994 were not covered by protective legislation. Students constituted a small part of the flexible workforce, but here there was considerably more equality between the women and men who were employed alongside being a full-time student since they were virtually all in similar flexible jobs.

Some of the changes in working patterns which have been occurring have tended to decrease the amount to which women and men are in separate jobs and thus to reduce gender inequalities. These include: the increased number of men taking part-time jobs; the pressure on unemployed men to take low paid part-time jobs; the reduction of overtime and unsocial hours payments, and the removal of premium payments for weekend work; the trend towards equality in the conditions attached to part-time jobs, and the growth in numbers of women following continuous employment patterns, sometimes with very long hours.

On the other hand there are developments which are tending to work towards greater inequalities. The pressure on unemployed men to take part-time jobs has not improved the status or pay of such jobs. There are now greater variations in pay because of decentralised bargaining to set against some of the legal cases which are helping to create better conditions for part-time work (IRS, 1992). There is increasing polarisation between those women with continuous and those with discontinuous careers, because of the differential access to maternity leave of highly educated and highly paid women compared with those women without any qualifications who are often low paid (Dex et al., 1996). Finally, the introduction of some of the new flexible working arrangements, for example annualised hours and performance related pay, will disadvantage women since they will reward those who are prepared to work very long hours.

Prior to our analysis, the conclusion reached by other studies on whether flexible work was good or bad for gender inequalities was that there were both positive and negative elements in the changes for women. There has been a move towards inequalities being more closely related to the conditions of employment and possibly less to gender divisions. This change has arisen from men being pressured to take flexible jobs.

FLEXIBLE WORK AND UNEMPLOYMENT

Is flexible work linked to unemployment? One of themes which has kept recurring in this book is that of the relationship between unemployment and flexible jobs. A large number of points have been made about this relationship. We draw these points together in this section of our conclusions alongside some of the results from our analysis of the unemployment histories in the British Household Panel Study (Dex and McCulloch, 1995a).

Flexible Careers

First there is the issue of whether some individuals have careers of flexible work and unemployment. Given that a man had had some flexible work experience, it was less likely that he would have experienced unemployment or multiple periods of unemployment, as the time he spent in flexible work increased. In some ways, we might have expected this result, since if individuals are spending more and more time in flexible work, they cannot also be spending more and more time in another state, for example, in unemployment. All women were less likely than men to have had any unemployment experience. In other respects, the findings for women were slightly different from those for men. Women who had spent up to one-third of their working lives in flexible jobs were equally likely to have also had some periods of unemployment as those women who had never had a flexible job. However, having spent longer in flexible jobs was associated, for women, with having had slightly less experience of unemployment, as it was for men.

For both men and women, having spent some time in temporary jobs was always associated with having had more periods of unemployment, irrespective of the amount of time spent unemployed. But again, as the amount of time spent in temporary jobs increased, the number of periods of unemployment did not necessarily increase.

For men, the risk of unemployment went up as the number of flexible jobs held increased but this relationship primarily applied to temporary jobs, rather than to all types of flexible jobs. Also, the risk of multiple spells of unemployment increased as the number of temporary jobs increased. For women, there was no relationship between the number of flexible jobs held and the experience of periods of unemployment or multiple periods of unemployment. However, women exhibited a similar increase in past unemployment periods and multiple experiences of temporary jobs. Unemployment was not related to women's numbers of part-time or self-employed jobs.

In answer to the original question, 'Do some individuals have careers of flexible work and unemployment?', the answer is 'Yes' but fairly small proportions. Those most likely to fit this description are the individuals who have had temporary jobs and, to a much lesser extent, some of the men who have had part-time jobs. In the analysis of BHPS unemployment histories, less than 2 per cent of men of working age had two or more temporary jobs in addition to two or more periods of unemployment (Dex and McCulloch, 1995). For women the same percentage was less than 1 per cent of women. An examination of the amounts of time individuals spent in unemployment found that 6 per cent of men in temporary jobs had spent between one- and two-thirds of their working lives unemployed. These figures are likely to be minimum estimates. The true figures are likely to be greater because the statistics are based on individuals' recall and this is likely to mean that short periods of temporary employment and unemployment have been under-recorded. However, the answer stands that a relatively small proportion of people have careers of flexible jobs and unemployment.

Unemployment Leading to Flexible Work

Does a past experience of unemployment make it more or less likely that an individual will be in a flexible job? Our earlier analysis showed that the past unemployment experiences of the self-employed were often less than those of employees, although this was less the case for women than it was for men. Also, flows out of unemployment into flexible jobs were over-represented as compared with their percentage distributions in the working population, as were flows into inactivity.

Men in temporary jobs were the most likely to have had an unemployment period in the past: 60 per cent of temporarily employed men had experienced at least one previous period of unemployment. Men in temporary jobs were also more likely than men in other jobs to have had three or more previous periods of unemployment. This relationship of past unemployment and a temporary job was also evident for women, although smaller than they were between men. An examination of the percentages of their past working life which individuals had spent unemployed suggested that there was a small group of men who had a career of unemployment interspersed with temporary jobs. Again, men (and women to a far lesser extent) in temporary jobs stand out by having a far higher proportion who had ever had a past period of long term unemployment. In the case of men, this is approximately double the experience of long term unemployment found in the other groups.

Flexible Jobs Leading to Recurrent Unemployment

Does the ending of a temporary job lead to recurrent unemployment? Studies have noted that the ending of temporary work can often be the reason for becoming unemployed. Dex and McCulloch (1995a) and analyses earlier in this book examined the flows into unemployment from different origin states. The figures suggest that temporary jobs had the highest risk of transitions into unemployment. Of those who were in temporary jobs at one wave, 14 per cent of the men in temporary jobs and 5 per cent of the women were unemployed by the next wave. These percentages are considerably higher than the percentage flows into unemployment from other states.

The analysis described in earlier chapters suggests that multiple unemployment spells were more common among those men and, to a lesser extent, women who had held a temporary job, than they were following other types of flexible work, or full-time permanent jobs. This was additional evidence that temporary jobs carry an increased risk of recurrent unemployment, as compared with other kinds of job. The proportions of men and women who experienced recurrent unemployment following temporary jobs was relatively small in this study.

Dex and McCulloch (1995a) found no evidence that men's or women's durations of unemployment were linked to their prior state of economic activity. In particular, having been in a temporary job did not appear to lead to either longer or shorter durations of unemployment. The same was true for the other flexible work states. In the case of temporary work, this finding was confirmed in a multivariate analysis which controlled for a wide range of other influences.

Temporary Jobs as a Stepping Stone to a Better Job?

Earlier analyses in this book also considered the issue of whether taking a temporary job is a good way to leave unemployment, and a stepping-stone to a more permanent position. Temporary jobs were found to be disproportionately represented in the jobs held by those who flowed out of unemployment. Men who had gone from a period of unemployment to a temporary job were less likely than those who had just had temporary jobs to go from that temporary job to a full-time permanent job. One-third of men who had gone from unemployment to a temporary job did find a full-time permanent job after the temporary job. The group with a prior experience of unemployment were also far more likely to go back into unemployment after their temporary job and far less likely to go on to another temporary job than other men in temporary jobs. Forty-one per cent of the men who had gone from unemployment into temporary jobs ended up back in unemployment after their temporary job compared with 12 per cent of men who had had a temporary job which was not preceded by unemployment. The same result can be seen in the women's results. In the case of men and women, the sample sizes on which these findings rest are very small.

It was found that those in temporary jobs would probably have less employer-related training experience. For a temporary job with no training attached, the chances of individuals using this job as a stepping-stone to a better job were much reduced.

There was some evidence that temporary jobs were more likely to lead to recurrent experiences of unemployment, as had been found by earlier studies. Leaving unemployment to go to a temporary job held therefore this risk. Taking a temporary job as a route out of unemployment led to full-time permanent jobs for approximately one-third of the men who had gone this route. However, this was a lower proportion than the men who made this successful move from temporary to full-time permanent jobs where the temporary job had not been preceded by unemployment. In addition the probability that fewer temporary jobs provided any training might help to turn temporary work and recurrent unemployment into a career for some. However, as indicated above, a relatively small proportion of men had this set of experiences.

HOW DOES THE UK COMPARE WITH OTHER INDUSTRIALISED COUNTRIES?

Examination of a selection of other industrialised countries revealed something of how the UK fits into a broader picture. While recent declines in union membership were common to many industrialised countries, deregulation was not as widespread as might be thought. The UK was found to be in the group with high proportions of its women's workforce in part-time employment. The growth of part-time employment across Europe appears to be most closely related to recruitment problems rather than to a desire for flexibility. Changes in part-time work cannot be put down to labour supply or to the adoption of new human resources strategies for flexibility largely because the growth in part-time employment in Britain preceded the more recent trend towards deregulation. In addition, the UK was unusual in having, at the same time, a strong growth in men's part-time employment, and an enormous growth in both men's and women's self-employment. It is difficult to explain these unusual elements of the UK's position without considering the role that recent government policy has had to play in promoting self-employment and part-time employment for men.

The UK was rated low among industrialised countries in its proportion of temporary employment, although it was in the middle ranges for short duration jobs. These temporary and short term jobs may be less likely than in some other countries to be linked to training posts and for this reason they may be more likely to be low quality flexible jobs, as compared to some countries. The UK's lack of regulation about temporary and part-time employment is probably not so responsible for its position. Commentators have suggested that fiscal incentives, industrial structures and public sector policies have had the most effects on part-time and temporary employment. The UK appears to be untypical in having strong growth of flexible employment alongside deregulation. Other economies with high proportions of flexible employment, especially part-time women's employment, tend to have highly regulated labour markets. This is a further reason not to accept that the longer term growth of flexible employment in Britain has been caused by deregulation. On the other hand, deregulation in Britain in the 1980s may well have contributed to a worsening of the position of flexible employees and created an environment where the conditions of employment in these jobs can fall even further. Also, a strong argument could be made for British government policy in the 1980s hav-

ing had an important role to play in bringing about some of the changes
which have been occurring; namely, the growth in self-employment,
the reductions in men's full-time employment, the growth in men's
part-time employment, and the appearance of more disadvantaged forms
of flexible employment.

IS FLEXIBLE WORK ACHIEVING ITS AIMS?

A number of studies have considered whether labour market restructuring towards flexible employment has changed the performance of
the British labour markets and economy since the end of the 1970s.
Beatson's (1995) analysis of employment and wage flexibility for the
government suggests that the British labour market has become more
flexible and that there are some encouraging signs of this having had
a beneficial effect on performance. However, Beatson does not provide any evidence on indicators of performance. Blanchflower and
Freeman (1994) carried out a before and after analysis of the British
economy taking 1979, the start of the Thatcher reforms, as their pivotal
point. They concluded that the Thatcherite reforms succeeded in their
goals of weakening union power. They may also have slightly increased
the responsiveness of employment and wages to market conditions as
well as increasing self-employment. They thought that the reforms failed
to improve the responsiveness of real wages to unemployment. They
suggested that higher inequality and poverty, and lower levels of full-
time employment, especially among men, were often outcomes and it
could hardly be argued that these were ideal preconditions for economic success. Blanchflower and Freeman claimed that their analysis
was preliminary. Indeed, while they provided a picture of the British
economy in the 1980s, their study has not proved that the labour market restructuring policies caused the changes which are now visible.
One other conclusion they drew was that the 1980s was a decade of
substantial improvement in the labour market position of women. Unfortunately they presented very little data on women's employment.
Women's full-time employment followed a similar pattern to men's
full-time employment over the 1980s. We must presume, therefore,
that their conclusion about women rests on the continued growth of
part-time women's work through the 1980s. The idea that increasing
part-time employment represented a substantial improvement for women
would be disputed by many, especially given the relatively low levels
of non-wage benefits attached to part-time employment.

Robinson (1994) and to a lesser extent Rubery (1989) were seeking to address the popular argument that standard full-time permanent jobs (for men) have been replaced by low paid part-time jobs (for women) which men are unable or unwilling to take. They set out to examine whether labour market restructuring towards flexible jobs and women's jobs helps to explain the rising aggregate level of unemployment since 1979 and the concomitant increasing pay inequalities between men and between women. The conclusion they reached was that it did not, but that polarisation in the labour market had been growing. The introduction of flexible forms within the public sector and some industrial sectors appears to have gone alongside the protection of status, conditions, contracts and union collective bargaining for a privileged core workforce (Rubery, 1989). Flexible work has created tiers of workers. However, as Rubery (1989) argues, it may still be the stronger group who determine pay levels and who keep real wage growth high in Britain. Thus flexibility may be a sign of growing inequalities between workers as some have argued (McLaughlin, 1994) and it may be having damaging effects on efficiency.

Rubery (1989) points out that there is no single way to organise a labour market in order to achieve economic objectives. For example, Japan with its lifetime employment commitments and the USA with its hire and fire policies, provide quite different models for achieving flexibility in labour markets.

As reported in OECD (1994) the OECD and the ILO requested national governments to outline their views about the impact of labour market deregulation. The response of the British government was that deregulation had successfully reduced both short term and long term unemployment, after controlling for cyclical effects, and had created a faster rate of growth of jobs in Britain in the 1980's than elsewhere in the European Union. The TUC analysed this response in a document (TUC, 1995) produced for the ILO. It examined the government's four claims in turn and disputed each of the conclusions. The claims were that there had been an earlier than expected fall in unemployment and an earlier than expected increase in employment; that there was a lower peak in the numbers of unemployed than in the previous recession and a fall in the peak numbers of long term unemployed compared with the previous recession; that there has been a fall in the incidence of long term unemployed compared with the previous peak; and that there has been a faster rate of job growth in the 1980s compared to previous economic cycles, an increase in the number of people in work, and a higher rate of labour force participation than in most other EU states.

On the claim relating to the faster growth of employment over the 1980s as a result of deregulation, the TUC argue that the changes in self-employment and temporary work do not constitute a radical change in the overall structure of the labour market although temporary employment has been important as a source of net employment growth over the 1990s recovery. Also, changes in part-time employment have been occurring over a longer period and cannot be attributed to deregulation. Calculations by Rubery and Fagan (1994) suggest that 82 per cent of the growth in women's part-time employment can be explained by changes in the industrial sectors.

Labour mobility has been suggested to be an indicator of the extent to which a labour market is flexible. 'In a flexible labour market, labour should be mobile' (Beatson, 1995, p. 54). However high turnover can impose costs on firms as well as affecting productivity of other workers and morale (IDS, 1995). A number of studies have begun to examine the extent to which labour turnover and job tenure have been changing over the 1980s and 1990s. The extent to which workers are in jobs of less than 12 months did change over the 1980s (Beatson, 1995). Average job tenure went down between 1975 and 1991 for most groups (Burgess and Rees, 1994) and job turnover did increase in the 1990s (IDS, 1995). The problem with all of these statistics is that they do not control for business cycle fluctuations. All of these measures of mobility would be expected to change over the cycle; for example, measures of job tenure appear to rise in the recession, probably because there are a relatively smaller proportion of short jobs in the stock of jobs. That mobility has increased in the 1990s, therefore, would be expected with the upturn in the economic cycle. It is not possible to attribute this increased mobility to deregulation, given the research results currently available.

While the climate of deregulation in the labour market over the 1980s may not have caused all of the growth in flexible employment in Britain, it has created an environment in which the low skilled sector and more vulnerable workers can be exploited. The fact that women are in the disadvantageous jobs to a greater extent than men is evidence that this is the case. Women who are employed in low-skilled part-time jobs are also often in jobs which are below their level of skill (Dex, 1992). The failure to utilise a significant part of the skills of its workforce is not a hallmark of an efficient economy.

THE FUTURE OF BRITAIN'S JOBS

What started out as a growth in women's employment in flexible jobs has gradually been spreading to encompass men. Young men in particular see very few opportunities to pursue a traditional full-time job (with training or apprenticeship) in the British labour market of the 1990s. Given we have identified some of the trends which have been occurring we can consider what their implications might be. Women's moves into part-time jobs are often associated with downward occupational mobility so that this often represents a loss of skill to the economy. This loss of skill is related to the lack of part-time jobs at the top end of the occupational hierarchy. Non-standard forms of employment are rarely providing training so this is another way in which the growth of such jobs is helping to lower the skill base of the British economy.

In addition, women's moves into part-time employment have the adverse consequence that they will have much reduced pension entitlements in old age. This implication also applies to those who have prolonged periods of any of the varieties of non-standard jobs, which have all been found to have considerably reduced entitlements to fringe benefits including statutory social security coverage. Since women are being more affected by non-standard forms of employment than men, the adverse consequences will be correspondingly greater for them in the future.

It is vital to consider some of the wider issues of these policies and the changes they imply. There may be a range of social consequences and long term inefficiencies resulting from dispossessing a high proportion of young men from traditional full-time jobs. Also, if workers and households are being made insecure, as well as affecting their mental health, increased insecurity will negatively affect workers' productivity at work; it could affect their voluntary job turnover and the costs of turnover to organisations. Neathey and Hurstfield (1995) found a few examples of employers who are beginning to realise that their policies are costly in these ways.

The growth which has been occurring in self-employment and part-time employment slowed down by the 1990s. Both the numbers and the percentages of the workforce in these jobs stopped growing in the early 1990s. Whether these forms of work will start to increase as the recession has eased remains to be seen. Projections on the employment structure of the economy in the year 2000 suggest that part-time employment will increase throughout the 1990s. Wilson (1994) estimated that there will be an increase of over 600 000 part-time jobs from 1991 to 2000; over 400 000 of these jobs were expected to be held by women. The main increase in jobs was forecast to come from business and miscellaneous services and from health and education. The jobs are allocated to women since women have been the predominant workforce in many of these industries in the 1980s.

In contrast to this view of continuing increases in women's part-time employment there is evidence which suggests a slightly different scenario. There is evidence from individuals' work histories, as described in this report, that women's part-time employment may have stabilised, especially that experienced over the family formation phase of women's lives. In addition, other sources are showing large increases in women's full-time employment when they have young children (*Employment Gazette*, 1993). These are presumably the increasingly highly educated women's workforce, some of whom have been delaying having children, who have been taking maternity leave in larger numbers. It is possible that the proportion of employed women in part-time employment may even go down in the future. Neathey and Hurstfield (1995) suggest that, because of business and financial pressures, some employers are now seeking more flexibility from employees of the sort that women part-timers with children are not in a position to offer. On the basis of these changes, we might expect therefore that in future there will be a growth in the full-time rather than part-time share of women's employment. This all points to increased competition between men and women for the better jobs. We also noted the increased occupancy of part-time jobs by those who are simultaneously in full-time education. This development is presumably linked to the fall in the real value of student grants. We may be in the process of moving to the US model of part-time employment, where the rates of part-time are highest among the young who are in full-time education.

There is considerable scope and some institutional pressures for men's part-time employment to continue to increase. Men's part-time employment may well therefore continue to increase. Temporary employment is also likely to continue to fluctuate, as it always has. The fixed-term component of temporary employment has been increasing, and may well continue to do so, given the changes which have been occurring in the public sector.

On the basis of the changes documented in this report and some of their implications we can add another comment to the debate over whether the policy encouraging deregulation has a achieved its goals. Britain is sliding into being a low wage, low skill economy in which the quality of its jobs is declining. It may be that women's skills are being lost more, disproportionately, than men's in this process. This loss of skill is not being replaced because non-standard jobs provide little training. The potential of the workforce is therefore being wasted. Neathey and Hurstfield (1995) did find an example of an employer who had reversed the hours and contract changes they had enacted because of the bad effect the changes had had on worker morale and productivity. Unfortunately, so far, this appears to be an isolated example. All this is making relatively little impact on unemployment, and labour mobility appears to be little changed. The young and the old are increasingly filling the most vulnerable positions in the labour market, but these changes are being felt across all age groups. It is debatable whether people who feel insecure and more vulnerable in their jobs will produce better performance and productivity. The case-study evidence suggests that these processes are far from being completed and are even getting worse with the advent of zero-hours contracts which might more aptly be called zero rights contracts. Does this picture show the increased efficiency we have been led to expect? I suggest not. Far more employers and the government need to realise that policies which are bad for workers are bad for business in the end. Britain needs to reverse these trends if it is not to slide even further into squandering the skills of its labour force. Are these jobs necessary if Britain is to survive? The question should be 'Will Britain survive if these are the jobs it seeks to create and provide its living?' The answer surely is 'No'.

Appendix

Appendix The British Household Panel Study Data (BHPS) and other sources

Definitions for the variables used from BHPS and the LFS are displayed in Table A1.1.

BHPS

The British Household Panel Study (BHPS) was started in 1991 by interviewing all the adult members (over 16) of 5500 British households. The survey contained approximately 10 000 individuals at its first wave; 9912 eligible adults provided a full interview at the first wave, and 352 proxy interviews were obtained, which represents a response rate of 74 per cent. A random sample was drawn from the small users file of the Postcode Address File which covers non-institutional residences in England, Wales and Scotland (north of the Caledonian Canal excluded).

The intention is that all adult members should be interviewed every year. The number of individuals who were interviewed at each of the first three waves are presented in Table A1.2.

Individuals were interviewed and asked a core of questions which remain constant from wave to wave. The design of the BHPS provides information not only about individuals' circumstances, but also contextual information about the households in which these individuals live. Since the BHPS samples at the household level, it is possible to match up responses of all the household members so that intra-household analyses can be carried out.

In addition, each wave contains a variable component. At Wave 2, the variable component was an employment status history for which respondents were asked to recall their periods of economic activity, with the start and end dates, from the point of leaving full-time education until the present. At Wave 3, the variable component was a job history in which respondents were asked to recall the details and dates of all of their jobs held since leaving full-time education, up to September 1990.

Wave 3 Job History Data

In the Wave 3 job history data, individuals recalled approximately 32 000 jobs. However, not all the details of these jobs were recalled. We summarise here the level of recall on particular aspects of these jobs (Table A1.3). The failure to recall details about jobs is not excessively high for individual items. For example, in 4 per cent of these jobs, a classification of whether the job was full-time, part-time or self-employed is missing. The industry classification and the contract status of jobs have higher missing values rates at 14–15 per cent. However, the rate of missing values grows when a classification of jobs is required which draws on several aspects of the job. Also, jobs where the information about them is complete constitute a much reduced sample of the total number of jobs: just under 20 per cent. The analysis of past jobs contained in this report uses this sample of jobs with nearly complete information.

FLEXIBLE JOBS IN BHPS

The extent to which flexible jobs were recorded in the BHPS Wave and retrospective data are displayed in Table A1.4. The retrospective work history accounts went from an individual leaving school up to October 1990. The Wave data analysed in this book covered the period from October 1990 to approximately October 1993.

FLEXIBLE JOBS IN LFS

The extent of flexible jobs is selected years of the Labour Force Survey are displayed in figures A1.1 to A1.3.

Figure A1.1   Involuntary part-time work, 1984–94, LFS (Spring)

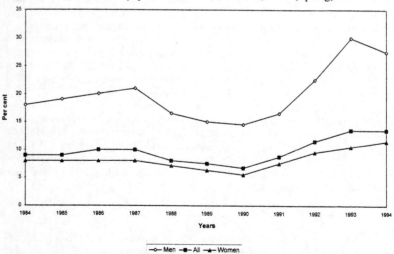

Source: Adapted from Robinson (1994), figure 11.

Figure A1.2 Temporary employment as a proportion of all employees, 1984–94, LFS (Spring)

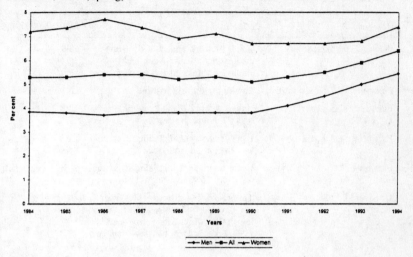

Source: Adapted from Robinson (1994), figure 12.

Figure A1.3 Involuntary temporary employment, 1984–94, LFS (Spring). Percentage of those in temporary work because unable to find permanent work

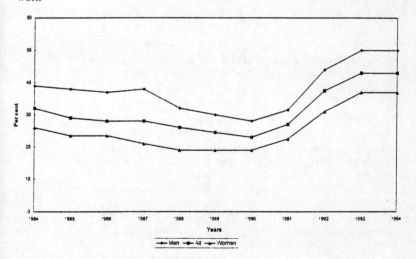

Source: Adapted from Robinson (1994), figure 12

Table A1.1 Definitions of categories of non-standard forms of employment created from LFS and BHPS data

Category	Definition	Data source
Full-time permanent	Hours of work and paid overtime greater than 30 per week and employee thinks of job as permanent	LFS
Part-time self-definition	Thinks of job as part-time	LFS
Part-time < 31 hours	Hours of work + paid overtime less than 31 hours per week	LFS
Part-time < 8 hours	Usual hours (not including overtime) less than eight hours per week	LFS
Part-time < 16 + < 2 yrs	Usual hours (not including overtime) less than 16 hours per week	LFS
Uncovered 1994	This represents groups which were not covered by employment protection legislation which was introduced in 1994 because they had less than two years tenure	
More than one PT job	Usual hours + paid overtime in main job plus a second job whose actual hours last week were less than 31 hours per week	LFS
Temporary full-time	Thinks of main job as temporary and thinks of hours as working full-time	LFS
Temporary part-time	Thinks of main job as temporary and thinks of hours as part-time	LFS
Self-employed	Thinks of self as self-employed	LFS
Self-employed full-time	Thinks of self as self-employed + thinks of hours as full time	LFS
Self-employed part-time	Thinks of self as self-employed + thinks of hours as part time	LFS
Any flexible	Any of part-time, temporary or self-employed (without employees)	LFS
Job change same firm/ different occupation	Employed in same firm as one year earlier but has different occupation this year from last year	LFS
Job change same firm/ FT to PT	Employed in same firm as one year earlier but has different hours this year from last year, FT became PT	LFS
Job change same firm/ employee to self-employed	Employed in same firm as one year earlier but has has changed from employee to self-employment in past year	LFS

Table A1.1 continued

Full-time permanent	Thinks of hours as full-time + thinks of job as permanent	BHPS retrospective data
Part-time permanent	Thinks of job as part-time + thinks of job as permanent	BHPS retrospective data
Temporary	Thinks of job as temporary (can be either full or part-time)	BHPS retrospective data
Self-employed	Thinks of self as self employed	BHPS

Table A1.2 BHPS wave responses of individuals

| | Respondent at | | | | |
	Wave 1	*New*	*Wave 2*	*New*	*Wave 3*
Wave 1	9912				
Died/out of scope	−139				
Eligible at Wave 2	9773				
Wave 2	8567	+892	9459		
Died/out of scope	−121		−336		
Eligible at Wave 3	8446		9123		
Wave 3	7617		8205	+812	9017

Table A1.3 Levels of missing values on selected aspects of jobs recalled as part of Wave 3 job listing

Aspect of job	Valid cases	Percent missing on item
FT/PT/self-employed	31 450	4
Permanent/temporary contract	27 819	15
Industry (SIC) of employer	28 092	14
Occupation (SOC)	30 858	6
RG Social class	30 366	7
Supervisor status	30 554	7
Month spell began	30 132	8
Year spell began	28 069	14
Month left employer	25 806	21
Year left employer	28 066	14
Reason left job	28 069	14
FT/PT/self-employed and contract status	27 730	15
FT/PT/self-employed + contract and dates	26 281	20
N	32 772	

RG – Registrar General
SIC – Standard Industrial Classification
SOC – Standard Occupational Classification

Table A1.4 Flexible jobs in the BHPS data up to Wave 3, per cent

	Retrospective data to 9.10.90		Wave data		Total	
	Men	Women	Men	Women	Men	Women
Full-time permanent	85.7	67.4	76.1	49.8	85.6	64.9
Full-time temporary	6.2	5.3	5.1	2.2	3.8	4.0
Part-time permanent	1.3	19.9	4.6	37.4	2.0	23.2
Part-time temporary	1.2	4.7	1.5	5.4	1.3	4.9
Self-employed permanent	4.9	2.2	11.3	4.5	6.4	2.6
Self-employed temporary	0.6	0.4	1.4	0.1	0.8	0.5
Total	100	100	100	100	100	100
N	11 704	14 577	3264	3081	14 634	17 520

Bibliography

Acker, J. (1992) 'The future of women and work: Ending the twentieth century', *Sociological Perspectives* 31(1) 53–68.

Acs, Z.J., Audretsch, D.B. and Evans, D.S. (1994) 'Why does the the self-employment rate vary across countries and across time?' Centre for Economic Policy Research Discussion Paper No. 871.

Advisory, Conciliation and Arbitration Service (ACAS), (1988) *Labour Flexibility in Britain: The 1987 ACAS Survey*, London: ACAS.

Allen, S. and Wolkowitz, C. (1986) 'The Control of Women's Labour: the Case of Homeworking', *Feminist Review*, 22, 25–51.

Allen, S. and Wolkowitz, C. (1987) *Homeworking: Myths and Realities*. London: Macmillan.

Amin, A. (ed.) (1994) *Post-Fordism – A Reader*, Oxford: Blackwell.

Atkinson, J. (1984) 'Flexibility, uncertainty and manpower management', Institute of Manpower Studies Report No. 89, Brighton, Sussex University.

Atkinson, J. and Meager, N. (1986) *New Forms of Work Organisation*, Institute of Manpower Studies Report No. 121, Brighton: IMS.

Beatson, M. (1993) 'Trends in pay flexibility', *Employment Gazette*, Vol. 101, No. 9, September, pp. 405–28.

Beatson, M. and Butcher, S. (1993) 'Union density across the employed workforce', *Employment Gazette*, Vol. 101, No. 1, January, pp. 673–89.

Beatson, M. (1995) *Labour Market Flexibility*, Employment Department Research Series No. 48.

Beechey, V. and Perkins, T. (1987) *A Matter of Hours*, Cambridge: Polity Press.

Bhavnani, R. (1994) *Black Women in the Labour Market: a Research review*, Equal Opportunities Commission Research Series.

Bird, D. and Corcoran, L. (1994) 'Trade union membership and density 1992–93', *Employment Gazette*, Vol. 102, No. 6.

Bisset, L. and Huws, U. (1984) *Sweated Labour: Homeworking in Britain Today*, London: Low Pay Unit.

Blanchflower, D. and Corry, B. (1986) *Part-time Employment in Great Britain: An Analysis using Establishment Data*, London: Department of Employment Research Paper No. 57.

Blanchflower, D. and Oswald, A. (1991) 'What makes an entrepreneur?' Institute of Economics and Statistics Discussion Paper No. 125.

Blanchflower, D.G. and Freeman, R.B. (1994) 'Did the Thatcher reforms change British labour market performance?' in R.Barrel (ed.) *The UK Labour Market: Comparative Aspects and Institutional Developments*, Cambridge University Press.

Bosworth, D. (1994) *Sunday Working: Analysis of an Employer Survey*, Employment Department Research Paper No. 33.

Brannen, J., Meszaros, G. and Moss, P. (1994) *Employment and Family Life: a Review of Research in the UK*, London: Employment Department Research Series No. 41.

Brown, W. (1987) 'The paradoxical role of pay in eliciting labour productivity'. Paper presented to the Second European Regional Congress on Industrial Relations, Israel.

Bruegel, I. and Hegewisch, A. (1994) 'Flexibilisation and part-time work in Europe', in Brown, P. and Crompton, R. (eds) (1994) *Economic Restructuring and Social Exclusion*, London: UCL Press.

Brunhes, B. (1988) 'Labour market flexibility in Europe: a comparative analysis of four countries'. Working Paper for the OECD Working Party on Industrial Relations. Paris: OECD.

Burchell, B. (1989) 'The impact on individuals of precariousness in the United Kingdom Labour Market', in G. Rodgers and J. Rodgers (eds) *Precarious jobs in Labour Market Regulation: the Growth of Atypical Employment in Western Europe,* Geneva: Internatioanl Institute of Labour Studies.

Burchell, B. (1994) 'The effects of labour market position, job insecurity, and unemployment on psychological health' in D. Gallie C. Marsh and C. Vogler (eds) *Social Change and the Experience of Unemployment*, Oxford: Oxford University Press.

Burgess, S. and Rees, H. (1994) 'Lifetime jobs and transient jobs', Discussion Paper, Department of Economics, University of Bristol.

Campbell, M. and Daly, M. (1992) 'Self-employment: Into the 1990s', in *Employment Gazette*, Vol. 100, No. 6, pp. 269–92.

Carter, S. and Cannon, T. (1988) *Female entrepreneurs: a study of female business owners: their motivations, experiences and strategies for success*, Employment Department Research Paper No. 65.

Casey, B. (1988) *Temporary Workers*, London: Policy Studies Institute.

Cragg, A. and Dawson, T. (1981) *Qualitative Research among Homeworkers*, Department of Employment Research Paper No. 21.

Curran, J. and Burrows, R. (1989) 'National profiles of the self-employed', in *Employment Gazette*, Vol. 99, No. 7.

Deakin, S. (1988) 'The comparative structure of labour law systems; state systems of regulation and harmonisation of labour standards in the EEC'. Paper prepared for the 10th Annual Conference of the International Working Party on Labour Markets Segmentation, sponsored by the EEC on the Internationalisation of Markets and Terms and Conditions of Employment, Oporto, Portugal.

Dex, S. (1988) *Women's Attitudes Towards Work*, London, Macmillan.

Dex, S. (1992) 'Labour force participation of women during the 1990s. Occupational mobility and part-time employment' in R. Lindley (ed.) (1992) *Women's Employment: Britain in the Single European Market*, Equal Opportunities Commission Research Series, London: HMSO.

Dex, S. (1995) 'The reliability of recall data: A literature review', *Bulletin de Methodologie Sociologique*, No. 49.

Dex, S. and Shaw, L.B. (1986) *British and American Women at Work*, London, Macmillan.

Dex, S., Walters, P. and Alden, D. (1993) *French and British Mothers at Work*, London, Macmillan.

Dex, S, Lissenburgh, S. and Taylor, M. (1994) *Women and Low Pay: Identifying the Issues*, Manchester: Equal Opportunities Commission.

Dex, S. and McCulloch, A. (1995) *Flexible Employment in Britain: A Statis-*

tical Analysis, Discussion Series No. 15. Manchester: Equal Opportunities Commission.

Dex, S. and McCulloch, A. (1995a) Unemployment histories in the British Household Panel Study. A Report to the Employment Department.

Dex, S. Joshi, H. and Macran, S. (1996) 'A widening gulf amongst Britain's mothers', *Oxford Review of Economic Policy*, Vol. 12, No. 1.

Dey, I. (1989) 'Flexible "parts" and rigid "fulls": The limited revolution in work-time patterns', *Work Employment and Society*, Vol. 3, No. 4, pp. 465–90.

Dickens, L. (1992) *Whose Flexibility? Discrimination and Equality Issues in Atypical Work*, London: Institute of Employment Rights.

Dolton, P.J. and Makepeace, G.H. (1990) 'Self-employment among graduates', *Bulletin of Economic Research*, 42:1, pp. 35–53.

Emerson, M. (1988) 'Regulation or deregulation of the labour market', *European Economic Review*, Vol. 32, pp. 775–817.

Employment Department Group (1991) *The Government's Expenditure Plans 1991–1992 to 1993–1994*, Cm 1506, HMSO.

Employment Department (1993) 'Women in the Labour Market' *Employment Gazette*, November, pp. 483–502.

Equal Opportunities Commission (EOC) (1993) *Women and Men in Britain*, Manchester: EOC.

Escott, K. and Whitefield, D. (1995) *The Gender Impact of CCT on Local Government*, Manchester: Equal Opportunities Commission Research Series.

European Commission (1992) *Employment in Europe 1992*, Luxembourg: Eurostat.

European Commission (1995) 'Flexibility and work organization', *Social Europe*, Supplement No. 1.

European Industrial Relations Review (EIRR) (1990) Non-standard forms of employment in Europe, EIRR Report No. 3.

Evans, D.S. and Leighton, L.S. (1989) 'Some empirical aspects of entrepreneurship', *American Economic Review* 79 (3) 519–35.

Felstead, A. (1991) 'The social organisation of the franchise: a case of "controlled self-employment"', *Work, Employment and Society*, 5, pp. 37–57.

Felstead, A. and Jewson, N. (1995) 'Working at home: estimates from the 1991 Census' in *Employment Gazette*, Vol. 103, No. 3 pp. 95–100.

Gershuny, J. and Brice, J. (1994) 'Looking backwards: family and work 1900 to 1992' in N. Buck, J. Gershuny, D. Rose and J. Scott, *Changing Households: the British Household Panel Survey, 1990–1992*, Colchester: ESRC Centre on Micro-social Change, University of Essex.

Goldberg, D. (1972) *The Detection of Psychiatric Illness by Questionnaire*, Maudsley Monograph No. 21, Oxford University Press.

Gottfried, H. (1992) 'In the margins: flexibility as a mode of regulation in the temporary help service industry' in *Work Employment and Society* Vol. 6, pp. 443–60.

Gottfried, H. and Graham, L. (1993) 'Constructing difference: the making of gendered subcultures in a Japanese automobile plant', *Sociology* Vol. 7 (4).

Gregory, A. (1987) 'The growth of part-time work in grocery in Britain and France' in *Retail and Distribution Management*, Vol. 15, 14–18.

Haddon, L. and Lewis, A. (1994) 'The experience of teleworking: an anno-
tated review', *International Journal of Human Resource Management*, Vol.
5, No. 1.

Hakim, C. (1985) *Employers' Use of Outwork*, London: Department of Employment Research Paper No. 44.

Hakim, C. (1987) 'Trends in the flexible workforce', *Employment Gazette*,
Nov. pp. 549–60.

Hakim, C. (1993) 'Grateful slaves and self-made women: Fact and fantasy in
women's work orientations', *European Sociological Review*, Vol. 7, No. 2,
101–21.

Hart, R. (1987) *Working Time and Employment*, London: Allen & Unwin.

Hill, S. Blyton, P. and Gorham, A. (1989) 'The economics of manpower flexibility', *Royal Bank of Scotland Review*, Number 163, 15–26.

Hunter, L.C. and MacInnes, J. (1991) *Employers' Labour Use Strategies –
Case Studies*, Employment Department Group Research Paper No. 87.

Hutchinson, S. (1993) 'Annual hours working in the UK', Institute of Personnel Management Issues in People Management Series, No. 5.

Hutton, W. (1995) *The State We're In*, London: Jonathan Cape.

Huws, U. (1994) 'Teleworking in Britain', *Employment Gazette*, Vol. 102,
No. 2, pp. 51–60.

Huws, U. (1994a) *Home Truths: Key Findings from the National Survey of
Homeworkers*. National Group on Homeworking, Report No. 2.

Incomes Data Services, (1994) *Teleworking*, IDS Study 551.

Incomes Data Services, (1995) *Managing Labour Turnover*, IDS Study 577.

Industrial Relations Services (IRS) (1992) *Pay and Gender in Britain: 2*, London:
IRS. A research report for the Equal Opportunities Commission.

Industrial Relations Services, (1994a) *Diversity and Change – Survey of Non-
standard Working*, IRS Employment Trends No. 570, October.

Industrial Relations Services, (1994b) *Non-standard Working Under Review*,
IRS Employment Trends No. 565, August.

IM (1994) *Survey of Long-term Employment Strategies*, London: Institute of
Management.

Laurie, H. and Taylor, M. (1992) Homeworkers in Britain. Report to the Employment Department. ESRC Centre for Research on Micro-social Change
Working Paper, University of Essex.

McGregor, A. and Sproull, A. (1991) *Employer Labour Use Strategies: Analysis
of a National Survey*, Employment Department Group Research Paper No.
83.

McLaughlin, E. (1994) 'Flexibility or polarisation?' in M.White (ed.) (1994)
Unemployment and Public Policy in a Changing Labour Market, Policy
Studies Institute.

McRae, S. (1991) *Maternity Rights in Britain*, London: Policy Studies Institute.

Marsh, C. (1991) *Hours of Work of Women and Men in Britain*, Manchester:
Equal Opportunities Commission Research Series.

Martin, J. and Roberts, C. (1994) *Women and Employment: A Lifetime Perspective*, London: HMSO.

Marullo, S. (1995) *A Comparison of Regulations on Part-time and Temporary
Employment in Europe*, Employment Department Research Paper Series,
No. 52.

Meager, N. Court, G. and Moralee, J. (1994) *Self-employment and the Distribution of Income*, Brighton: Institute of Manpower Studies Report 270.

Meulders, D. and Plasman, R. (1994) *Atypical Work in the EC*, Dartmouth Publishing.

Millward, N. (1995) *Targeting Potential Discrimination*, Manchester: Equal Opportunities Commission Discussion Series No. 11.

Naylor, K. (1994) 'Part-time working in Great Britain – an historical analysis', *Employment Gazette*, Vol. 102, No. 12, pp. 473–84.

Neathey, F. and Hurstfield, J. (1995) *Flexibility in Practice: Women's Employment and Pay in Retail and Finance, London, Industrial Relations Services*, EOC Research Division Series No. 16.

OECD (1991; 1992; 1994) *Employment Outlook*, Paris: Organisation of Economic Cooperation and Development.

OECD (1994) *Economic Outlook*, Paris: Organisation of Economic Cooperation and Development.

O'Reilly, J. (1994) 'What flexibility do women offer? Comparing the use of and attitudes to part-time work in Britain and France in retail banking, *Gender, Work and Organization*, Vol. 1, No. 3.

Owen, D. (1994) *Ethnic Minority Women and the Labour Market: Analysis of the 1991 Census*, Equal Opportunities Commission Research Series.

Page, B. (1995) 'Corporate teleworking: business transactions at a distance' in *Managing Information*, May, pp. 33–5.

Phizacklea, A. (1990) *Unpacking the Fashion Industry*, London and New York: Routledge.

Piore, M. and Sabel, C.F. (1984) *The Second Industrial Divide: Possibilities for Success*, New York: Basic Books.

Pollert, A. (1991) (ed.) *Farewell to Flexibility?* Oxford: Blackwell.

Proctor, S.J. Rowlinson, M. McArdle, L. Hassard, J. and Forrester, P. (1994) 'Flexibility, politics and strategy: In defence of the model of the flexible firm', *Work Employment and Society*, Vol. 8 (2) pp. 221–42.

Rainbird, H. (1990) *Self-employment: A Form of Disguised Wage Labour?* in A. Pollert (ed.) *Farewell to Flexibility?: Restructuring Work and Employment*. Oxford, Blackwell.

Reed Personnel Services (1995) *The Shape of Work to Come*, Tolworth: Reed Personnel Services.

Rees, H. and Shah, A. (1986) 'An empirical analysis of self employment in the UK', *Journal of Applied Econometrics*, Vol. 1, pp. 95–108.

Robinson, P. (1994) 'The British labour market in historical perspective: changes in the structure of employment and unemployment', Centre for Economic Performance Discussion Paper, No. 202.

Robinson, P. (1995) 'Evolution not revolution: Have UK labour market changes been vastly overstated?' *New Economy* (UK), October.

Rose, D. Dex, S. Taylor, M. and Perren, K. (1994) 'Changes in economic activity', in N. Buck, J. Gershuny, D. Rose, and J. Scott, *Changing Households*, University of Essex: ESRC Research Centre in Micro-social Change.

Rubery, J. (1989) 'Labour market flexibility in Britain', in F. Green (ed.) *Restructuring and the UK Economy*, Brighton: Harvester-Wheatsheaf.

Rubery, J. (1992) *The Economics of Equal Value*, Manchester: Equal Opportunities Commission.

Rubery, J. (1994) *Changing Patterns of Work and Working Time: towards the integration or the segmentation of the labour market in the UK*. Manchester: Manchester School of Management, UMIST.

Russell, R. (1983) 'Class formation in the workplace: the role of sources of income', *Work and Occupations*, Vol. 10, pp. 349–72.

Scase, R. and Goffee, R. (1982) *The Entrepreneurial Middle Class*, London: Croom Helm.

Scase, R. and Goffee, R. (1987) *The Real World of the Small Business Owner*, London: Croom Helm.

Smith, V. (1993) 'Flexibility in work and employment: The impact on women', *Research in the Sociology of Organizations*, Vol. 11.

Taylor, M. (1994) 'Earnings, independence or unemployment: Why become self-employed?' ESRC Research Centre on Micro-social Change Working Paper No. 26.

TUC (1995) 'Has deregulation delivered the jobs?' Report to the ILO Committee of Experts. London: Congress House, Trades Union Congress.

Walby, S. (1989) 'Flexibility and the changing division of labour', in S. Wood (ed.) *The Transformation of Work? Skill, Flexibility and the Labour Process*, London: Unwin Hyman.

Wareing, A. (1992) 'Working arrangements and patterns of working hours in Britain', *Employment Gazette*, March, pp. 88–100.

Watson, G. (1994) 'The flexible workforce and patterns of working hours in the UK', *Employment Gazette*, Vol. 102, No. 7, 239–48.

Watson, G. and Fothergill, B. (1993) 'Part-time employment and attitudes to part-time work', *Employment Gazette*, Vol. 101, No. 5, pp. 213–20.

Wilson, R. (1994) 'Sectoral and occupational change: Prospects for women's employment' in R. Lindley (ed.) (1994) *Labour market structures and prospects for women*, Manchester: Equal Opportunities Commission Research Series.

Index

absenteeism 25
ACAS (Arbitration, Conciliation and
  Advisory Service) 9, 12, 23
age of workers 54, 58, 64–7, 87, 97–9,
  101, 103, 111–18, 118–19, 128, 170,
  188
agriculture industry 22, 28, 29, 30, 32,
  33, 41
attitudes 6, 47, 50, 70–2

bargaining 7, 154–7, 177
benefits 3, 6, 9, 16, 17, 18, 53
BHPS (British Household Panel Study)
  details 10–11, 50, 63, 64, 70, 72, 74,
  89, 191–2, 194–6
  retrospective data 10–11, 104, 132,
  191–2, 195–6
bureaucracy 5
business cycle 23, 39, 48, 92, 95, 97,
  101, 102, 103, 112, 115, 169, 170,
  184, 185, 186
business services industry 23, 24, 48, 187

carers 84
casual work 1, 36, 38, 77, 91, 96
casualisation 1
childbirth effects 46–7
child care 6, 21, 46–7, 50, 53, 63,
  82–4, 88, 187
clerical work 22
cohort differences 111–18
collective bargaining 7, 154–7, 177,
  183–5
company cars 18
competitiveness 1, 2, 3, 5, 15, 20, 24,
  26, 172
CCT (Compulsory Competitive
  Tendering) 7
conditions of work 2, 7
construction industry 23, 28, 29, 53
contracts 9, 20, 24
  fixed term 1, 3, 22
  permanent 2, 19
cross-national comparisons 5, 20, 47,
  153–72
custom and practice 9

Data Archive 89

demand
  for labour 4
  for products 4, 19, 23
  customer 26
demarcations 4
demographic change 23
DFEE (Department for Education and
  Employment) 45
dependent children effects 82–4, 88,
  138, 140, 175
deregulation 1, 2, 9, 100, 153, 154,
  156, 182, 183–5, 187
discrimination 8–9, 60, 69
dismissed 126
distribution industry 23, 28, 41
divorced 68
domestic commitments 46, 49, 98, 126

economic performance 183–5
economy
  Britain 1, 2, 153–72, 173, 183–5
  growth 39
  industrialised countries 153–72
  macro goals 2
education
  full-time 59, 64, 65, 66, 88, 98, 112,
  115, 175, 187,
  industry 41, 187
  qualifications 47, 48, 75–6, 88, 128,
  131, 171, 177
elderly 6, 50, 84, 138
employee rights 8
employers 1, 2, 3, 10, 12, 15–27,
  159–60
  costs 7, 16–19, 20, 21
  strategies 15, 19–27, 159–60, 163–4,
  165, 166–7, 168, 169, 171–2, 186–8
ELUS (Employers Labour Use
  Strategies) survey 20, 22
employment
  casual 1, 36, 38, 77, 91, 96,
  conditions 1, 176–7
  core 9, 15, 184
  forecasts 12, 186–7
  French 20, 47
  growth 185, 186
  labour force 3
  legislation 3, 7–10

lifetime 1
low hours 3, 11
manufacturing 2, 5, 21, 23, 24, 26
part-time (see part-time work)
periphery 15
permanent 2, 16, 18, 19, 23
policies 12
reasons for leaving 41, 52, 104, 122, 125–7
regulations 1, 5, 6–10, 153, 164, 171, 182
self-employment (see self-employment)
services 2, 21, 29, 30, 40, 41, 48, 168, 187
structure 1, 3, 6, 102, 174, 185
temporary (*see* temporary work)
Employment Protection Acts 8, 27
energy and water industry 30
engineering industry 23
entry to flexible jobs 118–27
equal opportunities 9
Equal Opportunities Commission (EOC) 9
ethnic minorities 48, 49, 50, 68–70, 87, 175
European Commission 2
Directives 9
European Labour Force Survey (ELUS) 161, 163, 168
European Union 2, 8–9, 25, 153, 166, 168, 184
Court of Justice 9, 19
exit from flexible jobs 118–27, 127–31

factor prices 15
family business 49, 50
family policy 6
family-friendly practices 24
fashion industry 24
feel-bad factor 2, 173
feel-good factor 1
finance industry 20, 21, 24, 26, 48
financial dependence 47
firms 10, 15
capital usage 21, 23, 24
competitiveness 21, 24
size 6, 21, 23, 26, 167
fiscal system 6, 10, 22, 47, 49
fixed costs 16
fixed-term contracts 1, 3, 11, 29, 30, 32, 33, 38, 40, 52, 58, 77, 92, 102, 103, 165, 187
flexible career 178–9

flexibility
functional 4
numerical 4
labour market 4
place of work 4
working time 4
flexitime 4
franchising 53
freelancers 1, 23, 24, 93
fringe benefits 10, 15, 18, 21, 27, 52, 53, 176, 183, 186

gender inequalities 2, 5, 51, 62–3, 172–8, 184, 186, 187
GHQ (General Health Questionnaire) 74–5, 88, 89, 145–6
global economy 5, 12, 15
government schemes 45, 51, 55, 172

health services 30, 32, 33, 40, 187
holidays 18, 52
homework 4, 24–5, 27, 50–1, 52, 53, 54, 63, 92, 154, 167
hotel industry 23, 41
hours of work (*see* part-time work)
households 2, 3, 4, 10, 11, 135–49, 175
income 53, 84–7, 88, 89, 147–9, 176, 187
surveys 10–11
type 138–40, 175
housing
associations 146
employment related 18
tenure 82–3, 88, 146–7
human capital 88
human resources management 15, 19–27, 153, 159–60, 163–4, 165, 166–7, 168, 169, 171–2, 186–8.

ill-health effects 50, 127, 176
importance of work 47, 72, 73–4
incentives 7
income 84–7, 147–9, 176
income distribution 48
indirect discrimination 9
industrial districts 5
industrial relations 10, 22, 154–7
industrial system 6
industries 4, 22, 23, 24, 25, 185
of flexible work 28–30, 39–41
informal networks 5
Institute of Personnel Development (IPD) 52

insurance industry 25, 26
International Labour Organization
(ILO) 184
involuntary quits 41

job demarcation 4
job satisfaction 46, 47, 51, 72–4
job security 2, 72, 177
job sharing 4, 62

Labour Force Survey (LFS) 18, 22, 28,
45, 46, 51, 54, 55, 63, 64, 90, 168,
194
description of 10–11, 192–3
labour market
competitiveness 2, 183–5
conditions 6, 39, 41, 72, 88
deregulation 1, 2, 9, 100, 153, 154,
156, 182, 183–5, 187
efficiency 2
institutions 6–10
mobility 4
regulations 6–10
role of government 7
labour supply 6
legislation
custom and practice 9
employment protection 3, 8, 22, 26,
27, 53
European Union 19, 153
local government 22
local labour market 39
local authority housing 82, 146
lone parents 84, 88, 138
long hours 47, 177
low pay 47, 48, 50, 53, 177

macro-economic goals 2
manufacturing industry 2, 21, 23, 24,
26
managerial duties 34
manager occupations 30, 32, 33, 128
marginal work 1
married men 67–8, 88, 120–1
married women 21, 67–8, 88, 120–1
marital status effects 67–8, 87, 88
maternity leave 8, 16, 17, 115, 177,
187
meal subsidies 18
medical insurance 18
mortgages 82, 146

National Insurance 3, 10, 16, 17, 47,
186

National Opinion Polls (NOP) 46
niche markers 5, 41
night work 7
non-standard work definition 1
non-manual work 128
numbers of jobs 106–9, 127–8

occupation differences 30–4, 39–41,
128–30
occupational mobility 46, 186
on-call work 4, 5, 18, 21, 26, 27, 52,
92, 177, 188
OECD (Organisation for Economic
Cooperation and Development) 10,
101, 153, 154, 155, 156, 157, 158,
159, 160, 161, 169, 170, 171, 172
outwork 24
overtime 4, 7, 18, 52, 54, 55

partner's employment 46, 48–9, 82,
138–44, 145–6, 149, 175–6
part-time hours 1, 2, 3, 9, 10, 11, 15,
20–1, 26, 27, 28, 29, 32, 33, 35, 38,
39, 40, 41, 45, 46–7, 51, 54, 58, 59,
60; 62, 63, 154
by age 64–7, 97–9, 118–19
by attitudes 70–2
by caring responsibilities 84
by cohort 111–12, 115
by dependent children 82–3, 88
by education 75–6, 88
by ethnic origin 68–70
by GHQ 74–5, 88, 89
by household income 84–7, 88, 89
by housing tenure 82, 88
by lone parent 84, 88
by marital status 67–8, 119–21
by past employment 121–2
by past unemployment 80–1, 122,
123–4
by pay 77–9, 88
by training 76–7, 88
changes over time 91–6, 98, 99,
102–3, 173–4
definitions 158–9
in households 135–49
OECD countries 157–60, 172, 182–3
over lifetime 104, 105–11
previous jobs 122
second jobs 99
subsequent activity 123, 124–5
pay
decentralised bargaining 7, 154–7,
177

differentials 7, 52, 53, 77–9, 88,
177, 184
  real wage 8
pensions 17, 18, 19, 52, 53, 176, 186
performance-related pay 177
permanent work 2, 16, 18, 19, 34, 35,
36, 39, 40, 41, 51, 52, 53, 54, 60, 64,
72, 74, 104, 112–14, 122, 140, 143,
176
personal services industry 32, 33, 40,
41, 48
policy implications 3, 12
Post-Fordism 5
preferences 1, 46, 47
Price Waterhouse and Cranfield
survey 153–4, 159–60, 163–4, 165,
166– 7, 168, 169
private medical insurance 18
productivity 5, 8, 19, 20, 25, 188
professional occupations 22, 30, 32,
33, 40, 41
profit sharing 18
promotion 53
public sector 7, 9, 20, 22, 24, 29, 41,
160, 165, 172, 184

real wage 8
recall reliability 104
recreation facilities 18
recruitment costs 17, 19
redundancy 126
regeneration 1
regional differences 4, 21, 23, 24, 36–9
Registrar General Social Class 128
regulations of employment 1, 5, 6–10,
153, 164, 171, 182
  costs of 16–19
  voluntary 6, 9, 16, 18
restructuring 27, 183–5
retail industry 20, 21, 26, 30, 32, 40,
168
retirement 41, 51, 55, 66, 126, 127

sales occupation 32, 33, 40, 41
seasonal work 1, 4, 36, 38, 58, 77, 91,
96
second jobs 99, 102, 173, 174
security 2
segregated work 28
self employment 2, 3, 5, 10, 22–3, 27,
28, 29, 30, 32, 33, 34, 35, 36, 38, 39,
40, 41, 45, 48–50, 52
  by age 64–7, 97–9, 118–19
  by attitudes 70–2

by caring responsibilities 84
by cohort 111–12, 115
by dependent children 82–3, 88
by education 75–6
by ethnic origin 68–70
by GHQ 74–5
by household income 84–7, 88, 89
by housing tenure 82, 88
by lone parent 84, 88
by marital status 67–8, 119–21
by past employment 121–2
by past unemployment 80–1, 122,
123–4
by pay 77–9, 88
by training 76–7, 88
changes over time 91–6, 97, 99,
102–3, 173–4
in households 135–49
OECD countries 165–7, 182–3
over lifetime 104, 105–11
previous jobs 122
reasons for 49–50, 53, 54, 55, 58,
154
subsequent activity 123, 124–5
services industry 2, 21, 29, 30, 40, 41,
48, 168, 187
share schemes 18, 52
shift work 4, 52, 62, 92, 93
sick pay 10, 16, 17, 52
single status 68
skilled trades 30, 32, 128–9
Social Charter 2
social reproduction 6
social security 3, 10, 16, 17, 47, 186
stress 74, 145–6, 177
subcontracting 3, 5, 7, 22–3, 52, 92,
154, 165–7
Sunday work 4, 154, 167–8, 177
supervision 34, 51
surveys 3, 5

tax 6, 22, 47, 49
taxi driving 53
teaching occupation 32, 33
technology 5, 6, 15, 23
telecottages 24
telework 4, 24–5, 27, 50–1, 92
temporary work 1, 2, 3, 5, 9, 10, 11,
15, 17, 18, 19, 21–2, 26, 28, 30, 32,
33, 35, 36, 38, 39, 40, 41, 45, 49,
51–2, 53, 54, 55, 59, 154
  agency 21, 22, 52, 92
  by age 64–7, 97–9, 118–19
  by attitudes 70–2

by caring responsibilities 84
by cohort 111–12, 115–18
by dependent children 82–3, 88
by education 75–6, 88
by ethnic origin 68–70
by GHQ 74–5
by household income 84–7, 88, 89
by housing tenure 82, 88
by marital status 67–8, 119–21
by past employment 121–2
by past unemployment 80–1, 122, 123–4
by pay 77–9, 88
by training 76–7, 88
changes over time 91–6, 96–7, 102–3, 173–4
durations 127
fixed-term 1, 3, 11, 29, 30, 32, 33, 38, 40, 52, 58, 77, 92, 102, 103, 165, 187
in households 135–49
OECD countries 160–5, 172, 182–3
over lifetime 104, 105–12
previous jobs 122
reasons for 60–1
subsequent activity 123, 124–5, 127–31
unemployment 178–81
tenure of jobs 35–6, 41, 49, 59, 99–102, 104, 127, 130, 154, 169–71, 173, 185
term-time work 4, 61
TUC (Trades Union Congress) 184, 185
Trade Union Reform and Employment Rights Act 8
training 6, 53, 76–7, 88, 171, 177, 181, 186

schemes 45, 51, 55, 172
turnover 19, 25, 35, 36, 169, 185, 186

unemployment 2, 6, 9, 23, 39, 48, 52, 72, 95, 97, 104, 132, 143, 165, 177, 178–81, 183–5, 188
benefits 9, 17
long-term 80–1, 184
past 80, 122, 128
recurrent 180–1
uncertainty 16, 72
unfair dismissal 8, 9, 17
unions 2, 6, 9, 10, 16, 21, 153
coverage 156
flexible work 34–5
mark-up 8
membership 34–5, 154–7, 182
secondary action 7
unpaid family workers 45, 55, 62

vertical integration 6

Wages Councils 7
weekend work 154, 167–8, 177
welfare state 7
widowed status 68, 120
Women and Employment Survey (WES) 47
women returners 49
work incentives 7
working time 109–11
Workplace Industrial Relations Survey (WIRS) 21, 23

zero-hours contracts 4, 5, 18, 21, 26, 27, 52, 92, 177, 188